WITHDRAWN
HARVARD LIBRARY
WITHDRAWN

The Political Morality of Liberal Democracy

In this important new work in political and constitutional theory, Michael J. Perry elaborates and defends an account of the political morality of liberal democracy: the moral convictions and commitments that in a liberal democracy should govern decisions about what laws to enact and what policies to pursue. The fundamental questions addressed in this book concern (1) the grounding, (2) the content, (3) the implications for one or another moral controversy, and (4) the judicial enforcement of the political morality of liberal democracy. The particular issues discussed include whether government may ban previability abortion, whether government may refuse to extend the benefit of law to same-sex couples, and what role religion should play in the politics and law of a liberal democracy.

Michael J. Perry holds a Robert W. Woodruff Chair at Emory University, where he teaches in the law school. Previously, Perry held the Howard J. Trienens Chair in Law at Northwestern University, where he taught for fifteen years, and the University Distinguished Chair in Law at Wake Forest University. Perry has written on American constitutional law and theory; law, morality, and religion; and human rights theory in more than sixty articles and ten books, including *The Idea of Human Rights*; *We the People: The Fourteenth Amendment and the Supreme Court*; *Under God? Religious Faith and Liberal Democracy*; *Toward a Theory of Human Rights: Religion, Law, Courts*; and *Constitutional Rights, Moral Controversy, and the Supreme Court.*

The Political Morality of Liberal Democracy

MICHAEL J. PERRY
Emory University, School of Law

CAMBRIDGE UNIVERSITY PRESS
Cambridge, New York, Melbourne, Madrid, Cape Town, Singapore,
São Paulo, Delhi, Dubai, Tokyo

Cambridge University Press
32 Avenue of the Americas, New York, NY 10013-2473, USA

www.cambridge.org
Information on this title: www.cambridge.org/9780521115186

© Michael J. Perry 2010

This publication is in copyright. Subject to statutory exception
and to the provisions of relevant collective licensing agreements,
no reproduction of any part may take place without the written
permission of Cambridge University Press.

First published 2010

Printed in the United States of America

A catalog record for this publication is available from the British Library.

Library of Congress Cataloging in Publication data
Perry, Michael J.
The political morality of liberal democracy / Michael J. Perry.
p. cm.
Includes bibliographical references and index.
ISBN 978-0-521-11518-6 (hardback)
1. Democracy – Moral and ethical aspects.   2. Human rights.   3. Civil rights.   I. Title.
JC423.P368   2010
172–dc22   2009026769

ISBN 978-0-521-11518-6 Hardback

Cambridge University Press has no responsibility for the persistence or
accuracy of URLs for external or third-party Internet Web sites referred to in
this publication and does not guarantee that any content on such Web sites is,
or will remain, accurate or appropriate.

*To my friends and colleagues at Emory Law School's
Center for the Study of Law and Religion,
and to the memory of the great master of "law and religion,"
Hal Berman,
who graced the Center with his inspiring presence for more than twenty years*

Contents

Introduction   *page* 1

Part I. Liberal Democracy, Human Rights, and Religious Faith

1. Liberal Democracy and Human Rights   9
2. Liberal Democracy and Religious Faith   27

Part II. First Principles

3. The Right to Moral Equality   61
4. The Right to Religious Freedom   65
5. Beyond Religious Freedom: The Right to Moral Freedom   88
6. Religion as a Basis of Lawmaking   100

Part III. First Principles Applied

7. Abortion   123
8. Same-Sex Unions   138

Part IV. The Constitution of Liberal Democracy

9. Protecting Constitutionally Entrenched Rights: The Courts' – In Particular, the U.S. Supreme Court's – Proper Role   159

Conclusion: In the Matter of the Adoption of John Doe and James Doe   198

Index   205

Introduction

My overarching aim in this book is to elaborate and to defend an account – an understanding – of the political morality of liberal democracy.[1] By "political" morality, I mean the moral convictions and commitments that govern decisions about what laws to enact (or to maintain on the books), what policies to pursue, such as:[2]

- Should we retain capital punishment – or abolish it? (By "we," I mean here "we the citizens of a liberal democracy, acting through our elected representatives.")
- Should we ban abortion – or permit it?
- Should we ban physician-assisted suicide – or permit it?
- Should we refuse to extend the benefit of law to same-sex unions – or should we create civil unions for same-sex couples, and if so, should we call such unions "marriages"?
- Should we affirm, as a fundamental human right, freedom from severe poverty?

And so on. (I discuss abortion and same-sex unions in Chapters 7 and 8.) Such questions are not just moral questions, but they are, in part, moral questions: questions about what is morally right or morally wrong for us to do or not to do. And the political morality of liberal democracy, as I explain in this book, bears directly on such questions.

This book is my contribution to the Christian Jurisprudence Project, sponsored by the Center for the Study of Law and Religion at Emory Law School. As I originally conceived it, the book was to be about, and only about, an issue I have addressed in some of my

---

[1] Aidan O'Neill uses the term "post-Nuremberg democracy." Aidan O'Neill, "Roman Catholicism and the Temptation of *Shari'a*," 15 COMMON KNOWLEDGE 269, 297 et seq. (2009).

[2] Not that considerations other than moral convictions and commitments – including, of course, "political" considerations, in the popular sense of the term – don't govern such decisions.

Introduction

previous books: the proper role of religion in the politics and law of a liberal democracy. As I began to draft the book, however, my focus broadened to include several other issues that have engaged me over the years.

In the mid-1970s, at the beginning of my career as a law professor, I was principally engaged by – and I remain engaged by – constitutional controversies that are closely aligned with moral controversies: the constitutional controversy, for example, over laws banning abortion.[3] (I have also been engaged by the related question of the courts' proper role – especially the U.S. Supreme Court's proper role – in resolving such controversies.[4]) I was soon confronted by the question of the proper relationship of morality to constitutional law.[5] Because for most citizens of the United States morality is religiously grounded, another question – one that would become for me a scholarly obsession – quickly came into view: the proper role of religion in the politics and law of a liberal democracy.[6] Before long I was in the grip of this large question: Can any worldview that is not religious support – embed – the twofold claim to which liberal democracy is, as such – as *liberal* democracy – committed, namely, that each and every human being has equal inherent dignity and is inviolable?[7]

I can now see, in retrospect, that each of the principal questions that have engaged me over the course of my career concerns one or another aspect of the political morality of liberal democracy; in particular, each question concerns the grounding, the content, the implications for one or another moral controversy, or the judicial enforcement of the political morality of liberal democracy. In this

---

[3] My first article was "Abortion, the Public Morals, and the Police Power: The Ethical Function of Substantive Due Process," 23 UCLA L. REV. 689 (1976).

[4] See Michael J. Perry, *The Constitution, the Courts, and Human Rights* (1982); Michael J. Perry, *The Constitution in the Courts: Law or Politics?* (1994); Michael J. Perry, *We the People: The Fourteenth Amendment and the Supreme Court* (1999); Michael J. Perry, *Constitutional Rights, Moral Controversy, and the Supreme Court* (2009).

[5] See Michael J. Perry, *Morality, Politics, and Law* (1988).

[6] See Michael J. Perry, *Love and Power: The Role of Religion and Morality in American Politics* (1991); Michael J. Perry, *Religion in Politics: Constitutional and Moral Perspectives* (1997); Michael J. Perry, *Under God? Religious Faith and Liberal Democracy* (2003).

[7] See Michael J. Perry, *The Idea of Human Rights* (1998); Michael J. Perry, *Toward a Theory of Human Rights: Religion, Law, Courts* (2007).

book, I address all four aspects: grounding, content, implications, and judicial enforcement.[8]

Although broader in scope than I first conceived it, this remains a book about – although, now, only partly about – the proper, *and properly limited*, role of religious faith in the politics and law of a liberal democracy. The religious faith I know best is Christianity; my religious tradition is Roman Catholic. The liberal democracy I know best is the United States. Most of what I say in this book, however, is meant to speak to citizens of every liberal democracy – and to speak to them without regard to whether they are Christians or even religious believers. Nonetheless, the particular perspective from which this book is written – *my* perspective – is that of a citizen of the United States who, like most citizens of the United States, is a Christian.

Of the world's liberal democracies, the United States is one of the most religious.[9] Moreover, the United States, although predominantly Christian, has become one of the most religiously diverse countries in the world.[10] According to a survey published in 2008 by the Pew Forum on Religion and Public Life, three out every four adult Americans identify as members either of a Protestant church or of the Catholic Church: 26.3% as members of "evangelical Protestant churches"; 18.1%, "mainline Protestant churches"; 6.9%, "historically black churches"; and 23.9%, the Catholic Church. Mormons account for only 1.7% of the adult population; Jehovah's Witnesses, 0.7%; Orthodox Christians, 0.6%; and "other Christians," 0.3%. Jews account for 1.7%; Buddhists, 0.7%; Muslims, 0.6%; and Hindus, 0.4%. Adherents of "other world religions" account for less than 0.3%; adherents of "other faiths," 1.2%. Those who identify as "unaffiliated" – a group that includes atheists (1.6%), agnostics (2.4%), and those claiming "nothing in particular" (12.1%) – account for

---

[8] Along the way, I borrow from and develop earlier work.
[9] See Jeffrey L. Sheler, "Faith in America," U.S. NEWS, May 6, 2002, at 40, 42: "The United States may well be, as many experts claim, the most religious of the Western democracies."
[10] See Diana Eck, *A New Religious America: How a "Christian Country" Has Become the World's Most Religiously Diverse Nation* (2001). See also Sheler, n. 9, at 42: "Since the Immigration Act of 1995 eliminated quotas linked to national origin, Muslims, Buddhists, Hindus, Sikhs, Jains, Zoroastrians, and others have arrived in increasing numbers, dramatically altering the religious landscape of many communities.... Nationwide, there are now more Buddhists than Presbyterians and nearly as many Muslims as Jews."

Introduction

16.1%; those who "don't know," 0.8%.¹¹ That the country is both so religious and so religiously diverse helps to explain why in the United States the question of the proper role of religion in politics and law remains hugely controversial even after more than a generation of sustained debate.¹²

During the time I was writing this book, I would occasionally read something – a book, an article, an op-ed piece, or a blog – and get a whiff of a sentiment to the effect that persons of deep religious faith can be, *at best*, only weakly (halfheartedly) committed to liberal democracy.¹³ ("*All* religion is toxic to the liberal project, something we should have learned from the events of September 11, 2001.... Enlightenment rationalism, not religion, made liberal democracy possible."¹⁴) I hope this book demonstrates just how confused and mistaken – indeed, how ignorant – such a sentiment is.¹⁵

---

¹¹ http://religions.pewforum.org/pdf/affiliations-all-traditions.pdf.

¹² Since the early 1980s, a large literature has emerged, principally in the United States, about the legitimacy *vel non* of religiously grounded morality as a basis of law – in particular, of *coercive* law – in a liberal democracy. That literature includes three books of my own. See n. 6. For some other, important contributions to the literature, see Richard John Neuhaus, *The Naked Public Square: Religion and Politics in America* (2d ed. 1986); Kent Greenawalt, *Religious Convictions and Political Choice* (1988); Stephen L. Carter, *The Culture of Disbelief* (1993); Robert Audi & Nicholas Wolterstorff, *Religion in the Public Square: The Place of Religious Convictions in Political Debate* (1997); Kent Greenawalt, *Private Consciences and Public Reasons* (1997); Paul J. Weithman, ed., *Religion and Contemporary Liberalism* (1997); Robert Audi, *Religious Commitment and Secular Reason* (2000); Symposium, "Religiously Based Morality: Its Proper Place in American Law and Public Policy?" 36 WAKE FOREST L. REV. 217–570 (2001); Christopher J. Eberle, *Religious Convictions in Liberal Politics* (2002); Paul J. Weithman, *Religion and the Obligations of Citizenship* (2002); Terence Cuneo, ed., *Religion in the Liberal Polity* (2005).

Not everything I say in this book is consistent with everything I have said in my earlier writings. (For example, in Chapter 6, I argue *for* a position I argued *against* in chapter 2 of *Under God?*, n. 6.) "Only the hand that erases can write the true thing," said Meister Eckhart.

¹³ See, e.g., Mark Lilla, "The Politics of God," NEW YORK TIMES, Aug. 9, 2007; Mark Lilla, *The Stillborn God: Religion, Politics, and the Modern West* (2007); Stanley Fish, "Liberalism and Secularism: One and the Same," NEW YORK TIMES online, http://fish.blogs.nytimes.com/2007/09/02/liberalism-and-secularism-one-and-the-same/.

¹⁴ This is how Thomas F. Farr summarizes the sentiment – which he rejects – in his book *World of Faith and Freedom: Why International Religious Liberty Is Vital to American National Security* (2008), at xi.

¹⁵ In commenting on Lilla's *The Stillborn God* (see n. 13), Damon Linker writes:

> Lilla appears to have been led to this extreme and unconvincing position [that the authenticity of a political-theological view is determined entirely by its willingness to challenge by force of arms the legitimacy of all governments that fall short of complete conformity to divine law] by his desire to place the United

Introduction

Religious believers, no less than nonbelievers, can, and many do, enthusiastically affirm the political morality of liberal democracy; moreover, many religious believers affirm the political morality of liberal democracy partly *on the basis of their religious faith*. Of course, given that the citizenry of liberal democracies – not least, the citizenry of the United States – includes many religious believers, no elaboration of the political morality of liberal democracy according to which religious faith is, as such, necessarily illiberal would be a plausible elaboration.

Again, this book is my contribution to the Christian Jurisprudence Project, sponsored by Emory Law School's Center for the Study of Law and Religion, funded by the Alonzo L. McDonald Family Agape Foundation, and directed by my colleagues (and friends) John Witte Jr. and Frank S. Alexander. I am grateful to John and Frank for inviting me to participate in the project and to the Foundation – in particular, to Ambassador Alonzo McDonald, his son Peter, and the other Foundation Trustees – for generous financial support. I am also grateful, for helpful discussion, to the other participants in the project. Of course, nothing I say in this book necessarily reflects the views of the Foundation or of the Center for the Study of Law and Religion, where I am privileged to be a Senior Fellow.

> States, along with the world's other liberal democracies, firmly on the opposite shore from political theology. . . . The reality, however, is more complicated than this. Not only does the United States need to cope with the political theologies that dominate the Islamic world. Americans who engage in political reflection without reference to religion also need to come to grips with the presence of political theology right here at home – with the fact that millions of their fellow citizens are perfectly comfortable making theological assumptions about the political foundations of the nation, its principles, and its institutions.

Damon Linker, "Political Theology in America," *Cato Unbound*, http://www.cato-unbound.org/2007/10/10/damon-linker/political-theology-in-america/. Micah Watson makes a similar criticism:

> The American constitutional experiment in religious liberty was made possible in part not only by those who adhered to Hobbes's "great separation," but by many who saw religious toleration and church–state separation as themselves reflective of God's will for politics. In other words, Lilla does not consider the possibility that the most authentic *Christian* understanding of the New Testament may very well be congruent with much of the American approach to religion and politics.

Micah Watson, Book Review, 50 J. CHURCH & STATE 158, 159 (2008). See also Daniel Philpott, "Political Theology and Liberal Democracy, The Immanent Frame," http://www.ssrc.org/blogs/immanent_frame/2008/01/23/political-theology-liberal-democracy/.

Introduction

I owe a special word of thanks to the fourteen scholars – philosophers, theologians, and professors of law – who gathered in Atlanta in April 2008, for a roundtable sponsored by the Center for the Study of Law and Religion, to discuss several chapters of this book.

And, as always, I am greatly indebted to my perennially indispensable conversation partners: my students, who in this case include not only my students at Emory Law, where I have taught since August 2003, but also my students at the University of Western Ontario (Canada) School of Law, where I taught a January term course in 2009. While in productive conversation with my students at Western Law, I turned the penultimate draft of this book into the final draft.

Part I
Liberal Democracy, Human Rights, and Religious Faith

1

Liberal Democracy and Human Rights

Not every country that advertises (or advertised) itself as a democracy is (was) in fact a democracy. Two examples: The official name of North Korea, translated into English, is the Democratic People's Republic of Korea; the official name of East Germany, translated into English, was the German Democratic Republic.[1] And not every country that can plausibly advertise itself as a democracy[2] is a *liberal* democracy: a

---

[1] See Kenneth Roth, "Despots Masquerading as Democrats," in human rights watch, WORLD REPORT 1, 7 (2008): "As the Burmese junta rounded up protesting monks and violently suppressed dissent, it spoke of the need for 'disciplined democracy.' China has long promoted 'socialist democracy,' by which it means a top-down centrism that eliminates minority views." See Associated Press, "Report Says Democracies Enable Despots," NEW YORK TIMES, Jan. 31, 2008:

> Authoritarian rulers are violating human rights around the world and getting away with it largely because the U.S., European and other established democracies accepts their claims that holding elections makes them democratic, Human Rights Watch said in its annual report [today].
>
> By failing to demand that offenders honor their citizens' civil and political rights and other requirements of true democracy, Western democracies risk undermining human rights everywhere, the international rights watchdog said.
>
> Still, Kenneth Roth, Human Rights Watch's executive director, wrote in a segment of the report called "Despots Masquerading as Democrats": "It is a sign of hope that even dictators have come to believe that the route to legitimacy runs by way of democratic credentials."

[2] For a "modest" definition of democracy, see Andrew Koppelman, "Talking to the Boss: On Robert Bennett and the Counter-Majoritarian Difficulty," 95 NORTHWESTERN U. L. REV. 955, 956–57 (2001):

> [Joseph] Schumpeter ... proposes the following, more modest definition of democracy: "the democratic method is that institutional arrangement for arriving at political decisions in which individuals acquire the power to decide by means of a competitive struggle for the people's vote." The people influence political decisions by voting in elections and "do not control their political leaders in any way except by refusing to reelect them or the parliamentary majorities that support them." ...
>
> The politician is vulnerable to losing his office unless he continuously manages to attract votes. This creates an incentive for him to pay attention to what voters want. And this incentive guarantees that, in a democracy, the government

democracy committed, first, to the proposition that each and every human being has inherent dignity and is inviolable and, second, to certain human rights against government – that is, against lawmakers and other government officials – such as the right to freedom of religion.³ The union of the two most widely affirmed political-moral

> will not act in a way that attracts the wrath of an electoral majority – or, if it does, that it won't keep it up for long.
>
> (Quoting Joseph A. Schumpeter, *Capitalism, Socialism, and Democracy* [3d ed. 1950].) According to Koppelman, "[Joseph] Schumpeter is entirely free of ... mushy sentimentalism about majoritarianism...." Id. at 956. See also Richard A. Posner, "Enlightened Despot," NEW REPUBLIC, Apr. 23, 2007, at 53, 54: "Political democracy in the modern sense means a system of government in which the key officials stand for election at relatively short intervals and thus are accountable to the citizenry."

³ Not that this is the only way to conceive of what makes a democracy a *liberal* democracy: Not everyone who affirms liberal democracy also affirms the idea of "inherent human dignity." Nonetheless, the conception of liberal democracy articulated in the text is not only common; it is, for many, the most morally attractive conception. Philosopher Thomas Nagel has written that "[t]he term 'liberalism' applies to a wide range of political positions.... But all liberal theories have this in common: they hold that the sovereign power of the state over the individual is bounded by a requirement that individuals remain inviolable in certain respects.... The state ... is subject to moral constraints that limit the subordination of the individual to the collective will and the collective interest." Thomas Nagel, "Progressive but Not Liberal," NEW YORK REV. OF BOOKS, May 25, 2006. Similarly, philosopher Charles Larmore has argued that "our commitment to [liberal] democracy ... cannot be understood except by appeal to a higher moral authority, which is the obligation to respect one another as persons." Charles Larmore, "The Moral Basis of Political Liberalism," 96 J. PHILOSOPHY 599, 624–25 (1999). See also Jeffrey Stout, "A House Founded on the Sea: Is Democracy a Dictatorship of Relativism?," 13 COMMON KNOWLEDGE 385, 387 (2008): "[D]emocracy, rightly understood, derives its legitimacy in part from 'the affirmation that the human person, unlike animals and things, cannot be subjected to domination by others'" (quoting Pope John Paul II, *The Gospel of Life: Evangelium Vitae* 33 [1995]). Cf. Samuel Brittan, "Making Common Cause: How Liberals Differ, and What They Ought To Agree On," TIMES LIT. SUPP., Sept. 20, 1996, at 3, 4:

> [P]erhaps the litmus test of whether the reader is in any sense a liberal or not is Gladstone's foreign-policy speeches. In [one such speech,] taken from the late 1870s, around the time of the Midlothian campaign, [Gladstone] reminded his listeners that "the sanctity of life in the hill villages of Afghanistan among the winter snows, is as inviolable in the eye of almighty God as can be your own ... that the law of mutual love is not limited by the shores of this island, is not limited by the boundaries of Christian civilization; that it passes over the whole surface of the earth, and embraces the meanest along with the greatest in its unmeasured scope." By all means smile at the oratory. But anyone who sneers at the underlying message is not a liberal in any sense of that word worth preserving.

Listen, too, to Herman Melville: "But this august dignity I treat of, is not the dignity of kings and robes, but that abounding dignity that has no robed investiture. Thou shalt see it shining in the arm that wields a pick or drives a spike; that democratic dignity which, on all hands, radiates without end from God Himself! The great God absolute!

ideals of our time – democracy and human rights – yields a third great political-moral ideal: liberal democracy. Or, as Aidan O'Neill has termed it: post-Nuremberg democracy.[4]

To say that a democracy is committed to the proposition that every human being has inherent dignity and is inviolable is to say that in the political culture of the democracy, the proposition is axiomatic. To say that a democracy is committed to a human right against government is to say that in the legal system of the democracy, the right is recognized and protected as a fundamental legal right. More precisely, a democracy is committed to a human right against government, understood as a *moral* claim of a special sort – a moral claim about what government may not do to human beings, or about what government must do for human beings, given that every human being has inherent dignity and is inviolable – if in the legal system of the democracy the moral claim is recognized and protected as a fundamental *legal* claim.

Let's begin our inquiry into the political morality of *liberal* democracy by examining the proposition to which, as I said, liberal democracy is, as such – as *liberal* democracy – committed: Every human being has inherent dignity and is inviolable. I call that proposition, for a reason that will soon be apparent, "the morality of human rights."

I. THE MORALITY OF HUMAN RIGHTS

The name of my state of origin – Kentucky – is said by some to derive from a Native American word meaning "a dark and bloody ground." An apt name for our century of origin is a dark and bloody time – indeed, *the* dark and bloody time: The twentieth century "'was the bloodiest in human existence,' . . . not only because of the total number of deaths attributed to wars – 109 million – but because of the fraction of the population killed by conflicts, more than 10 times more than during the 16th century."[5] However, the list of twentieth-century horrors includes much more than wars. As the century began, King Leopold II of Belgium was presiding over a holocaust in the Congo;

The centre and circumference of all democracy! His omnipresence, our divine equality!" Herman Melville, *Moby Dick* 126 (Penguin Classics ed. 1992).

[4] See Aidan O'Neill, "Roman Catholicism and the Temptation of *Shari'a*," 15 COMMON KNOWLEDGE 269, 297 et seq. (2009).

[5] Kim A. McDonald, "Anthropologists Debate Whether War Is Inevitable among Humans," CHRONICLE OF HIGHER EDUCATION, Nov. 22, 1999 (quoting Carol Nordstrom, an anthropologist at the University of Notre Dame).

it is estimated that between 1880 and 1920, because of a system of slave labor, the population of the Congo "dropped by approximately ten million people."[6] From 1915 to 1923, the Ottoman Turks, who were Muslim, committed genocide against the Armenian minority, who were Christian.[7] Not counting deaths inflicted in battle, Stalin was responsible for the deaths of more than forty-two million people (1929–53); Mao, more than thirty-seven million (1923–76); Hitler, more than twenty million (1933–45), including more than ten million Slavs and about five and a half million Jews.[8] One need only mention these places to recall some more recent atrocities: Cambodia (1975–79), Bosnia (1992–95), Rwanda (1994), and the Darfur region of Sudan (present).[9] And, sadly, there is so much more.[10] For

[6] Adam Hochschild, *King Leopold's Ghost: A Story of Greed, Terror, and Heroism in Colonial Africa* 233 (1998). The causes – all of them related to the system of slave labor – were several: murder, starvation, exhaustion, exposure, disease, and a plummeting birth rate. See id. at 225–34. As Hochschild observes, this was "a death toll of Holocaust dimensions." Id. at 4. The holocaust in the Congo was not an isolated event. See, e.g., Giles Foden, "Rehearsal for Genocide," NEW YORK TIMES BOOK REV., Apr. 20, 2003; Ross A. Slotten, "AIDS in Namibia," 41 SOC. SCI. MED. 277 (1995):

> In 1884, Namibia formally became a German colony and was known as German South West Africa. During the time of annexation, the Herero and Nama peoples were the largest tribes, inhabiting the most desirable land, which the Germans gradually expropriated between 1893 and 1903. This expropriation led to many battles, culminating in the intentional genocide of 60% of the population. To this day, the Hereros and Namas have not recovered their original numerical strength.

[7] See Israel W. Charney, ed., *I Encyclopedia of Genocide* 61–105 (1999). See also Peter Balakian, *The Burning Tigris: The Armenian Genocide and America's Response* (2003).

[8] See Charney, n. 7, at 29 (Table 5). "[The Nazi] genocides likely cost the lives of about 16,300,000 people: nearly 5,300,000 Jews, 260,000 Gypsies, 10,500,000 Slavs, and 220,000 homosexuals, as well as another 10,000 handicapped Germans." Id. at 439. "The Nazi genocide against the Jews – the Holocaust, as it has generally come to be known as – is estimated to have resulted in the murder of about five and a half million Jews in Nazi-occupied Europe, around half the number targeted in the notorious Wannsee Conference of January 1942." Ian Kershaw, "Afterthought: Some Reflections on Genocide, Religion, and Modernity," in Omer Bartov & Phyllis Mack, eds., *In God's Name: Genocide and Religion in the Twentieth Century* 377 (2001).

[9] For a narrative of the failures of the United States to respond to recent genocides, see Samantha Power, *"A Problem from Hell": America and the Age of Genocide* (2002).

[10] See, e.g., Mark Danner, *The Massacre at El Mozote: A Parable of the Cold War* (1994); Iris Chang, *The Rape of Nanking: The Forgotten Holocaust of World War II* (1997); Philip Dray, *At the Hands of Persons Unknown: The Lynching of Black America* viii (2002): "Through 1944, when lynchings first began to decline strongly, [the Tuskegee Institute] recorded 3,417 lynchings of blacks.... Not until 1952 did a year pass without a single recorded lynching." See generally Jonathan Glover, *Humanity: A Moral History of the Twentieth Century* (1999).

an exhaustive and exhausting account of the grim details, one can consult the two-volume *Encyclopedia of Genocide*, which reports:

> In total, during the first eighty-eight years of [the twentieth] century, almost 170 million men, women, and children were shot, beaten, tortured, knifed, burned, starved, frozen, crushed, or worked to death; buried alive, drowned, hanged, bombed, or killed in any other of the myriad other ways governments have inflicted deaths on unarmed, helpless citizens and foreigners. Depending on whether one used high or more conservative estimates, the dead could conceivably be more than 360 million people. It is as though our species has been devastated by a modern Black Plague.[11]

In the midst of the countless grotesque inhumanities of the twentieth century, however, there is a heartening story, amply recounted elsewhere:[12] the emergence, after World War II, of the international law of human rights. ("Until World War II, most legal scholars and governments affirmed the general proposition, albeit not in so many words, that international law did not impede the natural right of each

---

[11] Charney, n. 7, at 28. "[G]enocide – intentional acts to elimate in whole, or in substantial part, a specific human population – [has] claimed the lives of some 60 million people in the 20th century, 16 million of them since 1945, when the watchword was 'Never again.' Genocide has, in fact, been so frequent, the number of victims so extensive, and serious attempts to prevent it so few, that many scholars have described the 20th century as 'the age of genocide.'" Roger W. Smith, "American Self-Interest and the Response to Genocide," CHRONICLE OF HIGHER EDUCATION, July 30, 2004.

It bears emphasis here that "religion has played an important role in several outbreaks of genocide since World War I." Omer Bartov & Phyllis Mack, "Introduction," in Bartov & Mack, n. 8, at 1. But the role religion has played is not invariably negative, as Bartov and Mack explain:

> Violence and religion have been closely associated in a variety of intricate, often contradictory ways, since the earliest periods of human civilization. Institutionalized religions have practiced violence against both their adherents and their real or imagined opponents. Conversely, religions have also been known to limit social and political violence and to provide spiritual and material comfort to its victims. Religious faith can thus generate contradictory attitudes, either motivating aggression or restraining it. Individual perpetrators and victims of violence can seek in religious institutions and personal faith both a rationale for atrocity, a justification to resist violence, or a means to come to terms with the legacy of destruction by integrating it into a wider historical or theological context.

Id. Cf. Os Guinness, "On Faith," WILSON QUARTERLY, Spring 2005: "It's a simple fact, for example, that, contrary to the current scapegoating of religion, more people were slaughtered during the 20th century under secularist regimes, led by secularist intellectuals, and in the name of secularist ideologies, than in all the religious persecutions in Western history."

[12] See, e.g., Louis B. Sohn, "The New International Law: Protection of the Rights of Individuals Rather Than States," 32 AMERICAN U. L. REV. 1 (1982); Robert F. Drinan, *Cry of the Oppressed: The History and Hope of the Human Rights Revolution* (1987).

equal sovereign to be monstrous to his or her subjects."[13]) Indeed, in the final decade of the twentieth century, the Security Council of the United Nations went so far as to establish two international criminal tribunals, one (in 1993) to deal with atrocities committed in the former Yugoslavia since 1991 and the other (in 1994) to deal with atrocities committed in Rwanda in 1994. (In 2001, pursuant to the Rome Statute of the International Criminal Court [1998], the International Criminal Court was established, with jurisdiction over the crime of genocide, crimes against humanity, war crimes, and the crime of aggression.[14]) The twentieth century, therefore, was not only the dark and bloody time; the second half of the twentieth century was also the time in which a growing number of states the world over responded to the savage horrors of the twentieth century by establishing the international law of human rights, thereby rendering the moral landscape of the twentieth century a touch less bleak.[15]

---

[13] Tom J. Farer & Felice Gaer, "The UN and Human Rights: At the End of the Beginning," in Adam Roberts & Benedict Kingsbury, eds., *United Nations, Divided World* 240 (2d ed. 1993).

[14] See Henry J. Steiner, Philip Alston, & Ryan Goodman, *International Human Rights in Context: Law, Politics, Morals* 1291–310 (3d ed. 2008); Benjamin N. Schiff, *Building the International Criminal Court* (2008).

[15] Much of the international law of human rights consists of rules contained in human rights treaties, which are legally binding only in the states that have become parties to the treaties. But some of the international law of human rights consists of rules that are legally binding in every state, such as the rules pertaining to the crime of genocide, crimes against humanity, war crimes, and the crime of aggression. On those four categories of crime, see the Rome Statute of the International Criminal Court, Arts. 6–8, which, like every other human rights law or document I refer to in this chapter, is available on the web and, thanks to Google, easily accessible.

Regrettably, the international law of human rights has been much less consequential than many hoped it would be. As I was drafting this book (May 2008), Amnesty International issued its 2008 Report, the foreword to which states:

> World leaders owe an apology for failing to deliver on the promise of justice and equality in the Universal Declaration of Human Rights, adopted 60 years ago [1948]. In the past six decades, many governments have shown more interest in the abuse of power or in the pursuit of political self-interest, than in respecting the rights of those they lead. This is not to deny that progress has been made.... But for all the good, the fact remains that injustice, inequality and impunity are still the hallmarks of our world today.

Amnesty International Report 2008, *State of the World's Human Rights* 3 (2008). Moreover, the Report "assailed the moral leadership of the United States, saying that, as 'the world's most powerful state' it 'sets the standard for government behavior globally.' But, Amnesty International said, the United States had 'distinguished itself in recent years through its defiance of international law.'" Alan Cowell, "Human Rights Report

The law of human rights is one thing, the morality of human rights, another. By "the morality of human rights," I mean the morality that, according to the International Bill of Human Rights, is the principal ground of – the principal warrant for – the law of human rights. The morality of human rights is not the only ground of the law of human rights,[16] but it is, according to the International Bill of Human Rights, the principal ground, as I am about to explain.

The International Bill of Human Rights, as it is known,[17] consists of three documents: the Universal Declaration of Human Rights, the International Covenant on Civil and Political Rights, and the International Covenant on Economic, Social, and Cultural Rights.[18] The Universal Declaration refers, in its preamble, to "the inherent dignity... of all members of the human family" and states, in Article 1, that "[a]ll members of the human family are born free and

---

Assails U.S.," NEW YORK TIMES, May 29, 2008. Cf. Samuel Moyn, "On the Genealogy of Morals," THE NATION, Apr. 16, 2007, at 25:

> Even those who retain an investment in human rights cannot treat them as an unquestionable good, mainly because the America that once seemed to many enthusiasts to be the prospective servant of universality abroad all too quickly became the America pursuing low-minded imperial ambitions in high-minded humanitarian tones. The effect on human rights as a public language and political cause has been staggering, and it is not yet clear whether they can recover.

It bears mention that one can affirm the international law of human rights *in general* without affirming each and every provision one finds in the international law of human rights. Indeed, one can affirm the international law of human rights in general while thinking that some of the provisions one finds there do not belong there. See, e.g., James Griffin, *On Human Rights* 191–211 (2008).

[16] See Michael J. Perry, *Toward a Theory of Human Rights* 25–26 (2007).
[17] See Office of the High Commissioner for Human Rights, Fact Sheet No. 2 (Rev. 1): The International Bill of Human Rights, http://www.unhchr.ch/html/menu6/2/fs2.htm.
[18] The Universal Declaration was adopted and proclaimed by the General Assembly of the United Nations on Dec. 10, 1948. The International Covenant on Civil and Political Rights (ICCPR) and the International Covenant on Economic, Social, and Cultural Rights (ICESCR), which are treaties and as such are binding on the several state parties thereto, were meant, in part, to elaborate the various rights specified in the Universal Declaration. The ICCPR and the ICESCR were each adopted and opened for signature, ratification, and accession by the General Assembly of the United Nations on Dec. 16, 1966. The ICESCR entered into force on Jan. 3, 1976, and as of January 2007 had 155 state parties. The ICCPR entered into force on Mar. 23, 1976, and as of January 2007 had 160 state parties. The United States is a party to the ICCPR but not to the ICESCR. In October 1977, President Jimmy Carter signed both the ICCPR and the ICESCR. Although the U.S. Senate has not ratified the ICESCR, in September 1992, with the support of President George H. W. Bush, the Senate ratified the ICCPR (subject to certain "reservations, understandings and declarations" that are not relevant here; see 138 CONG. REC. S 4781–84 [daily ed. Apr. 2, 1992]).

equal in dignity and rights... and should act towards one another in a spirit of brotherhood." The two covenants each refer, in their preambles, to "the inherent dignity... of all members of the human family" and to "the inherent dignity of the human person" – from which, the covenants insist, "the equal and inalienable rights of all members of the human family... derive."[19]

According to the International Bill of Human Rights, then – and also according to the constitutions of many liberal democracies[20] – the morality of human rights consists of two connected claims, the first of which is this: *Each and every (born) human being has equal inherent dignity.*[21]

- *The Oxford English Dictionary* gives this as the principal definition of "dignity": "The quality of being worthy or honourable; worthiness, worth, nobleness, excellence."[22]
- To say that every human being has "inherent" dignity is to say that the fundamental dignity every human being possesses, she possesses *not* as a member of one or another group (racial, ethnic, national, religious, etc.), *not* as a man or a woman, *not* as someone who has done or achieved something, and so on, *but simply as a human being*.[23]

[19] The relevant wording of the two preambles is as follows:
The State Parties to the present Covenant,
  Considering that... recognition of the inherent dignity and of the equal and inalienable rights of all members of the human family is the foundation of freedom, justice, and peace in the world.
  Recognizing that these rights derive from the inherent dignity of the human person.
    ...
  Agree upon the following articles:...

[20] See David Kretzmer & Eckart Klein, eds., *The Concept of Human Dignity in Human Rights Discourse* v–vi, 41–42 (2002); Vicki C. Jackson, "Constitutional Dialogue and Human Dignity: States and Transnational Constitutional Discourse," 65 MONTANA L. REV. 15 (2004); Mirko Bagaric & James Allan, "The Vacuous Concept of Dignity," 5 J. HUMAN RIGHTS 257, 261–63 (2006).

[21] As a descriptive matter, the morality of human rights holds not that every human being has inherent dignity, but only that every *born* human being has inherent dignity. See Perry, n. 16, at 54. Except when discussing abortion, I generally bracket the born/unborn distinction and say simply that according to the morality of human rights, every human being has inherent dignity. I have argued elsewhere that one who affirms that every born human being has inherent dignity has good reason to affirm as well that every unborn human being has inherent dignity. See id. at 54–59.

[22] *Oxford English Dictionary* (2d ed. 1991).

[23] The ICCPR, in Article 26, bans "discrimination on any ground such as race, colour, sex, language, religion, political or other opinion, national or social origin, property, birth

- To say that every human being has "equal" inherent dignity is to say that, like being pregnant, being "inherently dignified" is not a condition that admits of degrees: Just as no pregnant woman can be more – or less – pregnant than another pregnant woman, no human being can have more – or less – inherent dignity than another human being. According to the morality of human rights, "[a]ll members of the human family are born . . . equal in dignity. . . ." Hereafter, when I say "inherent dignity," I mean "equal inherent dignity."[24]

This is the second claim: *The inherent dignity of human beings has a normative force for us, in this sense: We should – every one of us – live our lives in accord with the fact that every human being has inherent dignity; we should respect – we have conclusive reason to respect – the inherent dignity of every human being.*

There is another way to state the second claim: *Every human being is "inviolable": not to be violated.*[25] According to the morality of human rights, one can violate a human being either explicitly or implicitly. One violates a human being *explicitly* if one explicitly denies that she (or he) has inherent dignity. (The Nazis explicitly denied that the

---

or other status." See Peter Berger, "On the Obsolescence of the Concept of Honor," in Stanley Hauerwas & Alasdair MacIntyre, eds., *Revisions: Changing Perspectives in Moral Philosophy* 172, 176 (1983): "Dignity . . . always relates to the intrinsic humanity divested of all socially imposed roles or norms. It pertains to the self as such, to the individual regardless of his position in society. This becomes very clear in the classic formulations of human rights, from the Preamble to the Declaration of Independence to the Universal Declaration of Human Rights of the United Nations." Cf. Charles E. Curran, *Catholic Social Teaching: A Historical and Ethical Analysis 1891–Present* 132 (2002): "Human dignity comes from God's free gift; it does not depend on human effort, work, or accomplishments. All human beings have a fundamental, equal dignity because all share the generous gift of creation and redemption from God. . . . Consequently, all human beings have the same fundamental dignity, whether they are brown, black, red, or white; rich or poor, young or old; male or female; healthy or sick."

[24] For a discussion of the concept of human dignity, and of the role the concept has played in various contexts (Western thought, legal discourse, judicial discourse, and transnational judicial conversations), see Christopher McCrudden, "Human Dignity" (2006), http://ssrn.com/abstract=899687. See also Doron Shultziner, "Human Dignity – Functions and Meanings," *Global Jurist Topics* (2003), http://www.bepress.com/gj/topics/vol3/iss3/art3. For a skeptical account of talk about human dignity, see Bagaric & Allan, n. 20. "Dignity is a vacuous concept." Id. at 269.

[25] For a general definition of what it means to say that one is "inviolable," see *Oxford English Dictionary* (2d ed. 1991): "not to be violated; not liable or allowed to suffer violence; to be kept sacredly free from profanation, infraction, or assault."

Jews had inherent dignity.²⁶) One violates a human being *implicitly* if one treats her as if she lacks inherent dignity, either by doing to her what one would not do to her, or by refusing to do for her what one would not refuse to do for her, if one genuinely perceived her to have inherent dignity. (Even if the Nazis had not explicitly denied that the Jews had inherent dignity, they would have implicitly denied it: The Nazis did to the Jews what no one who genuinely perceived them to have inherent dignity, would have done.) In the context of the morality of human rights, to say that (1) every human being has inherent dignity and we should live our lives accordingly (namely, in a way that respects that dignity) is to say that (2) every human being has inherent dignity and is inviolable: not to be violated, in the sense of "violate" just indicated. To affirm the morality of human rights is to affirm that every human being has inherent dignity and is inviolable.

II. FROM MORALITY TO LAW

Again, by the morality of human rights I mean the morality that, according to the International Bill of Human Rights, is the principal ground of the law of human rights.²⁷ How, precisely, does the morality of human rights ground the law, including the international law, of human rights?

The morality of human rights holds that every human being has inherent dignity and is inviolable. So we who affirm the morality of human rights, *because* we affirm it, should do what we can, all things considered – we have conclusive reason to do what we can, all things considered – to prevent human beings, including government officials, from doing things that violate human beings either explicitly or implicitly.²⁸ (The "doing" may be a not-doing, a refusal to help.)

---

[26] See Michael Burleigh & Wolfgang Wipperman, *The Racial State: Germany, 1933–1945* (1991); Johannes Morsink, "World War Two and the Universal Declaration," 15 HUMAN RIGHTS Q. 357, 363 (1993); Claudia Koonz, *The Nazi Conscience* (2003).

[27] See Griffin, n. 15, at 156, referring to "the ground of human rights that the United Nations has adopted: the dignity of the human person." Actually, the ground of human rights the United Nations has adopted, in the International Bill of Human Rights, is the equal inherent dignity of the (born) human being.

[28] The "all things considered" will be, in many contexts, indeterminate. What Amartya Sen, borrowing from Immanuel Kant, calls the distinction between "perfect" and "imperfect" duties is relevant here – although I would mark the distinction with different terms: "determinate" and "indeterminate" duties. As Sen remarks, "[t]he perfectly specified demand not to torture anyone is supplemented by the more general, and less easily

Moreover, we who affirm the morality of human rights, *because* we affirm it, have conclusive reason to do what we can, all things considered, to *do more than* prevent human beings from doing things that violate human beings: We also have conclusive reason to do what we can, all things considered, to prevent human beings from doing things that, even if they do not violate human beings, even implicitly, nonetheless cause them unwarranted suffering (or other harm). (I am referring here to serious, not trivial, human suffering. Although some serious suffering is physical in nature, much serious suffering is not physical but, for want of a better word, emotional.[29]) In Germany during World War II, Dietrich Bonhoeffer observed that "[w]e have for once learned to see the great events of world history from below,

> specified, requirement to consider the ways and means through which torture can be prevented and then to decide what one should, thus, reasonably do." Amartya Sen, "Elements of a Theory of Human Rights," 32 PHILOSOPHY & PUBLIC AFFAIRS 315, 322 (2004). Sen elaborates:
>> Even though recognition of human rights (with their associated claims and obligations) are ethical affirmations, they need not, by themselves, deliver a complete blueprint for evaluative assessment. An agreement of human rights does involve a firm commitment, to wit, to give reasonable consideration to the duties that follow from that ethical endorsement. But even with agreement on these affirmations, there can still be serious debates, particularly in the case of imperfect obligations, on (i) the ways in which the attention that is owed to human rights should be best paid, (ii) how the different types of human rights should be weighed against each other and their respective demands integrated together, (iii) how the claims of human rights should be consolidated with other evaluative concerns that may also deserve ethical attention, and so on. A theory of human rights can leave room for further discussions, disputations and arguments. The approach of open public reasoning ... can definitively settle some disputes about coverage and content (including the identification of some clearly sustainable rights and others that would be hard to sustain), but may have to leave others, at least tentatively, unsettled. The admissibility of a domain of continued dispute is no embarrassment to a theory of human rights.
>
> Id. at 322–23.

[29] It is easy enough to identify the kind of suffering government imposes on human beings, or threatens to impose on them, in consequence of their violating, for example, a criminal ban on their practicing their religion: at the very least, the suffering that attends one's loss of liberty. But, of course, not everyone will choose to violate the ban. What kind of suffering is endured by human beings in consequence of their choosing not to violate the ban – in consequence, that is, of their bowing to the ban and not practicing their religion? It is the serious and sometimes traumatic emotional (psychological) suffering that attends one's being prevented from living a life of religious *integrity* – that is, from living one's life in harmony with the yield of one's religious conscience, with one's religious convictions and commitments. The kind of suffering endured by human beings in consequence of being prevented from practicing their religion is, in that sense, the dis-integration of their lives.

from the perspective of the outcast, the suspects, the maltreated, the powerless, the oppressed, the reviled – in short, from the perspective of those who suffer."[30] If we refuse to do what we can (all things considered) to prevent human beings from violating others or otherwise causing them unwarranted suffering – and by "we" I mean here primarily the collective we, as in "We the People," acting through our elected representatives – we refuse to do what we can to protect the victims *and thereby violate them*: We treat them – "those who suffer" – as if they lack inherent dignity by refusing to do for them what no one who genuinely perceived them to have inherent dignity would refuse to do. Primo Levi wrote that "if we see the severe torment that pain is causing, and do nothing, then we ourselves are the Tormenter."[31] Martin Luther King, Jr., declared, in the same spirit, that "[m]an's inhumanity to man is not only perpetrated by the vitriolic actions of those who are bad. It is also perpetrated by the vitiating inaction of those who are good."[32] Sometimes we violate a human being not by doing something to hurt her but by refusing to do something to protect her. "Sins against human rights are not only those of commission, but those of omission as well."[33]

To say, in the present context, that an instance of human suffering is "unwarranted" is to say that the act that causes the suffering – even if it is a refusal to act, a refusal to intervene to diminish the suffering – is not warranted, that it is not justified. It is scarcely surprising that those whose act is in question judge, or pretend to judge, the act, and therefore the suffering it causes, to be justified. However, we who enounter the suffering – who come face to face with "those who suffer" – must decide what, if anything, we should do, or try to do, about the suffering, and in the course of making that decision, we must reach our own judgment about whether the suffering is warranted.

We can now see how the morality of human rights grounds the law, including the international law, of human rights – how, that is, a

---

[30] Dietrich Bonhoeffer, "After Ten Years: A Letter to the Family and Conspirators," in Dietrich Bonhoeffer, *A Testament to Freedom* 482, 486 (Geoffrey B. Kelly & F. Burton Nelson, eds.; rev. ed.; HarperSanFrancisco 1995). "After Ten Years" bears the date "Christmas 1942."
[31] I have not been able to locate the source of this statement.
[32] Quoted in Nicholas D. Kristof, "The American Witness," NEW YORK TIMES, Mar. 2, 2005.
[33] Charles L. Black, Jr., *A New Birth of Freedom: Human Rights, Named and Unnamed* 133 (1999).

commitment to the morality of human rights – to the inherent dignity and inviolability of every human being – grounds a commitment to recognizing and protecting certain moral rights as fundamental legal rights: We who affirm the morality of human rights, *because* we affirm it, should press our elected representatives not to violate human beings – *any* human beings – or otherwise cause them unwarranted suffering; *but we should also press them to recognize and protect certain moral claims as fundamental legal claims: moral claims about what may not be done to human beings, or about what must be done for human beings, especially by government, given that every human being has inherent dignity and is inviolable.* As we have learned in the period since the end of World War II, the law of human rights is one way of trying to prevent governments – and others[34] – from violating human beings or otherwise causing them unwarranted suffering.[35]

III. UNDERSTANDING RIGHTS-TALK: LEGALITY, MORALITY, UNIVERSALITY

When talking about rights, including human rights, either as legal or as moral concepts, to say that one has a "right" is to say that one has a justified claim. To say "A has a legal right that B not do X to him" is to say "A has a justified claim that B's doing X to him is legally forbidden." (To say "A has a legal right that B do Y for him" is to say "A has a justified claim that B's doing Y for him is legally required.") Similarly, to say "A has a moral right that B not do X to him" is to

---

[34] See Henry J. Steiner, "Human Rights: The Deepening Footprint," 20 HARVARD HUMAN RIGHTS J. 7, 9 (2007):

> Increasingly, international norms and institutions are reaching beyond the state to regulate large categories of non-state actors, from political associations and business corporations to ordinary individuals. They do so directly under international law, through treaty norms defining personal international crimes like crimes against humanity that cover state and non-state actors. They also do so indirectly, and far more broadly, by requiring state parties to protect their population against rights-violating conduct of non-state actors, often through treaties that specify what non-state activity – such as discriminatory corporate employment, or family violence – the state must proscribe and act against. Whatever its accuracy at the movement's foundation, the notion that the human rights movement regulates only state conduct is at best an historical observation. As it develops, human rights law continues to erode the long-standing notion of a public – private divide, in the sense of state and non-state actors, where only the former is subject to regulation under international law.

[35] See Thomas Buergenthal, "The Evolving International Human Rights System," 100 AMERICAN J. INT'L L. 783 (2006).

say "A has a justified claim that B's doing X to him is morally wrong." Morally "wrong," that is, in the sense of morally forbidden: forbidden by true morality, correctly informed.

"A has a justified claim that B's doing X to him is legally forbidden." Such a claim can be translated, and typically is translated, into the language of rights – the language, that is, of *legal* rights: "A has a legal right that B not do X to him." (Such a claim can also be translated into the language of legal duties: "B has a legal duty not to do X to A.") Many people talk about human rights not only as legal concepts but also as moral concepts. "A has a justified claim that, because he has inherent dignity, B's doing X to him is morally wrong." That way of talking leads naturally to: "B's not doing X to A is morally right (because A has inherent dignity)." And *that* way of talking, in turn, leads naturally to: "A has a moral right – a moral human right – that B not do X to him. "[T]he idea of a [moral] human right grew out of a transmutation of the discourse of *what is* actually [morally] right into the discourse of *having* a natural right."[36]

However, some people are wary about translating claims about what it is morally wrong to do (and the equivalent claims about what it is morally right to do) into the language of rights – the language, that is, of moral rights. (Or, correlatively, into the language of moral duties.) As James Nickel has observed, "[i]t is often claimed that a 'right' is mainly a legal notion, ... and that non-legal rights are mainly phony rights."[37] The sentiment to which Nickel refers brings to mind Jeremy Bentham's famous dismissal of the language of "natural" rights:

> Of a natural right who has any idea? I, for my part, have none: a natural right is a round square – an incorporeal body. What a legal right is I know. I know how it was made. I know what it means when made. To me a right and a legal right are the same thing.... Right and law are correlative terms: as much so as son and father. Right is with me the child of law: from different operations of the law result different sorts of rights.[38]
>
> *Right*, the substantive *right*, is the child of law: from *real* laws come *real* rights, but from laws of nature, fancied and invented by poets, rhetoricians,

---

[36] Griffin, n. 15, at 94. But cf. id. at 272: "[I]t is distinctly counter-intuitive to express *all* [moral] claims in terms of rights."
[37] James W. Nickel, *Making Sense of Human Rights* (2d ed., 2007).
[38] Jeremy Bentham, "Supply Without Burthen or Escheat *Vice* Taxation," in Jeremy Waldron, ed., *Nonsense Upon Stilts: Bentham, Burke and Marx on the Rights of Man* 70, 72–73 (1987).

and dealers in moral and intellectual poisons come *imaginary* rights, a bastard brood of monsters, "gorgons and chimeras dire."³⁹

Natural rights is simple nonsense: natural and imprescriptible rights, rhetorical nonsense – nonsense upon stilts.⁴⁰

As Amartya Sen has observed, "[Bentham's] suspicion remains very alive today, and despite the persistent use of the idea of human rights in practical affairs, there are many who see the idea of human rights as no more than 'bawling upon paper,' to use another of Bentham's barbed portrayals of natural rights claims."⁴¹

Again, Nickel: "If legal rights provide the model, moral rights may be thought of as phony rights, as lacking key features that real rights have." What "key features" may moral rights, as distinct from legal rights, be thought to lack? The principal such feature is enforceability. Legal rights are, as such, enforceable (even if, for good reasons or bad, legal rights are not always enforced) by the political community that has established the rights. Social rights too – rights that, although they do not have the status of law in a particular community, are nonetheless widely regarded by members of the community as authoritative for the community – are, as such, enforceable by the social community: by shaming, for example, or by shunning. In what way, if any, are moral rights – that is, moral rights as such, and not, for example, as social rights – enforceable?

For one who believes that God enforces, or can enforce, true moral rights, by somehow holding accountable those who violate the rights, moral rights too are enforceable. But for one who is not a theist – or for a theist who does not believe that God holds accountable those who violate true moral rights – moral rights are not, as such, enforceable. Some who fit that profile – not a theist, or a theist but not one who believes that God holds rights violators accountable – concur in Raymond Geuss's position that "essential to the existence of a set of 'rights' [is] that there be some specifiable and more or less effective mechanism for enforcing them."⁴² Consider, too, Alasdair

---

³⁹ Jeremy Bentham, "Anarchical Fallacies," in id. at 46, 69.
⁴⁰ Id. at 53.
⁴¹ Sen, n. 28, at 316.
⁴² Raymond Geuss, *History and Illusion in Politics* 143 (2001). For a critique of Geuss's position, see John Tasioulas, "The Moral Reality of Human Rights," in Thomas Pogge, ed., *Freedom from Poverty as a Human Right: Who Owes What to the Very Poor?* 75, 79–88 (2007).

MacIntyre's statement: "[W]henever [there is] good reason for describing transactions in [the language of rights], it is always in virtue of the existence ... of some particular set of institutional arrangements requiring description in those terms, and the rights in question therefore will always be institutionally conferred, institutionally recognized and institutionally enforced rights."[43] (Shouldn't MacIntyre have said "socially" rather than "institutionally"?)

Some even suggest that nothing of consequence is lost if we stop translating claims about what it is morally wrong (not) to do into the language of moral rights:

> [T]he ancients and the medievals did not have the notion of a right – was their moral life stunted in some way as a result? Did they lack the tools for dealing with certain aspects of the moral enterprise? Among them moral questions were dealt with in terms of what is [morally] right and wrong, what is in accordance with or required by the natural law, what people ought to do or are obliged to do, but not in terms of what someone has a right to, or has a right to do.[44]

Now, contrast to the foregoing statement what John Finnis has said, in *Natural Law and Natural Rights*, about the utility of moral-rights-talk:

> [T]he modern vocabulary and grammar of rights is [an] instrument for reporting and asserting the requirements of other implications of a relationship of justice *from the point of view of the person(s) who benefit(s) from that relationship*. It provides a way of talking about "what is just" from a special angle: the viewpoint of the "other(s)" to whom something (including, *inter alia*, freedom of choice) is owed or due, and who would be wronged if denied that something. . . . The modern language of rights provides a supple and potentially precise instrument for sorting out and expressing the demands of justice.[45]

---

[43] Quoted in Nicholas Wolterstorff, *Justice: Rights and Wrongs* 32 (2008).

[44] Theodore M. Benditt, RIGHTS 3 (1982). See also John Finnis, *Natural Law and Natural Rights* 209–10 (1980): "[I]t is salutary to bear in mind that the modern emphasis on the power of the right-holder, and the consequent systematic bifurcation between 'right' (including 'liberty') and 'duty', is something that sophisticated lawyers were able to do without for the whole life of classical Roman law." Cf. Griffin, n. 15, at 94: "Ethics ... could do without the discourse of [human] rights and still say all that is necessary to it."

[45] Finnis, n. 45, at 205, 210. However, Finnis adds, as a cautionary note, that moral rights-talk "is often, though not inevitably or irremediably, a hindrance to clear thought when the question is: What are the demands of justice?" Id. at 210.

James Griffin makes a more focused point: not about moral-rights-talk generally but about a particular kind of moral-rights-talk: human-rights-talk:

> [T]he discourse [of moral human rights] has distinct merits. It focuses and gives prominence to obligations that arise, not from social status or special talents and skills, but from the dignity of human status itself. The dignity of human status itself is not the only, or the most, important moral status that human beings have. The case for singling it out is largely practical. Ring-fencing this particular status gives it prominence, ease of transmission, enhanced effectiveness in our social life, and indeed in our moral life, and so on.[46]

I concur in Finnis's statement – and in Griffin's.

In any event, moral-rights-talk – the expression of moral claims in the language of moral rights – will no doubt continue to be a common feature not only of moral discourse about human rights but also of moral discourse generally.[47] And I can't see that there's anything to be gained by refusing to make peace with that state of affairs.[48]

Now, a brief comment on the sense in which human rights – both human rights of the legal sort and human rights of the moral sort – are, as such, universal, and on the different sense in which human rights are not necessarily universal.

A right, whether moral or legal, is universal in scope if it specifies what A is not to do to *any* human being, or what A is to do for *every* human being. Most of the legal rights that constitute the international law of human rights – the human right not to be tortured – are universal in scope: A is not to torture any human being. However, some of the legal rights that constitute the international law of human rights specify what A is not to do to *some* human beings – children,[49] for example, or prisoners; and some specify what A is to do for *some* human beings – for example, impoverished human beings living in

---

[46] Griffin, n. 15, at 94.
[47] See Bagaric & Allan, n. 20, at 257: "[T]here is today, more than ever before, a strong tendency to advance virtually all moral claims and arguments in terms of rights. The assertion of [moral] rights has become the customary means for most of us – at least in the developed world – to express our moral sentiments...."
[48] But cf. Griffin, n. 15, at 95: "We have constantly to remind ourselves of the destructive modern tendency to turn all important moral matters into matters of rights, especially of human rights."
[49] See the Convention on the Rights of the Child.

an affluent society. It is implicit in the international law of human rights, therefore, that what makes a legal right a *human* right is not the right is universal in scope: Again, some of the legal rights that constitute the international law of human rights are not universal in scope. What makes a legal right, even a legal right that is not universal in scope, a *human* right is that establishing and protecting the right as a legal right is a way of taking seriously the morality of human rights; it is a way of taking seriously, that is, the proposition that *all* human beings – *even* children, *even* prisoners, *even* the impoverished – have inherent dignity and are inviolable; establishing and protecting the right as a legal right is a way of protecting human beings, *whether all human beings or just some*, from being violated or otherwise subjected to unwarranted suffering. It is because children (*even* children) and prisoners (*even* prisoners) and the impoverished (*even* the impoverished) have inherent dignity and are inviolable that we must protect them. According to the international law of human rights, that a legal right is not universal in scope does not entail that the right is not a human right. And, for the same reason, that a moral right is not universal in scope does not entail that the right is not a human right. Some nonuniversal (in scope) moral rights are human rights, namely, those that specify what is owed to *some* human beings in virtue of the fact that *all* human beings have inherent dignity and are inviolable.[50]

---

[50] It is common to think that the fact that a right is not universal in scope entails that the right is not truly a human right. See, e.g., Wolterstorff, n. 43, at 313–16. At one point in his book on human rights, James Griffin seems to acknowledge that human rights can be nonuniversal in scope; he refers to both to "basic, universal human rights" and to "derived, non-universal human rights got by applying basic rights to particular circumstances." Griffin, n. 15, at 39. But at another point in his book, Griffin states that "[a] human right is a claim of all human agents against all other human agents." Id. at 177.

It bears mention that Griffin's statement that "a human right is a claim . . . against all other human agents" is plainly false: Many human rights (of the moral as well as the legal sort) are claims against only some other human agents – for example, government officials. Assuming that the right not to be deprived of one's liberty without (what Americans call) due process of law is a human right, it is a right one has, not against "all other human agents," but against those government officials authorized (under certain conditions) to deprive one of one's liberty.

2

Liberal Democracy and Religious Faith

[The] affirmation of universal human rights [that characterizes] modern liberal political culture [represents an] authentic development[] of the gospel....
– Charles Taylor[1]

One sometimes encounters the ignorant sentiment that persons of deep religious faith cannot truly embrace liberal democracy.[2] Again, my principal focus in this book is the liberal democracy of which I am a citizen: the United States. Most citizens of the United States are religious believers,[3] and for most of them, their religious faith gives them a powerful reason to hold liberal democracy within their embrace:

1. It is a part of the content of the religious faith of most citizens of the United States that every human being has inherent dignity and is inviolable.
2. A liberal democracy is, as such – as a *liberal* democracy – committed to the proposition that every human being has inherent dignity and is inviolable.
3. So the religious faith of most citizens of the United States gives them a powerful reason to embrace liberal democracy.

Let me elaborate.

---

[1] Charles Taylor, *A Catholic Modernity?* 16 (1999). Taylor then hastens to add "that modern culture, in breaking with the structures and beliefs of Christendom, also carried certain facets of Christian life further than they ever were taken or could have been taken within Christendom. In relation to the earlier forms of Christian culture, we have to face the humbling realization that the breakout was a necessary condition of the development." Id. For Taylor's development of this point, with particular reference to modern liberal political culture's affirmation of universal human rights, see id. at 18–19. Cf. Charles Taylor, "Closed World Structures," in Mark A. Wrathall, ed., *Religion after Metaphysics* 47, 53–54, & 61 (2003).
[2] See introduction, n. 13.
[3] See introduction, n. 11.

The morality of human rights is as close to a global morality as we human beings have ever achieved (or probably will ever achieve); and, relatedly, the language of human rights has become the moral *lingua franca*.[4] Nonetheless, this fundamental question remains: Is the morality of human rights true?

Recall from the preceding chapter that the morality of human rights consists of two connected claims:

1. Every human being has (equal) inherent dignity.
2. Every human being is inviolable; that is, the inherent dignity that every human being has, has a normative force for us, in this sense: We should – every one of us – live our lives in accord with the fact that every human being has inherent dignity; we should respect – we have conclusive reason to respect – the inherent dignity of every human being.

If it is true, *why* is it true – *in virtue of what* is it true – both that every human being has inherent dignity and that we should live our lives accordingly? That the International Bill of Human Rights is (famously) silent on that question is not surprising, given the plurality of religious and nonreligious views that existed among those who bequeathed us the Universal Declaration and the two covenants.[5]

---

[4] See Jürgen Habermas, *Religion and Rationality: Essays on Reason, God, and Modernity* 153–54 (Eduardo Mendieta, ed., 2002): "Notwithstanding their European origins, ... [i]n Asia, Africa, and South America, [human rights now] constitute the only language in which the opponents and victim of murderous regimes and civil wars can raise their voices against violence, repression, and persecution, against injuries to their human dignity."

The morality of human rights is not new; in one or another version, it is a very old morality. See Leszek Kolakowski, *Modernity on Endless Trial* 214 (1990):

> It is often stressed that the idea of human rights is of recent origin, and that this is enough to dismiss its claims to timeless validity. In its contemporary form, the doctrine is certainly new, though it is arguable that it is a modern version of the natural law theory, whose origins we can trace back at least to the Stoic philosophers and, of course, to the Judaic and Christian sources of European culture. There is no substantial difference between proclaiming "the right to life" and stating that natural law forbids killing. Much as the concept may have been elaborated in the philosophy of the Enlightenment in its conflict with Christianity, the notion of the immutable rights of individuals goes back to the Christian belief in the autonomous status and irreplaceable value of the human personality.

[5] See Jacques Maritain, "Introduction," in *UNESCO, Human Rights: Comments and Interpretation* 9–17 (1949). Maritain wrote: "[W]e agree about the rights but on condition that no one asks us why." Id. at 9. However, Maritain was wrong: There was agreement not only about "the rights" but also about a part of the "why": namely, that every human being has inherent dignity. Again, the Declaration explicitly refers, in its preamble, to

I am about to articulate a religious response to the question. For purposes of exposition, I attribute the religious response to an imaginary "Sarah," who is a religious believer. No one who is not a religious believer will accept Sarah's response (or any other religious response); indeed, even some who *are* religious believers will not accept it. Nonetheless, Sarah's response is an intelligible, coherent response to the question, a response that for many religious believers is conclusive reason to live the kind of life the morality of human rights claims they (and we) should live.

Although she is a Christian, Sarah is sufficiently familiar with Judaism and Islam to know that her religious response, which she is about to elaborate, is not one that just Christians (not all Christians, but many) affirm; many religious Jews and Muslims affirm it too.[6] So, notwithstanding her Christian vocabulary and scriptural references, Sarah's religious response is ecumenical as among the three great monotheistic faiths.[7]

"the inherent dignity ... of all members of the human family" and states, in Article 1, that "[a]ll members of the human family are born free and equal in dignity and rights ... and should act towards one another in a spirit of brotherhood." So Maritain should have said something to this effect: "We agree not only about the rights but also that every human being has inherent dignity – but on condition that no one asks us *why* every human being has inherent dignity."

[6] On Islam, democracy, and human rights, see Abdullahi Ahmed An-Na'im, *Islam and the Secular State: Negotiating the Future of Shari'a* (2008). See also Khaled Abou El Fadl, "Islam and the Challenge of Democratic Commitment," in Elizabeth M. Bukar & Barbara Barnett, eds., *Does Human Rights Need God?* 58 (2005); Recep Senturk, "'I Am Therefore I Have Rights': Human Rights and Islam between Universalistic and Communalistic Perspectives," 2 MUSLIM WORLD J. HUMAN RIGHTS (2005), http://www.bepress.com/mwjhr/vol2/iss1/art11/.

On Judaism and human rights, see Asher Maoz, "Can Judaism Serve as a Source of Human Rights?," 64 HEIDELBERG J. INTL' L. 677 (2004); Michael Lerner, "Jesus the Jew," TIKKUN, May/June 2004, at 33:

Jesus' message of love is ... an intrinsic part of Torah Judaism.... It was the Torah, not Jesus, that first taught "Thou shalt love thy neighbor as thyself" and "Thou shalt love the Lord your God with all your heart, with all your soul, and with all your might." It was this same Judaism that taught a truly revolutionary message: "Thou shalt love the stranger (Hebrew: ger, which might also be translated as "The Other" or "the Powerless one," based on the follow-up point made in Torah, "Remember that you were a Ger in Egypt" when the Jewish people were enslaved).

See generally Robert Traer, *Faith in Human Rights: Support in Religious Traditions for a Global Struggle* (1991).

[7] If we listen carefully to what Sarah is about to say – and if we refrain from imputing to Sarah standard Christian positions on theological issues Sarah does not address, such as the divinity of Jesus – we will not assume that Sarah identifies herself as a Christian in the conventional sense (although for all we know she may).

Liberal Democracy, Human Rights, and Religious Faith

Sarah affirms that every human being has inherent dignity and that we should live our lives accordingly. (For a reason that will soon be apparent, Sarah prefers to say that every human being "is sacred." Nonetheless, for Sarah, each predicate – "has inherent dignity," "is sacred" – is fully equivalent to the other; Sarah translates each predicate into the other without remainder.) In affirming this, Sarah affirms the morality of human rights. Predictably, Sarah's affirmation provokes this question: "Why – in virtue of what – does every every human being have inherent dignity?" Sarah gives a religious explanation: Speaking the words of *The First Letter of John*, Sarah says that "God is love." ("Whoever fails to love does not know God, because God is love." 1 John 4:8.[8] "God is love, and whoever remains in love remains in God and God in him." 1 John 4:16.)[9] Moreover, God's act of creating and sustaining the universe is an act of love,[10] and we

---

[8] The translations of biblical passages here and elsewhere in this book are those of *The New Jerusalem Bible* (1985).

[9] See John D. Caputo, "The Experience of God and the Axiology of the Impossible," in Mark A. Wrathall, ed., *Religion after Metaphysics* 123, 138 (2003):

> There is no name more closely associated in the Christian Scriptures with "God" than love. That is what God is, and this comes as close as the New Testament does to a "definition" of God, as opposed to defining God onto-theo-logically in terms of possibility and actuality, essence and existence. Even so, it would be at best a quasi-definition because in saying that God is love one is not de-fining God in the sense of setting forth God's limits and boundaries, but saying that God is unbounded and unlimited and unconditional excess, for love is love only in excess and overflow, not in moderation.
>
> So the experience of God is given in the experience of love. But love is perfect not when love is drawn around a closed circle of friends and intimates, which makes perfect sense and is perfectly possible, but precisely when love is stretched to the breaking point of loving when love is mad and impossible. The God of love and the God of the impossible seem like a nice fit, a kind of pre-fit.

[10] Simone Weil wrote: "God created through love and for love. God did not create anything except love itself, and the means to love." Simone Weil, *Waiting for God* 123 (Emma Craufurd, tr., 1951).

Sarah doesn't mean to put much weight on the distinction between (a) God's "creating" and (b) God's "sustaining" the universe. See Brian Davies, "Creationism and All That," TABLET [London], May 11, 2002, at 16:

> In the thirteenth century, St Thomas Aquinas, though himself believing that the world had a beginning, argued that this is seriously irrelevant to the doctrine of creation. He said that to believe that the world is created is chiefly to believe that its being there at all and at any time is God's doing.
>
> And this, too, is what we find biblical authors teaching.... In these texts God is intimately involved with the world as its ever-present cause.

. . .

human beings are the beloved children of God and sisters and brothers to one another.[11] (As Hilary Putnam has noted, the moral image central to what Putnam calls the Jerusalem-based religions "stresse[s] equality and also fraternity, as in the metaphor of the whole human race as One Family, of all women and men as sisters and brothers."[12]) Every human being has inherent dignity, says Sarah, in the sense that every human being is a beloved child of God and a sister/brother to every other human being.[13] Sarah is fully aware that she is speaking analogically, but that's the best anyone can do, she insists, in

> At the end of his *Tractatus Logico-Philosophicus* Ludwig Wittgenstein wrote: "Not *how* the world is, is mystical, but *that* it is." For Wittgenstein, *how the world* is a scientific matter with scientific answers (even if we do not have all the answers yet). But, he insists, even when the scientific answers are in, we are still left with the *thatness* of the world, the fact *that* it is. And it is with this fact that we surely need to grapple if we are reasonably to arrive at the notion of creation apart from the testimony of scripture.

[11] Cf. Kristen Renwick Monroe, *The Heart of Altruism: Perceptions of a Common Humanity* 216 (1996):
> [I]t is the [altruistic] perspective itself that constitutes the heart of altruism. Without this particular perspective, there are no altruists.... [The perspective] consists of a common perception, held by all altruists, that they are strongly linked to others through a shared humanity. This self-perception constitutes such a central core to altruists' identity that it leaves them with no choice in their behavior toward others. They are John Donne's people. All life concerns them. Any death diminishes them. Because they are a part of mankind.

[12] Hilary Putnam, *The Many Faces of Realism* 60–61 (1987). In an essay on "The Spirituality of the Talmud," Ben Zion Bokser and Baruch M. Bokser state: "From this conception of man's place in the universe comes the sense of the supreme sanctity of all human life. 'He who destroys one person has dealt a blow at the entire universe, and he who sustains or saves one person has sustained the whole world.'" Ben Zion Bokser & Baruch M. Bokser, "Introduction: The Spirituality of the Talmud," in *The Talmud: Selected Writings* 7 (1989). They continue:
> The sanctity of life is not a function of national origin, religious affiliation, or social status. In the sight of God, the humble citizen is the equal of the person who occupies the highest office. As one talmudist put it: "Heaven and earth I call to witness, whether it be an Israelite or pagan, man or woman, slave or maidservant, according to the work of every human being doth the Holy Spirit rest upon him."... As the rabbis put it: "We are obligated to feed non-Jews residing among us even as we feed Jews; we are obligated to visit their sick even as we visit the Jewish sick; we are obligated to attend to the burial of their dead even as we attend to the burial of the Jewish dead."

Id. at 30–31.

[13] Cf. Daniel C. Dennett, *Darwin's Dangerous Idea: Evolution and the Meanings of Life* 474 (1995) (quoting Lee Khan Yew, senior minister of Singapore, on the outcry over the sentence of flogging given to Michael Fay for vandalism): "To us in Asia, an individual is an ant. To you, he's a child of God. It is an amazing concept."

speaking about who/what God is[14] – as in "Gracious God, gentle in your power and strong in your tenderness, you have brought us forth from the womb of your being and breathed into us the breath of life."[15]

Sarah's explanation provokes a yet further question, about the ground of the normativity – of the "should" – in the claim that we *should* live our lives in a way that respects the inherent dignity of every human being: "I'll assume, for the sake of our discussion, that every human being has inherent dignity in the sense that every human being is a beloved child of God and a sister/brother to every other human being. So what? Why should it matter to me – to the way I live my life – that every human being has inherent dignity, that every human being is a beloved child of God and a sister/brother to me? Why should I respect – why should I want to be a person who respects – the inherent dignity of every human being?" In responding to this important question about the ground of

---

[14] See Richard P. McBrien, ed., *The HarperCollins Encyclopedia of Catholicism* 43 (1995):
  analogy, A comparison in the form of "A is to B as C is to D," e.g., God is to the world as the artist is to her work."
   All theological language is analogous since we can compare God only to the created things we know; we cannot speak of God except in human terms. The Fourth Lateran Council (1215) declared that "No similarity can be found so great but that the dissimilarity is even greater" (DS 806). Thus every similarity between God and creatures (God is wise; humans are wise) is understood to include a greater dissimilarity (God's wisdom is unlike human wisdom in that it infinitely surpasses it). Thomas Aquinas (d. 1274) is particularly well known for developing the role of analogy in theological discourse.
  (Not all theological language is analogical, however; *some* is negative: e.g., God is not finite, God is not comprehensible.) Continuing to speak analogically, Sarah says that every human being is created "in the image of God." See id. at 654:
  imago Dei (Lat., "image of God"), theological concept that denotes the likeness of the human creature to God. According to Gen 1:26, humanity was created "in [God's] image, according to [God's] likeness." Found sparsely in the Hebrew Scriptures, the word "image" was often used in Pauline writings in the NT to interpret Christ's work and became central to early Christian reflections on the human condition, the meaning of redemption in Christ, and hope for humankind....
   Early theologians did not consistently separate "image" from "likeness" in interpreting human existence, and they saw the image of God variously in God's intellect, the capacity for moral decision, and the ability to rule over creation; but these theologians usually agreed that it implied a kinship between God and humankind and a call for the imitation of God.
  For a discussion of different understandings and uses of the "image of God" language, see Roger Ruston, *Human Rights and the Image of God* 269–91 (2004).

[15] *United Church of Christ, Book of Worship* 111 (1983).

normativity, Sarah – who "understands the authority of moral claims to be warranted not by divine dictates but by their contribution to human flourishing"[16] – states her belief that the God who loves us has created us to love one another.[17] (We are created not only to achieve union, in love, with one another; we are also created, Sarah believes, to achieve union, in love, with God. Sarah understands that state to be "not an ontological unity such that either the lover or the beloved ceases to have his own individual existence [, but rather] a unity at the level of affection or will by which one person *affectively* takes the other to be part of himself and the goods of the other to be his own goods."[18]) Given our created nature – given what we have been created *for* – the most fitting way of life for us human beings, the most deeply satisfying way of life of which we are capable, as children of God and sisters and brothers to one another, is one in which we embrace Jesus' "new" commandment, reported in John 13:34, to "love one another... just as I have loved you."[19] By becoming persons of a certain sort – persons who discern one another as bearers of inherent dignity and love one another as such – we

---

[16] See Jean Porter, *Nature as Reason: A Thomistic Theory of the Natural Law* 144–45 (2005):

In the course of reviewing recent work on the biological roots of morality, Stephen Pope contrasts divine command approaches to ethics to the revised natural law theory currently being developed by some contemporary Catholic moral theologians, including himself, observing that this latter approach "understands the authority of moral claims to be warranted not by divine dictates but by their contribution to human flourishing." The Thomistic theory of natural law to be developed here shares in this fundamental approach, insofar as it takes happiness to be the aim of, and correlatively the ultimate criterion for, moral behavior.

(Quoting Stephen Pope, "The Evolutionary Roots of Morality in Theological Perspective," 33 ZYGON 545, 554 [1998].)

[17] In an e-mail discussion, Steve Smith characterized Sarah's views this way: "Human fulfillment generally, and my own fulfillment, will be served by learning to love and respect that which is sacred. Human beings are sacred. Therefore, human fulfillment is served by... etc. As Smith observes: "In this presentation, the claims that (a) my fulfillment is served by learning to love Bill, Jane, et al. and (b) Bill, Jane, et al. are sacred are hardly independent claims, or independent reasons to care about others.... Both the 'fulfillment' and the 'sacredness' parts are necessary to the argument. But at the same time, they are not just different phrasings of the same claim."

[18] David M. Gallagher, "Thomas Aquinas on Self-Love as the Basis for Love of Others," 8 ACTA PHILOSOPHICA 23 (1999) (emphasis in original).

[19] For Christians, the basic shape of the good life is indicated by the instruction given by Jesus at a Passover seder on the eve of his execution: "I give you a new commandment: love one another; you must love one another just as I have loved you" (John 13:34). See also John 15:12, 17.

fulfill our created nature.[20] "We are well aware that we have passed over from death to life because we love our brothers. Whoever does not love, remains in death" (1 John 3:14).[21] Indeed, Sarah believes that in some situations, we love most truly and fully – and therefore

---

[20] In his book *After Theory* (2003), Terry Eagleton writes that "Aristotle thought that there was a particular way of living which allowed us... to be at our best for the kind of creatures we are. This was the life conducted according to the virtues. The Judaeo-Christian tradition considers that it is the life of charity or love. What this means... is that we become the occasion of each other's self-realization. It is only through being the means of your fulfillment that I can attain my own." Quoted in David Lodge, "Goodbye to All That," NEW YORK REV., May 27, 2004, at 39, 41.

[21] In the Gospel, there are two great commandments, not one. See Matthew 22:34–40: "But when the Pharisees heard that he had silenced the Sadducees they got together and, to put him to the test, one of them put a further question, 'Master, which is the greatest commandment of the Law?' Jesus said to him, 'You must love the Lord your God with all your heart, with all your soul, and with all your mind. This is the greatest and the first commandment. The second resembles it: You must love your neighbor as yourself. On these two commandments hang the whole Law, and the Prophets too." See also Mark 12:28–34; Luke 10:25–28. Cf. J. L. Mackie, *Ethics: Inventing Right and Wrong* 243 (1977): "D.D. Raphael, in 'The Standard of Morals', in *Proceedings of the Aristotelian Society* 75 (1974–75) follows Edward Ullendorff in pointing out that whereas 'Thou shalt love thy neighbor as thyself' represents the Greek of the Septuagint (Leviticus 19:18) and of the New Testament, the Hebrew from which the former is derived means rather 'You shall treat your neighbor lovingly, for he is like yourself.'"

What is the relation between the two commandments? In the view of great German Catholic theologian Karl Rahner, not only is there no tension between the commandment to love God and the commandment to love one another, but there is "a radical identity of the two loves." Karl Rahner, *Theological Investigations*, vol. 6, 231, 236 (1969). In his "Reflections on the Unity of the Love of Neighbor and the Love of God," Rahner wrote: "It is radically true, i.e., by an ontological and not merely 'moral' or psychological necessity, that whoever does not love the brother whom he sees, also cannot love God whom he does not see, and that one can love God whom one does not see only *by* loving one's visible brother lovingly." Id. at 247. Rahner's reference is to a passage in John's First Letter in which it is written: "Anyone who says 'I love God' and hates his brother, is a liar, since whoever does not love the brother whom he can see cannot love God whom he has not seen" (1 John 4:20). In Rahner's view, it is only by loving one's neighbor that one achieves the ontological/existential state of being/consciousness that constitutes "love of God," even though one may not "believe in God." See Rahner, supra this note, at 238–39. If Rahner is right, then there is, in the following sense, not two great commandments, but one: Compliance with the first great commandment (to love God) requires compliance with the second (to love one another), and compliance with the second entails compliance with the first. See id. at 232. Consider, in that regard, the Last Judgment passage in Matthew's Gospel:

> When the Son of man comes in his glory, escorted by all the angels, then he will take his seat on his throne of glory. All nations will be assembled before him and he will separate people from one another as the shepherd separates sheep from goats. He will place the sheep on his right hand and the goats on his left. Then the King will say to those on his right hand, "Come, you whom my

we live most truly and fully – by taking the path that will probably or even certainly lead to our dying. "No one can have greater love than to lay down his life for his friends" (John 15:13).[22]

Sarah also believes that the ultimate fulfillment of our created nature – which, Sarah believes, is mystical union, in love, with God

> Father has blessed, take as your heritage the kingdom prepared for you since the foundation of the world. For I was hungry and you gave me food, I was thirsty and you gave me drink, I was a stranger and you made me welcome, lacking clothes and you clothed me, sick and you visited me, in prison and you came to see me." Then the upright will say to him in reply, "Lord, when did we see you hungry and feed you, or thirsty and give you drink? When did we see you a stranger and make you welcome, lacking clothes and clothe you? When did we find you sick or in prison and go to see you?" And the King will answer, "In truth I tell you, in so far as you did this to one of the least of these brothers of mine, you did it to me." Then he will say to those on his left hand, "Go away from me, with your curse upon you, to the eternal fire prepared for the devil and his angels. For I was hungry and you never gave me food, I was thirsty and you never gave me anything to drink, I was a stranger and you never made me welcome, lacking clothes and you never clothed me, sick and in prison and you never visited me." Then it will be their turn to ask, "Lord, when did we see you hungry or thirsty, a stranger or lacking clothes, sick or in prison, and did not come to your help?" Then he will answer, "In truth I tell you, in so far as you neglected to do this to one of the least of these, you neglected to do it to me." And they will go away to eternal punishment, and the upright to eternal life (Matthew 25:31–46).

> In Matthew's Gospel, these are Jesus' final words to his disciples before the beginning of the passion narrative. Matthew 26:1–2 states: "Jesus had now finished all he wanted to say, and he told his disciples, 'It will be Passover, as you know, in two days' time, and the Son of Man will be handed over to be crucified.'"

> It seems to follow, from Rahner's view, that it is a mistake, a confusion, to say that we should love one another *because* we love, or should love, God and God wants us to – or *because* we fear, or should fear, God and God wants us to. We should say, instead, that for us to love one another is also for us to love God – and that we should achieve the ontological/existential state of being/consciousness that constitutes "love of one another" (= "love of God") because that state is the highest human good; to have achieved that radically unalienated condition is to have become *truly, fully* human.

[22] Dietrich Bonhoeffer wrote that "when Christ calls us, his call leads to death." Dietrich Bonhoeffer, *The Cost of Discipleship* 41 (R. H. Fuller, tr., 1995; originally published 1937). Cf. Helmut Gollwitzer et al., *Dying We Live: The Final Messages and Records of the Resistance* (New York: Pantheon Books, Inc. 1956); Terry Eagleton, "Lunging, Flailing, Mispunching," LONDON REV. OF BOOKS, Oct. 19, 2006) (reviewing Richard Dawkins, *The God Delusion* [2006]):

> The central doctrine of Christianity... is, in the words of the late Dominican theologian Herbert McCabe, that if you don't love you're dead, and if you do, they'll kill you. Here, then, is your pie in the sky and opium of the people. It was, of course, Marx who coined that last phrase; but Marx, who in the same passage described religion as the "heart of a heartless world, the soul of soulless conditions," was rather more judicious and dialectical in his judgment on it than the lunging, flailing, mispunching Dawkins.

and with one another[23] – can be neither fully achieved nor even fully understood in our earthly life.[24] "Now we see only reflections in a mirror, mere riddles, but then we shall be seeing face to face. Now, I can know only imperfectly; but then I shall know just as fully as I am myself known" (I Corinthians 13:12). But in our earthly life, Sarah believes, we can make an important beginning.[25]

The "love" in Jesus' counsel to "love one another" is not *eros* or *philia*, but *agape*.[26] To love another in the sense of *agape* is to *see her (or him) in a certain way* (namely, as child of God and sister/brother to oneself) and, therefore, *to act toward her in a certain way*.[27] *Agape* "discloses to us the full humanity of others. To become properly aware

---

[23] Cf. Charles Taliaferro, "Why We Need Immortality," 6 MODERN THEOLOGY 367 (1990).

[24] See Byron L. Sherwin, "Jews and the World to Come," FIRST THINGS, June/July 2006, at 13. Cf. Graham Greene, *Monsignor Quixote* 221 (1982): "The Mayor didn't speak again before they reached Orense; an idea quite strange to him had lodged in his brain. Why is it that the hate of a man – even of a man like Franco – dies with his death, and yet love, the love which he had begun to feel for Father Quixote, seemed now to live and grow in spite of the final separation and the final silence – for how long, he wondered with a kind of fear, was it possible for that love of his to continue? And to what end?"

[25] Compare, to Sarah's eschatological vision, the view of Jürgen Habermas:
> [By confronting] the conscientious question about deliverance for the annihilated victims[,] we become aware of the limits of that transcendence from within which is directed to this world. But this does not enable us to ascertain the *countermovement* of a compensating transcendence from beyond. That the universal covenant of fellowship would be able to be effective retroactively, toward the past, only in the weak medium of our memory, of the remembrance of the living generations, and of the anamnestic witnesses handed down falls short of our moral need. But the painful experience of a deficit is still not a sufficient argument for the assumption of an "absolute freedom which saves in death."

Habermas, *Religion and Rationality*, n. 4, at 80.

[26] The literature in Christian ethics on agape is voluminous. Some recent titles include: Colin Grant, *Altruism and Christian Ethics* (2001); Garth L. Hallett, *Christian Neighbor-Love: An Assessment of Six Rival Versions* (1989); Stephen J. Pope, *The Evolution of Altruism and the Ordering of Love* (1994); Edmund N. Santurri & William Werpehowski, eds., *The Love Commandments: Essays in Christian Ethics and Moral Philosophy* (1992); Edward Collins Vacek, SJ, *Love, Human and Divine: The Heart of Christian Ethics* (1994); Timothy P. Jackson, *Love Disconsoled: Meditations on Christian Charity* (1999); André Comte-Sponville, *A Small Treatise on the Great Virtues* 222–90 (Catherine Temerson, tr., 2001); Timothy P. Jackson, *The Priority of Love: Christian Charity and Social Justice* (2003).

[27] For Sarah, to love another, in the sense of *agape*, is not to *feel* a certain way but to act in a certain way. Cf. Jeffrie G. Murphy, "Law Like Love," 55 SYRACUSE L. REV. 15, 21 (2004):
> There are, of course, many fascinating questions that can be asked about the love commandment. Does it command love as an emotion or simply that we act in a certain way? Kant, convinced that we can be morally bound only to that which is in our control, called emotional love pathological love and claimed that it could

of that full humanity is to become incapable of treating it with contempt, cruelty, or indifference. The full awareness of others' humanity that love involves is an essentially motivating perception."[28]

The "one another" in Jesus' counsel is radically inclusive: "You have heard how it was said, You will love your neighbor and hate your enemy. But I say this to you, love your enemies and pray for those who persecute you; so that you may be children of your Father in heaven, for he causes his sun to rise on the bad as well as the good, and sends down rain to fall on the upright and the wicked alike.... You must therefore set no bounds to your love, just as your heavenly Father sets none to his" (Matthew 5:43–48).[29]

> not be our duty to feel it. What is actually commanded he called practical love – which is simply acting morally as Kant conceived acting morally.
>
> Murphy explained to me that by "pathological" (which is the English word commonly used to translate the German word Kant used), Kant did not mean diseased or sick but simply something from our passions with respect to which we are passive and thus not in voluntary control.

[28] Timothy Chappell, Book Review, 111 MIND 411, 412 (2002) (reviewing Raimond Gaita, *A Common Humanity: Thinking About Love and Truth and Justice* [2000]). Chappell is here describing "Gaita's view" and says that it is "reminiscent of course of Simone Weil and Iris Murdoch." Id. See Gaita, supra this note, at xxxiii:

> Iris Murdoch said that understanding the reality of another person is a work of love, justice and pity. She meant, I believe, that love, justice and pity are *forms* of understanding rather than merely conditions that facilitate understanding – conditions like a clear head, a good night's sleep, an alcohol-free brain. Real love is hard in the sense of hardheaded and unsentimental. In ridding oneself of sentimentality, pathos and similar afflictions, one is allowing justice, love and pity to do their cognitive work, their work of disclosing reality. It is the same love, [Simone] Weil tells us, that sees what is invisible.

Compare Alain Finkielkraut, *In the Name of Humanity: Reflections on the Twentieth Century* 5–6 (2000) (commenting on Primo Levi's encounter, at Auschwitz, with the German chemist Doktor Engineer Pannwitz): "To Doktor Pannwitz, the prisoner standing there [Levi], before the desk of his examiner, is not a frightened and miserable man. He is not a dangerous or inferior or loathsome man either, condemned to prison, torture, punishment, or death. He is, quite simply, not a man at all."

[29] See also Luke 6:27–35. Recall here the Parable of the Good Samaritan (Luke 10:29–37):

> But the man was anxious to justify himself and said to Jesus, "And who is my neighbour?" In answer Jesus said, "A man was once on his way down from Jerusalem to Jericho and fell into the hands of bandits; they stripped him, beat him and then made off, leaving him half dead. Now a priest happened to be travelling down the same road, but when he saw the man, he passed by on the other side. In the same way a Levite who came to the place saw him, and passed by on the other side. But a Samaritan traveller who came on him was moved with compassion when he saw him. He went up to him and bandaged his wounds, pouring oil and wine on them. He then lifted him onto his own mount and took him to an inn and looked after him. Next day, he took out two denarii and handed them to

As it happens, Sarah embodies Jesus' extravagant counsel to "love one another just as I have loved you." She loves all human beings. Sarah loves even "the Other": She loves not only those for whom she has personal affection, or those with whom she works or has other dealings, or those among whom she lives; she loves even those who are most remote, who are unfamiliar, strange, alien, those who, because they are so distant or weak or both, will never play any concrete role, for good or ill, in Sarah's life.[30] Sarah loves even those from whom she is most estranged and toward whom she feels most antagonistic: those whose ideologies and projects and acts she judges to be not merely morally objectionable, but morally abominable.[31] Sarah loves even her enemies; indeed, Sarah loves even those who have violated her, who have failed to respect her inherent dignity. Sarah is fond of quoting Graham Greene to her incredulous friends: "When you visualized a man or a woman carefully, you could always begin to feel pity.... When you saw the corners of the eyes, the shape of the mouth, how the hair grew, it was impossible to hate. Hate was just a failure of imagination."[32]

> the innkeeper and said, 'Look after him, and on my way back I will make good any extra expense you have.' Which of these three, do you think, proved himself a neighbour to the man who fell into the bandits' hands?" [The man] replied, "The one who showed pity towards him." Jesus said to him, "Go, and do the same yourself."
>
> In *The New Jerusalem Bible*, a note attached to "Samaritan" explains that "[t]he contrast is between the element in Israel most strictly bound to the law of love, and the heretic and stranger,... from whom normally only hate could be expected."

[30] See Norman Geras, *The Contract of Mutual Indifference: Political Philosophy after the Holocaust* 67 (1998): "The claims of the intimate circle are real and important enough. Yet the movement from intimacy, and to faces we do not know, still carries the ring of a certain local confinement. For there are the people as well whose faces we never encounter, but whom we have ample means of knowing *about*.... [T]heir claims too, in trouble, unheeded, are a cause for shame."

[31] See Gaita, n. 28, at xviii–xix: "[T]he language of love...compels us to affirm that even...the most radical evil-doers...are fully our fellow human beings."

[32] Graham Greene, *The Power and the Glory* 131 (Penguin ed. 1940). See also Denise Levertov, *The Poet in the World* 53 (1973): "Man's capacity for evil...is less a positive capacity...than a failure to develop man's most fundamental human function, the imagination, to its fullness, and consequently a failure to develop compassion."

For a dissenting view on hate, see Meir Y. Soloveichik, "The Virtue of Hate," FIRST THINGS, February 2003, at 41. As the CHRONICLE OF HIGHER EDUCATION stated, in an e-mail notice on this article dated Feb. 13, 2003: "Rabbi Soloveichik asks: 'Is an utterly evil man...deserving of a theist's love?' and, reflecting on his conversations with Christian clergymen, concludes that there is 'no minimizing the difference between Judaism and Christianity on whether hate can be virtuous.' He examines the 'theological

Such love – such a state of being, such an orientation in the world – is, obviously, an ideal. Moreover, it is, for most human beings, an extremely demanding ideal; for many persons, it is also an implausible ideal.[33] Why should anyone embrace the ideal? Why should anyone want to be (or to become) such a person – a person who, like Sarah, loves even the Other? This is, existentially if not intellectually, the fundamental moral question for anyone: Why should I want to be the kind of person who makes the choices, who does the things, I am being told I should make/do? And, in fact, Sarah's interlocutor presses her with this question: "Why should I want to be the kind of person who, like you, loves the Other? What reason do I have to do *that*?" Because that is essentially the question about the ground of the normativity in the claim that we should live our lives in a way that respects the inherent dignity of every human being, Sarah is puzzled; she thought that she had already answered the question. Sarah patiently rehearses her answer, an answer that appeals ultimately to *one's commitment to one's own authentic well-being*: "The most deeply satisfying way of life of which we are capable is one in which we 'love one another just as I have loved you.' By becoming persons who love one another, we fulfill – we perfect – our created nature and thereby achieve our truest, deepest, most enduring happiness."[34] It is now Sarah's turn to

---

underpinnings' for each faith's approach to hate and notes that 'the crucifixion is a story of a loving God seeking humanity's salvation,' but that 'not a single Jewish source asserts that God deeply desires to save all humanity.'" For vigorous criticism, by religious Jews and others, of Soloveichik's essay, and a response by Soloveichik, see "Correspondence: Jews and Christians, Hate and Forgiveness," FIRST THINGS, May 2003, at 2–9.

[33] It seems to have been an implausible ideal for Ivan Karamazov:
> I have never been able to understand how it was possible to love one's neighbors. And I mean precisely one's neighbors, because I can conceive of the possibility of loving those who are far away. I read somewhere about a saint, John the Merciful, who, when a hungry frozen beggar came to him and asked him to warm him, lay down with him, put his arms around him, and breathed into the man's reeking mouth that was festering with the sores of some horrible disease. I am convinced that he did so in a state of frenzy, that it was a false gesture, that this act of love was dictated by some self-imposed penance. If I must love my fellow man, he had better hide himself, for no sooner do I see his face than there's an end to my love for him.

Fyodor Dostoevsky, *The Brothers Karamazov*, opening of ch. 5, IV (Norton ed. 1976).

[34] Thus, Sarah rejects as false Vacek's distinction between "natural-law ethics" and "mutual-love ethics." See Edward Collins Vacek, SJ, "Divine-Command, Natural-Law, and Mutual-Love Ethics," 57 THEOLOGICAL STUDIES 633 (1996): "In natural-law ethics, something is right because it fulfills human nature, and the task is to discover and realize that nature. In mutual-love ethics, something is finally right because it is appropriate to our

ask a question of her interlocutor: "What further reason could you possibly want for becoming (or remaining) the kind of person who loves the Other?"

> When he was deliberating about how to live, St. Augustine asked, "What does anything matter, if it does not have to do with happiness?" His question requires explanation, because he is not advising selfishness nor the reduction of other people to utilities, and even qualification, because other things can have some weight. All the same, the answer he expects is obviously right: only a happy life matters conclusively. If I had a clear view of it, I could have no motive to decline it, I could regret nothing by accepting it, I would have nothing about which to deliberate further.[35]

A clarification may be helpful here. Does Sarah do what she does for the Other – for example, does she contribute to Bread for the World as a way of feeding the hungry – for a *self-regarding* reason? Does she do so, say, because it makes her happy to do so? No. Although feeding the hungry does make Sarah happy, that isn't why she does it. Given the kind of person she is, the reason – the *other-regarding* reason – Sarah feeds the hungry is this: "The hungry are my sisters and brothers; I love them." Now, a different question: Why is Sarah committed to being the kind of person she is, and why does she believe that everyone should want to be such a person? *Pace* Augustine, Sarah's answer to that question is self-regarding: "As persons who love one another, we fulfill our created nature and thereby achieve our

> love relationship with God, and the fundamental moral task is to live in accord with this relationship." For Sarah, what fulfills human nature is to live in a relationship of love with God and with other human beings. Vacek's "mutual-love ethics" seems to me better understood not as an alternative to, but as a version of, "natural-law ethics." For an excellent explication of Aquinas's understanding of the relation between self-love and other-love (and also between self-love and love of God), see Gallagher, n. 18; see also Porter, *Nature as Reason*, n. 16, at 209–10.

[35] Stephen Scott, "Motive and Justification," 85 J. PHILOSOPHY 479, 499 (1988). On the term "happiness," see Julia Annas, "Virtue and Eudaimonism," 15 SOCIAL PHILOSOPHY & POLICY 37, 53 n. 35 (1998): "Despite the differences between *eudaimonia* and happiness which I have explored in this essay, and which are striking to philosophers reflecting on virtue and happiness, 'happiness' is clearly the correct translation for *eudaimonia* in ancient literature of all kinds, and it would be a mistake to conclude that we should translate *eudaimonia* by some other term." Compare Richard Taylor, "Ancient Wisdom and Modern Folly," 13 MIDWEST STUDIES IN PHILOSOPHY 54, 57, 58 (1988): "The Greek *eudaimonia* is always translated '*happiness*,' which is unfortunate, for the meaning we attach to the word happiness is thin indeed compared to what the ancients meant by *eudaimonia*. *Fulfillment* might be a better term, though this, too, fails to capture the richness of the original term.... The concept of happiness in modern philosophy, as well as in popular thinking, is superficial indeed in comparison."

truest, deepest, most enduring happiness."³⁶ According to Sarah, it is not individual acts of love that necessarily make one happy; it is, rather, becoming a person who loves the Other "just as I have loved you." "[S]elf-fulfillment happens when we are engaged from beyond ourselves. Self-fulfillment ultimately depends on self-transcendence. This is essentially the claim that is made by religion, that the meaning of our lives is to be found beyond ourselves."³⁷

It bears emphasis that Sarah does not believe that she should be the kind of person she is because God has issued a command to her to be that kind of person – a command that, because God is entitled to rule, to legislate, she is obligated to obey. For Sarah, God is not best understood in such terms. A theistic religious vision does not necessarily include, although some conventional theistic religious visions do include, a conception of God as supreme legislator, issuing directives for human conduct.³⁸ For Sarah, for whom God is love, not supreme legislator, some choices are good for us to make (or not to make) – and, therefore, we should (or should not) make them – not because God commands (or forbids) them, but because God is who God is, because the universe – the universe created and sustained by God who is love in an act that is an expression of God/love – is what it is, and, in particular, because we human beings are who we are. For Sarah, "[t]he Law of God is not what God legislates but what God is, just as the Law of Gravity is not what gravity legislates

---

³⁶ Sarah's eudaimonistic, love-animated morality will not sit well with those whose thinking is under the influence of Kant. For an insightful, clarifying discussion of how sharply Kant's understanding of happiness differs from Aristotle's, see James Bernard Murphy, "Practical Reason and Moral Psychology in Aristotle and Kant," 18 SOCIAL PHILOSOPHY & POLICY 257, 273–76 (2001).

³⁷ Grant, n. 26, at xix. Sarah agrees with Grant. She understands Aquinas to have defended substantially the same position. See n. 34. Cf. David O. Brink, "A Puzzle about the Rational Authority of Morality," 6 PHILOSOPHICAL PERSPECTIVES 1, 22 (1992): "Unless agent-neutral reasons are necessarily superior reasons, the best solution would be to argue that agent-relative reasons, properly understood, support other-regarding moral requirements as well. So friends of agent-neutrality would do well to cultivate the resources of strategic and metaphysical egoists, even if they reject the rational egoist assumption that all reasons for action are agent-relative." (For Brink's discussion of "metaphysical egoism," see id. at 18–22. See also David O. Brink, "Self-Love and Altruism," 14 SOCIAL PHILOSOPHY & POLICY 122 [1997]. Augustine, Aquinas, and Sarah are all what Brink calls "metaphysical egoists." So too, apparently, are some "neo-Confucian" thinkers. See Yong Huang, "'Why Be Moral?' The Cheng Brothers' Neo-Confucian Answer," 36 J. RELIGIOUS ETHICS 321 [2008].)

³⁸ Indeed, for some religious believers, such a "God" is an idol. Cf. Charles Larmore, "Beyond Religion and Enlightenment," 30 SAN DIEGO L. REV. 799, 799–802 (1993).

but what gravity is."[39] Sarah believes that because God is who God is, because the universe is what it is, and because we are who we are, and not because of anything commanded by God as supreme legislator, the most fitting way of life for us human beings – the most deeply satisfying way of life of which we are capable – is one in which we children of God, we sisters and brothers, "love one another just as I have loved you."

Sarah's religious worldview reminds us that in the real world, if not in every academic moralist's study, fundamental moral questions are intimately related to religious (or metaphysical) questions; there is no way to address fundamental moral questions without also addressing, if only implicitly, religious questions.[40] (That is *not* to say that one must give a religious answer to a religious question, like the question, for example, Does God exist? Obviously many people do not give religious answers to religious questions.[41]) In the real world, one's

---

[39] John Dominic Crossan, "Case Against Manifesto," 5 LAW, TEXT, CULTURE 129, 144 (2000). For a version of Divine Command Theory – albeit, an unconventional version – that has a strong affinity with Sarah's moral "theory," see Martin Kavka & Randi Rashkover, "A Jewish Modified Divine Command Theory," 32 J. RELIGIOUS ETHICS 387 (2004). In discussion, Recep Senturk said that he does not see any conflict between a loving God and a legislating God. The holy scriptures of Judaism, Christianity, and Islam (Senturk said) always portray God as both a loving God and a legislating God. I don't mean to suggest that there is a conflict. For Sarah, nonetheless, "the Law of God is not what God legislates but what God is, just as the Law of Gravity is not what gravity legislates but what gravity is." Cf. id. at 411: "[W]e think that there is no philosophical ground for understanding 'obedience to God' in the sense [of] 'obedience to propositional sentences uttered by God.'"

[40] See Peter Geach, *God and the Soul* 127–28 (1969).

[41] Jürgen Habermas has acknowledged "that a philosophy that thinks postmetaphysically cannot answer the question that [David] Tracy ... calls attention to: why be moral at all?" Habermas, Religion and Rationality, n. 4, at 81. What Habermas then goes on to say is really quite remarkable:

> At the same time, however, this philosophy can show why this question does not arise meaningfully for communicatively socialized individuals. We acquire our moral intuitions in our parents' home, not in school. And moral insights tell us that we do not have any good reasons for behaving otherwise: for this, no self-surpassing of morality is necessary. It is true that we often behave otherwise, but we do so with a bad conscience. The first half of the sentence attests to the weakness of the motivational power of good reasons; the second half attests that rational motivation by reasons is more than nothing [*auch nicht nichts ist*] – moral convictions do not allow themselves to be overridden without resistance.

Id. Let's put aside the fact that "we" acquire our moral "intuitions" in many places besides (or in addition to) our parents' home – in the streets, for example. The more important point, for present purposes, is that we don't all acquire the same moral intuitions. Some of us acquire moral intuitions that enable us to ignore, and perhaps

Liberal Democracy and Religious Faith

response to fundamental moral questions has long been intimately bound up with one's response – one's answers – to certain other fundamental questions: Who are we? Where did we come from; what is our origin, our beginning? Where are we going; what is our destiny, our end?[42] What is the meaning of suffering? Of evil? Of death? And there is the cardinal question, the question that comprises many of the others: Is human life ultimately meaningful or, instead, ultimately bereft of meaning, meaning-less, absurd?[43] If any questions are fundamental, *these* questions – "religious or limit questions"[44] – are fundamental. Such questions – "naive" questions, "questions with no answers," "barriers that cannot be breached"[45] – are "the most serious

---

even to brutalize, the Other without any pangs of "conscience." It is incredible that in the waning days of this unbearably brutal century, Habermas – writing in Germany of all places – could suggest otherwise. We need not even look at the oppressors themselves; we need look only at those whose passivity makes them complicitors. The real world is full of what Primo Levi called "us-ism": "Those on the Rosenstrasse who risked their lives for Jews did not express opposition to anti-semitic policies per se. They displayed primarily what the late Primo Levi, a survivor of Auschwitz, called 'selfishness extended to the person closest to you . . . us-ism.' In most of the stories that I have heard of Aryans who risked their lives for Jews to whom they were married, they withdrew to safety, one by one, the moment their loved ones were released. Their protests bring home to us the iron limits, the tragically narrow borders, of us-ism." Nathan Stoltzfus, "Dissent in Nazi Germany," ATLANTIC, September 1992, at 87, 94.

[42] "In an old rabbinic text three other questions are suggested: '*Whence* did you come?' '*Whither* are you going?' 'Before *whom* are you destined to give account?'" Abraham J. Heschel, *Who Is Man?* 28 (1965). "All people by nature desire to know the mystery from which they come and to which they go." Denise Lardner Carmody & John Tully Carmody, *Western Ways to the Center: An Introduction to Religions of the West* 198–99 (1983). "The questions Tolstoy asked, and Gauguin in, say, his great Tahiti triptych, completed just before he died ('Where Do We Come From? What Are We? Where Are We Going?'), are the eternal questions children ask more intensely, unremittingly, and subtly than we sometimes imagine." Robert Coles, *The Spiritual Life of Children* 37 (1990).

[43] Communities, especially historically extended communities – "traditions" – are the principal matrices of religious answers to such questions: "Not the individual man nor a single generation by its own power, can erect the bridge that leads to God. Faith is the achievement of many generations, an effort accumulated over centuries. Many of its ideas are as the light of the star that left its source a long time ago. Many enigmatic songs, unfathomable today, are the resonance of voices of bygone times. There is a collective memory of God in the human spirit, and it is this memory which is the main source of our faith." From Abraham Heschel's two-part essay "Faith," first published in volume 10 of *The Reconstructionist*, Nov. 3 & 17, 1944. For a later statement on faith, incorporating some of the original essay, see Abraham J. Heschel, *Man is Not Alone* 159–76 (1951).

[44] David Tracy, *Plurality and Ambiguity: Religion, Hermeneutics, Hope* 86 (1987).

[45] In Milan Kundera's *The Unbearable Lightness of Being*, the narrator, referring to "the questions that had been going through Tereza's head since she was a child," says that "the only truly serious questions are ones that even a child can formulate. Only the most

and difficult... that any human being or society must face."[46] John Paul II was surely right in his encyclical, *Fides et Ratio*, that such questions "have their common source in the quest for meaning which has always compelled the human heart" and that "the answer given to these questions decides the direction which people seek to give to their lives."[47]

We can now see why it is that for most citizens of the United States, their religious faith gives them a powerful reason to hold liberal democracy within their embrace.

> naive of questions are truly serious. They are the questions with no answers. A question with no answer is a barrier than cannot be breached. In other words, it is questions with no answers that set the limits of human possibilities, describe the boundaries of human existence." Milan Kundera, *The Unbearable Lightness of Being* 139 (1984).

[46] David Tracy, *The Analogical Imagination* 4 (1981). Tracy adds: "To formulate such questions honestly and well, to respond to them with passion and rigor, is the work of all theology.... Religions ask and respond to such fundamental questions.... Theologians, by definition, risk an intellectual life on the wager that religious traditions can be studied as authentic responses to just such questions." Id.

[47] John Paul II, *On the Relation Between Faith and Reason: Fides et Ratio*, issued on Sept. 14, 1998. In the introduction to *Fides et Ratio*, John Paul II wrote:

> Moreover, a cursory glance at ancient history shows clearly how in different parts of the world, with their different cultures, there arise at the same time the fundamental questions which pervade human life: Who am I? Where have I come from and where am I going? Why is there evil? What is there after this life? These are the questions which we find in the sacred writings of Israel and also in the Veda and the Avesta; we find them in the writings of Confucius and Lao-Tze, and in the preaching of Tirthankara and Buddha; they appear in the poetry of Homer and in the tragedies of Euripides and Sophocles as they do in the philosophical writings of Plato and Aristotle. They are questions which have their common source in the quest for meaning which has always compelled the human heart. In fact, the answer given to these questions decides the direction which people seek to give to their lives.

Id. at introduction, pt. 1. See also id., chapter 3, pt. 26. (*Fides et Ratio* would more accurately be named *Fides et Philosophia*.) We find a similar statement in the Second Vatican Council's Declaration on the Relation of the Church to Non-Christian Religions (*Nostra Aetate*, 1):

> People look to their different religions for an answer to the unsolved riddles of human existence. The problems that weigh heavily on people's hearts are the same today as in ages past. What is humanity? What is the meaning and purpose of life? Where does suffering originate, and what end does it serve? How can genuine happiness be found? What happens at death? What is judgement? What reward follows death? And finally, what is the ultimate mystery, beyond human explanation, which embraces our entire existence, from which we take our origin and toward which we tend?

A powerful reason, but not by itself a sufficient one. Even if one affirms that every human being has inherent dignity and is inviolable and therefore has a strong reason to embrace liberal democracy, one may also have another and perhaps stronger reason(s) to reject liberal democracy. Consider, for example, the (imaginary) Elysians, whom I discuss in Chapter 3: They affirm that every human being has inherent dignity and is inviolable and therefore has a strong reason to embrace liberal democracy. But they also have an even stronger reason (stronger for them) to reject liberal democracy – to reject, that is, the right to freedom of religious practice, which is one of the human rights to which liberal democracy is, as such, committed. To reject the right to freedom of religious practice – or any of the other human rights to which a liberal democracy is, as such, committed – is to reject liberal democracy.

Unlike the Elysians, however, most U.S. citizens embrace liberal democracy, and their doing so is not only consistent with their religious faith *but strongly supported by it.*

Indeed, we may fairly wonder – as I do in the postscript to this chapter – what reason those who lack religious faith have for embracing liberal democracy's constitutive commitment to the inherent dignity and inviolability of every human being. Listen, in that regard, to Jürgen Habermas, who is *not* a religious believer:

> Christianity has functioned for the normative self-understanding of modernity as more than a mere precursor or a catalyst. Equalitarian universalism, from which sprang the ideas of freedom and social solidarity, of an autonomous conduct of life and emancipation, of the individual morality of conscience, human rights, and democracy, is the direct heir to the Judaic ethic of justice and the Christian ethic of love. This legacy, substantially unchanged, has been the object of continual critical appropriation and reinterpretation. To this day, there is no alternative to it. And in light of the current challenges of the postnational constellation, we continue to draw on the substance of this heritage. Everything else is just idle postmodern talk.[48]

---

[48] Jürgen Habermas, *Time of Transitions* 150–51 (2006). See also Habermas, *Religion and Rationality*, n. 4, at 162: "[T]he basic concepts of philosophical ethics, as they have developed up to this point, also fail to capture all the intuitions that have already found a more nuanced expression in the language of the Bible, and which we have only come to know by means of a halfway religious socialization." Listen, too, to Australian philosopher Raimond Gaita, who, like Habermas, is not a religious believer. See n. 31 and accompanying text.

Liberal Democracy, Human Rights, and Religious Faith

POSTSCRIPT TO CHAPTER 2

The Morality of Human Rights:
Is There a Secular Ground?
And What Difference Does It Make if There's Not?

> Few contemporary moral philosophers... have really joined battle with Nietzsche about morality. By and large we have just gone on taking moral judgements for granted as if nothing had happened. We, the philosopher watchdogs, have mostly failed to bark....
>
> – Philippa Foot[49]

Again, the morality of human rights consists of two connected claims:

1. The dignity claim: Every human being has inherent dignity.
2. The inviolability claim: Every human being is inviolable; that is, the inherent dignity that every human being has, has a normative force for us, in this sense: We should – every one of us – live our lives in accord with the fact that every human being has inherent dignity; we should respect – we have conclusive reason to respect – the inherent dignity of every human being.

Can any secular worldview warrant – embed – the dignity claim?[50] Is there anything one who is not a religious believer can say that is functionally equivalent to "the unashamedly anthropomorphic... claim

---

[49] Philippa Foot, *Natural Goodness* 103 (2001).
[50] Cf. Glenn Tinder, "Can We Be Good without God: The Political Meaning of Christianity," ATLANTIC, December 1989, at 69, 80 (passages rearranged and emphasis added):
> Nietzsche's stature is owing to the courage and profundity that enabled him to make all this unmistakably clear. He delineated with overpowering eloquence the consequences of giving up Christianity, *and every like view of the universe and humanity*. His approval of those consequences and his hatred of Christianity give force to his argument. Many would like to think that there are no consequences – that we can continue treasuring the life and welfare, the civil rights and political authority, of every person without believing in a God who renders such attitudes and conduct compelling. Nietzsche shows that we cannot. We cannot give up the Christian God – *and the transcendence given other names in other faiths* – and go on as before. We must give up Christian morality too. If the God-man is nothing more than an illusion, the same thing is true of the idea that every individual possesses incalculable worth. The standard of *agape* collapses. It becomes explicable only on Nietzsche's terms: as a device by which the weak and failing exact from the strong and distinguished a deference they do not deserve. Thus the spiritual center of Western politics fades and vanishes.

For Tinder's book-length treatment of the relevant issues, see Glenn Tinder, *The Political Meaning of Christianity: An Interpretation* (1989).

that we are sacred because God loves us, his children"?[51] Australian philosopher Raimond Gaita, who is an atheist,[52] has observed that "[i]f we are not religious, we will often search for one of the inadequate expressions which are available to us to say what we hope will be a secular equivalent of [the religious articulation that all human beings, as beloved children of God, are sacred]." Examples of the hoped-for secular equivalent: "We may say that all human beings are inestimably precious, that they are ends in themselves, that they are owed unconditional respect, that they possess inalienable rights, and, of course, that they possess inalienable dignity." In Gaita's reluctant judgment, "these are ways of trying to say what we feel a need to say when we are estranged from the conceptual resources we need to say it."[53]

Imagine a cosmology according to which the universe is, finally and radically, meaningless[54] – or, even if meaningful in some

---

[51] Gaita, n. 28, at 23–24.

[52] See John Haldane, "The Greatest of These Is Love, as an Atheist Reminds Us," TABLET [LONDON], Dec. 9, 2000, at 1678.

[53] Gaita, n. 28, at 23–24. See also Habermas, *Religion and Rationality*, n. 4, at 162: "[T]he basic concepts of philosophical ethics, as they have developed up to this point, also fail to capture all the intuitions that have already found a more nuanced expression in the language of the Bible, and which we have only come to know by means of a halfway religious socialization." Cf. Gaita, n. 28, at 5: "Religious traditions speak of the sacredness of each human being, but I doubt that sanctity is a concept that has a secure home outside those traditions."

[54] Bruce Ackerman has announced: "There is no moral meaning hidden in the bowels of the universe." Bruce A. Ackerman, *Social Justice in the Liberal State* 368 (1980). See also Bertrand Russell, *Mysticism and Logic* 47–48 (1917):

> That man is the product of causes which had no prevision of the end they were achieving; that his origin, his growth, his hopes and fears, his loves and his beliefs, are but the outcome of accidental collocations of atoms; that no fire, no heroism, no intensity of thought and feeling, can preserve an individual life beyond the grave; that all the labor of the ages, all the devotion, all the inspiration, all the noonday brightness of human genius, are destined to extinction in the vast death of the solar system, and that the whole temple of man's achievement must inevitably be buried beneath the debris of a universe in ruins – all these things, if not quite beyond dispute, are yet so certain that no philosophy which rejects them can hope to stand. Only within the scaffolding of these truths, only on the firm foundation of unyielding despair, can the soul's habitation henceforth be safely built.

Ackerman's declaration, like Russell's before him, brings to mind one of Nietzsche's sayings:

> Man a little, eccentric species of animal, which – fortunately – has its day; all on earth a mere moment, an incident, an exception without consequences, something of no importance to the general character of the earth; the earth

sense, not meaningful in a way hospitable to our deepest yearnings for what Abraham Heschel called "ultimate relationship, ultimate belonging."⁵⁵ Consider, for example, Clarence Darrow's bleak vision (as recounted by Paul Edwards):

> Darrow, one of the most compassionate men who ever lived, . . . concluded that life was an "awful joke." . . . Darrow offered as one of his reasons the apparent aimlessness of all that happens. "This weary old world goes on, begetting, with birth and with living and with death," he remarked in his moving plea for the boy-murderers Loeb and Leopold, "and all of it is blind from the beginning to the end." Elsewhere he wrote: "Life is like a ship on the sea, tossed by every wave and by every wind; a ship headed for no port and no harbor, with no rudder, no compass, no pilot; simply floating for a time, then lost in the waves." In addition to the aimlessness of life and the universe, there is the fact of death. "I love my friends," wrote Darrow, "but they all must come to a tragic end." Death is more terrible the more one is attached to things in the world. Life, he concludes, is "not worthwhile,"

>> itself, like every star, a hiatus between two nothingnesses, an event without plan, reason, will, self-consciousness, the worst kind of necessity, *stupid* necessity – Something in us rebels against this view; the serpent vanity says to us: "all that *must* be false, *for* it arouses indignation – Could all that not be merely appearance? And man, in spite of all, as Kant says."

> Friedrich Nietzsche, *The Will to Power* 169 (Walter Kaufmann & R. J. Hollingdale, trs., & Walter Kaufmann, ed., 1967).

55 For the person deep in the grip of, the person claimed by, the problem of meaning, "[t]he cry for meaning is a cry for ultimate relationship, for ultimate belonging," wrote Heschel. "It is a cry in which all pretensions are abandoned. Are we alone in the wilderness of time, alone in the dreadfully marvelous universe, of which we are a part and where we feel forever like strangers? Is there a Presence to live by? A Presence worth living for, worth dying for? Is there a way of living in the Presence? Is there a way of living compatible with the Presence?" Heschel, *Who Is Man?*, n. 42, at 75. See also Dostoevsky, n. 33, at 235: "For the secret of man's being is not only to live but to have something to live for. Without a stable conception of the object of life, man would not consent to go on living, and would rather destroy himself than remain on earth, though he had bread in abundance." (This is one of the Grand Inquisitor's statements in chapter 5 of Book Five.) Cf. W. D. Joske, "Philosophy and the Meaning of Life," in E. D. Klemke, ed., *The Meaning of Life* 248, 250 (1981) ("If, as Kurt Vonnegut speculates in *The Sirens of Titan*, the ultimate end of human activity is the delivery of a small piece of steel to a wrecked space ship wanting to continue a journey of no importance whatsoever, the end would be too trivial to justify the means."); Robert Nozick, *Philosophical Explanations* 586 (1981) ("If the cosmic role of human beings was to provide a negative lesson to some others ['don't act like them'] or to provide needed food to passing intergalactic travelers who were important, this would not suit our aspirations – not even if afterwards the intergalactic travelers smacked their lips and said that we tasted good.").

and he adds... that "it is an unpleasant interruption of nothing, and the best thing you can say of it is that it does not last long."[56]

One prominent contemporary proponent of a Darrowian cosmology, the physicist and Nobel laureate Steven Weinberg, "finds his own world-view 'chilling and impersonal'. He cannot understand people who treat the absence of God and of God's heaven as unimportant."[57]

Where is there a place in a cosmological view like Darrow's and Weinberg's for the idea that every human being has equal inherent dignity to gain a foothold? ("The masses blink and say: 'We are all equal. – Man is but man, before God – we are all equal.' Before God! But now this God has died."[58]) For one who believes that the universe is utterly bereft of transcendent meaning, why – in virtue of what – is it the case that every human being has inherent dignity? Richard Posner asks: "Thomas Nagel is a self-proclaimed atheist, yet he thinks that no one could *really* believe that 'we each have value only to ourselves and to those who care about us.' Well, to whom then? Who confers value on us without caring for us in the way that we care for friends, family, and sometimes members of larger human communities? Who else but the God in whom Nagel does not believe?"[59]

I am inclined to concur in R. H. Tawney's view (except that where Tawney says "all" morality, I would say something like "our" morality):

---

[56] Paul Edwards, "Life, Meaning and Value of," 4 *Encyclopedia of Philosophy* 467, 470 (Paul Edwards, ed., 1967). Whether Clarence Darrow was in fact "one of the most compassionate men who ever lived" is open to question. For a revisionist view of Darrow, see Gary Wills, *Under God: Religion and American Politics*, chs. 8–9 (1990).

[57] John Leslie, "Is It All Quite Simple? The Physicist's Search for a Theory of Everything," TIMES LIT. SUPP., Jan. 29, 1993, at 3 (reviewing, *inter alia*, Steven Weinberg, *Dreams of a Final Theory* [1992]). See Steven Weinberg, "Without God," NEW YORK BOOKS REV., Sept. 25, 2008. Cf. Paul Davies, "The Holy Grail of Physics," NEW YORK TIMES BOOK REV., Mar. 7, 1993 (reviewing, *inter alia*, Weinberg's book): "Reductionism [in physics] may be a fruitful research method, but it is a bleak philosophy.... If the world is but a collection of inert atoms interacting through blind and purposeless forces, what happens to ... the meaning of life?"

[58] This passage – quoted in George Parkin Grant, *English Speaking Justice* 77 (1985) – appears in Nietzsche's *Thus Spoke Zarathustra*, Part IV ("On the Higher Man"), near the end of section 1.

[59] Richard A. Posner, "The Problematics of Moral and Political Theory," 111 HARVARD L. REV. 1637, 1687 (1998) (citing Thomas Nagel, *The Last Word* 130 [1997]). Cf. James Boyd White, "Talking about Religion in the Language of Law: Impossible but Necessary," 81 MARQUETTE L. REV. 177, 197–99 (1998) (explaining why he has difficulty understanding what one who is not a religious believer might be saying in affirming the Declaration of Independence's insistence on the "equality" of all human beings).

"The essence of all morality is this: to believe that every human being is of infinite importance, and therefore that no consideration of expediency can justify the oppression of one by another. But to believe this it is necessary to believe in God."[60] One need not be a religious believer to concur in Tawney's view. Listen again to the atheist Gaita: "The secular philosophical tradition speaks of inalienable rights, inalienable dignity and of persons as ends in themselves. These are, I believe, ways of whistling in the dark, ways of trying to make secure to reason what reason cannot finally underwrite."[61]

Consider now the question about the truth of the inviolability claim: Even assuming that every human being has inherent dignity,[62] is it in fact the case that we – every one of us – should live our lives in accord with the (assumed) fact that every human being has inherent dignity, that we should respect – that we have conclusive reason to respect – the inherent dignity of every human being? Is there a plausible affirmative secular response to that question? What is the ground of normativity – the ground, that is, of the "should" – in the claim that we should live our lives in accord with the fact that every human being has inherent dignity?[63] Because the "should" in that

---

[60] J. M. Winter & D. M. Joslin, eds., *R.H. Tawney's Commonplace Book* 67 (1972). On Aug. 13, 1913, Tawney wrote, in his diary, the passage accompanying this note. Three days earlier, on Aug. 10, he quoted in his diary T. W. Price, Midland secretary of the Workers' Educational Association and lecturer at Birmingham University: "Unless a man believes in spiritual things – in God – altruism is absurd. What is the sense of it? Why shld [*sic*] a man recognize any obligation to his neighbor, unless he believes that he has been put in the world for a special purpose and has a special work to perform in it? A man's relations to his neighbors become meaningless unless there is some higher power above them both." Id. Cf. Dennis Prager, "Can We Be Good Without God?," 9 ULTIMATE ISSUES 3, 4 (1993): "If there is no God, you and I are purely the culmination of chance, pure random chance. And whether I kick your face in, or support you charitably, the universe is as indifferent to that as whether a star in another galaxy blows up tonight."

[61] Gaita, n. 28, at 5.

[62] Cf. Patrick Lee & Robert George, "The Nature and Basis of Human Dignity," 21 RATIO JURIS 173 (2008).

[63] I am assuming in this essay that all normative reasons – reasons for action – are agent-relative ("internal") rather than agent-neutral ("external"). See Richard Joyce, *The Myth of Morality* 106–34 (2001). See also Peter Geach, *God and the Soul* xix, 121–22 (1969). Cf. Henry B. Veatch, "Modern Ethics, Teleology, and Love of Self," 75 MONIST 52, 60 (1992):

> [T]he stock answer given to this question ["Why should I be moral?"] has long been one of trying to distinguish between a *reason* and a *motive* for being moral. For surely, it is argued, if I recognize something to be my duty, then surely I have a reason to perform the required action, even though I have no motive for performing it. In fact, even to ask for a motive for doing something, when

claim means "has (or have) conclusive reason to," we may ask the question this way: What conclusive reason do we have to live our lives in accord with the fact that every human being has inherent dignity? What answer can one give who is in the grip of what Bernard Williams called "Nietzsche's thought": "[T]here is not only no God, but no metaphysical order of any kind."[64]

The point is not that one cannot live one's life in accord with the fact (if it is a fact) that every human being has inherent dignity unless one believes in God.[65] Many who do not believe in God manage to live their lives in truly saintly ways, and many who do believe in God are anything but saintly.[66] The point is simply that it is open to serious question whether a secular worldview can bear the weight of the claim that we should – that we have conclusive reason to – live our lives in accord with the fact that every human being has inherent

> one already has a reason for doing it, would seem to be at once gratuitous and unnecessary – at least so it is argued. Unhappily, though, the argument has a dubious air about it at best. For does it amount to anything more than trying to prove a point by first attempting to make a distinction, implying that the distinction is no mere distinction, but a distinction with a difference – viz. the distinction between a reason and a motive. But then, having exploited the distinction, and yet at the same time insinuating that one might conceivably have a reason for doing something, but no motive for doing it, the argument draws to its conclusion by surreptitiously taking advantage of the fact that there possibly is no real distinction between a reason and a motive after all, so that if one has a reason for doing a thing, then one has a motive for doing it as well. In other words, it's as if the argument only succeeds by taking back with its left hand what it had originally given with its right.

[64] Bernard Williams, "Republican and Galilean," NEW YORK REV., Nov. 8, 1990, at 45, 48 (reviewing Charles Taylor, *Sources of the Self: The Making of Modern Identity* [1989]). Cf. John M. Rist, *Real Ethics: Rethinking the Foundations of Morality* 2 (2002): "[Plato] came to believe that if morality, as more than 'enlightened' self-interest, is to be rationally justifiable, it must be established on metaphysical foundations."

[65] Kristen Renwick Monroe's study of altruists and altruism is relevant here: *The Heart of Altruism: Perceptions of a Common Humanity* 216 (1996).

[66] See Jim Wurst, "Archbishop Tutu Examines Link Between Religion and Politics," U.N. WIRE, Mar. 18, 2004 (reporting on and quoting Archbishop Tutu's speech "God's Word and World Politics"):

> Religion... is neither automatically good or bad, it can be either depending on what it inspires its adherents to do. Religion has the capacity to produce saints, but it also has the capacity to produce rogues.... Christians need to be among the most modest because of the many ghastly things that Christians have perpetrated [e.g., slavery, apartheid, Nazi Germany and the Holocaust, fascism in Italy and Spain, the dropping of the atomic bombs on Hiroshima and Nagasaki, the Ku Klux Klan and the Rwanda genocide]. We who are Christians have much that should make us hang our heads in shame.

dignity.⁶⁷ It is obscure what ground one who is not a religious believer can give for the claim that every human being has conclusive reason to live her life in a way that respects the inherent dignity of every human being.⁶⁸ Listen, in that regard, to Charles Taylor:

> The logic of the subtraction story is something like this: Once we slough off our concern with serving God, or attending to any other transcendent reality, what we're left with is human good, and that is what modern societies are concerned with. But this radically under-describes what I'm calling modern humanism. That I am left with only human concerns doesn't tell me to take universal human welfare as my goal; nor does it tell me that freedom is important, or fulfillment, or equality. Just being confined to human goods could just as well find expression in my concerning myself exclusively with my own material welfare, or that of my family or immediate milieu. The, in fact, very exigent demands of universal justice and benevolence which characterize modern humanism can't be explained just by the subtraction of earlier goals and allegiances.⁶⁹

Let's assume here what many secular enthusiasts of the law of human rights believe: No religious worldview is plausible. ("[T]here is not only no God, but no metaphysical order of any kind."⁷⁰) Let's also assume what many religious enthusiasts of the law of human rights believe: Even *if* there is a plausible secular argument for the dignity claim – that is, a plausible secular account of the sense in which,

---

⁶⁷ See Leszek Kolakowski, *Religion, If There Is No God: On God, the Devil, Sin, and Other Worries of the So-Called Philosophy of Religion* 191 (1982):
  When Pierre Bayle argued that morality does not depend on religion, he was speaking mainly of psychological independence; he pointed out that atheists are capable of achieving the highest moral standards... and of putting to shame most of the faithful Christians. That is obviously true as far as it goes, but this matter-of-fact argument leaves the question of validity intact; neither does it solve the question of the effective sources of the moral strength and moral convictions of those 'virtuous pagans.'
  See also Rist, n. 64, at 267: "Although a 'moral saint' may exist without realist (and therefore religious) beliefs, yet his stance as a moral saint cannot be *justified* without recourse to realism."
⁶⁸ Patrick Lee and Robert George argue that "all persons possess profound, inherent, and equal dignity," and that "[t]hus, every human being deserves full moral respect." Lee & George, n. 62, at 191. However, Lee and George's "thus" is a non sequitur: That A has inherent dignity does not entail that B should – that B has conclusive reason to – live B's life in a way that respects A's dignity. The dignity claim and the inviolability claim are separate claims. The passage by Charles Taylor accompanying the next footnote makes the point.
⁶⁹ Taylor, "Closed World Structures," n. 1, at 61.
⁷⁰ See n. 64.

and why, human beings (most of them, anyway[71]) have a significant moral status, whether it be called "inherent dignity" or something else – nonetheless there is no plausible secular argument for the inviolability claim: No plausible secular argument supports the claim that we should – that we have conclusive reason to – live our lives in accord with the fact that every human being has that status. (I have explained elsewhere why, in my judgment, several efforts to specify a secular ground of normativity are problematic.[72]) What follows from those two assumptions for one who affirms the law of human rights – in particular, for one who affirms the post-World War II internationalization of the law of human rights?[73]

---

[71] For example, all human beings who are "normative agents." See James Griffin, *On Human Rights* (2008).
> The sense of "human dignity" that I am invoking must be specified, because there are several acceptable senses of "dignity" not relevant to human rights: for example, the dignity that quite properly should be accorded to a person deep in dementia or even to a dead person's body. The sense of dignity relevant to human rights, however, is that of a highly prized status: that we are normative agents.

Id. at 151–53. "What human rights guarantee is that one be able to live the life of a normative agent." Id. at 162. "On my account, of course, very young children do not yet have any human rights to be infringed." Id. at 165. "[E]mbryos and foetuses do not have human rights, though there may be moral considerations other than human rights that serve to prohibit abortions." Id. at 220.

[72] See Michael J. Perry, "Morality and Normativity," 13 LEGAL THEORY 211, 236–48 (2008); Michael J. Perry, *Toward a Theory of Human Rights* 18–25 (2007). See also Nicholas Wolterstorff, *Justice: Rights and Wrongs* 325–40 (2008).

[73] Cf. Amartya Sen, "Elements of a Theory of Human Rights," 32 PHILOSOPHY & PUBLIC AFFAIRS 35, 317 (2004):
> Human rights activists are often quite impatient with such critiques. The invoking of human rights tends to come mostly from those who are concerned with changing the world rather than interpreting it (to use a classic distinction made famous, oddly enough, by that overarching theorist, Karl Marx). It is not hard to understand their unwillingness to spend time trying to provide conceptual justification, given the great urgency to respond to terrible deprivations around the world. This proactive stance has its practical rewards, since it has allowed immediate use of the colossal appeal of the idea of human rights to confront intense oppression or great misery, without having to wait for the theoretical air to clear.

Sen then adds:
> However, the conceptual doubts must also be satisfactorily addressed, if the idea of human rights is to command reasoned loyalty and to establish a secure intellectual standing. It is critically important to see the relationship between the force and appeal of human rights, on the one hand, and their reasoned justification and scrutinized use, on the other.

Id.

Here are three options. (Are there others?)

1. One can say: "For me, the claim that every human being has inherent dignity and is inviolable is bedrock; 'this is where my spade is turned.'[74] I have more confidence in that claim than I have in any imaginable argument, religious or secular, for the claim. That claim is, as it were, my 'religion'." That response will work for some, but others will be engaged – and troubled – by this question: If, as one's bedrock conviction holds, the Other, even the Other, truly does have inherent dignity and truly is inviolable, what *else* must be true; *what must be true for it to be true that the Other has inherent dignity and is inviolable?*[75]
2. One can say: "Let's abandon 'human rights foundationalism';[76] in particular, let's abandon the effort to ground – to argue for the truth of – the claim that every human being has inherent dignity and is inviolable. I and many others want to live our lives *as if* every human being has inherent dignity and is inviolable. Why? Because we much prefer living our lives according to that 'as if' to living them as if only some or even no human beings have inherent dignity and are inviolable; we much prefer living in a world that unfolds according to the former 'as if' rather than according to

---

74 "I have reached bedrock and this is where my spade is turned." Ludwig Wittgenstein, *Philosophical Investigations*, sec. 217 (1953), quoted in Hilary Putnam, *The Many Faces of Realism* 85 (1987).
75 In an e-mail discussion, Steve Smith wrote:
> Insofar as humans have the quality of "dignity" or (as I prefer) "sacredness," perceptive sincere persons may well be able to perceive that quality without even knowing or giving much thought to the "ground" of the quality. So they don't need to believe in God in order to accord this respect to human beings. Their understanding would be seriously incomplete, of course, but their moral commitment might still be perfectly sincere.
>
> The problems arise when (a) they try to give a secular account of this quality – because the account will be deficient – and/or (b) they affirmatively embrace a naturalist cosmology of the sort you associate with Darrow and Weinberg, because that cosmology will tend to subvert their initial more innocent perception of the sacredness of life. In other words, "sacredness" won't be intelligible in the naturalist ontological worldview, and so the worldview and the moral commitment will be inconsistent.
>
> But even so, insofar as people are able to maintain inconsistencies (and many of us are prodigiously talented at that), they can hold both to a naturalist worldview and to genuine moral commitments, including commitments to human rights.
76 The term *human rights foundationalism* is Richard Rorty's. See Richard Rorty, "Human Rights, Rationality, and Sentimentality," in Stephen Shute & Susan Hurley, eds., *On Human Rights: The Oxford Amnesty Lectures 1993* 111, 116 (1993).

the latter."[77] That response will work for some, but others will be troubled:

> Outside our philosophical study... we don't think we're merely "expressing our acceptance" of norms calling for mutual respect and social justice when we make (sometimes great) personal sacrifices in order to comply with these norms. We act as if we think that the authority of these norms is not "in our heads" or traceable only to social conventions and our (cognitive or affective) reactions to them, but "real."[78]

And what would happen – not this year, or next, but eventually – if we who embrace the cause of human rights were to stop believing that the inherent dignity and inviolability of every human being is "real"? Consider what the Polish poet and Nobel Laureate, Czeslaw Milosz, has suggested:

> What has been surprising in the post–Cold War period are those beautiful and deeply moving words pronounced with veneration in places like Prague and Warsaw, words which pertain to the old repertory of the rights of man and the dignity of the person.
>
> I wonder at this phenomenon because maybe underneath there is an abyss. After all, those ideas had their foundation in religion, and I am not over-optimistic as to the survival of religion in a scientific-technological civilization. Notions that seemed buried forever have suddenly been resurrected. But how long can they stay afloat if the bottom is taken out?[79]

---

[77] I have criticized a version of the second response – Richard Rorty's version – elsewhere. See Perry, *Toward a Theory of Human Rights*, n. 72, at 26–28.

[78] Jean E. Hampton, *The Authority of Reason* 120 (Richard Healey, ed., 1998). Thanks to George Wright for calling this passage to my attention.

[79] Czeslaw Milosz, "The Religious Imagination at 2000," NEW PERSPECTIVES QUARTERLY, Fall 1997, at 32. See also Gaita, n. 28, at xviii–xix:
> [T]he language of love... compels us to affirm that even those who suffer affliction so severe that they have irrevocably lost everything that gives sense to our lives, and the most radical evil-doers, are fully our fellow human beings. On credit, so [to] speak, from this language of love, we have built a more tractable structure of rights and obligations. If the language of love goes dead on us, however, if there are no examples to nourish it, either because they do not exist or because they are no longer visible to us, then talk of inalienable natural rights or of the unconditional respect owed to rational beings will seem lame and improbable to us. Indeed, exactly that is happening.

Cf. Timothy P. Jackson, "The Theory and Practice of Discomfort: Richard Rorty and Pragmatism," 51 THOMIST 270, 284–85 (1987):
> [T]he loss of realism... means the loss of any and all realities independent of or transcendent to inquiry. In this respect, God must suffer the same fate as any other transcendent subject or object. Because faith makes sense only when

3. One can say: "Let's stop trying to ground – to justify – the international law of human rights on the basis of 'the inherent dignity and inviolability of every human being'. Let's justify it instead on a different basis, namely, on the basis of 'selfish' – that is, self-regarding – reasons: Let's explain why from this point on, we and our families and friends and other loved ones will be much better off, in the long run, living in a world in which every country both refrains from doing to its citizens (and others) what the international law of human rights tells it not to do to them and does for its citizens what the international law of human rights tells it to do for them."[80] That response will work for some, but others will wonder whether it is in fact the case that from this point on we and our loved ones will be much better off, in the long run, inhabiting a world in which every country lives in accord with the international law of human rights.

The reasons the International Bill of Human Rights gives in support of the international law of human rights include not only "the inherent dignity... of all members of the human family" but also this historically based consideration, which, whatever else it is, is profoundly self-regarding: that "disregard and contempt for human rights" undermine "peace in the world" and "friendly relations among nations."[81] Along those lines, U.S. Secretary of State Warren Christopher, in June 1993, argued before the World Conference on Human

> accompanied by the possibility of doubt, Rorty's distancing of scepticism means a concomitant distancing of belief in "things unseen." He, unlike Kant, denies both knowledge and faith; but for what, if anything, is this supposed to make room? Faith may perhaps be given a purely dispositional reading, being seen as a tendency to act in a certain way, but any propositional content will be completely lost. The pull toward religious faith is at best a residue of metaphysical realism and of the craving for metaphysical comfort. The taste for the transcendent usually associated with a religious personality will find little place in a Rortian world. Similarly, hope and love, if thought to have a supernatural object or source, lose their point. The deconstruction of God must leave the pious individual feeling like F. Scott Fitzgerald after his crackup: "a feeling that I was standing at twilight on a deserted range, with an empty rifle in my hand and the targets down." The deconstructed heart is ever restless, yet the theological virtues stand only as perpetual temptations to rest in inauthenticity. We live in a world without inherent *telos*; so there simply is no rest as Christianity has traditionally conceived it.

[80] For a fine example of such a response, see Dohrman W. Byers, "The Morality of Human Rights: An Egocentric Foundation" (unpublished ms. 2008).
[81] See the preambles to the Universal Declaration of Human Rights, the ICCPR, and the ICESCR.

Rights that "[a] world of democracies would be a safer world.... States that respect human rights and operate on democratic principles tend to be the world's most peaceful and stable. On the other hand, the worst violators of human rights tend to be the world's aggressors and proliferators. These states export threats to global security, whether in the shape of terrorism, massive refugee flows, or environmental pollution. Denying human rights not only lays waste to human lives; it creates instability that travels across borders."[82] In 2002, William Schulz, at the time the executive director of Amnesty International USA, argued that "respect for human rights both in the United States and abroad has implications for our welfare far beyond the maintenance of our ethical integrity. Ignoring the fates of human rights victims almost anywhere invariably makes the world – *our* world – a more dangerous place. If we learned nothing else from the horrific events of September 11, perhaps we learned that."[83]

Some will wonder, however, whether such arguments in support of the international law of human rights – and, in particular, in support of an American foreign policy that includes as one of its main goals the protection of human rights[84] – are mainly rhetoric and little substance. As one expert has put the point: "[Self-regarding] arguments are hard to prove and not fully persuasive. Despite considerable effort, it has been difficult to construct a wholly convincing 'selfish' rationale for major U.S. national commitments to promote the human rights of foreigners."[85]

---

[82] Warren Christopher, "Democracy and Human Rights: Where America Stands," 4 U.S. DEPARTMENT OF STATE DISPATCH 441, 442 (1993).

[83] William F. Schulz, *In Our Own Best Interests: How Defending Human Rights Benefits Us All* xix (2002). See also William W. Burke-White, "Human Rights and National Security: The Strategic Connection," 17 HARVARD HUMAN RIGHTS J. 249 (2004).

[84] Cf. William F. Schulz, ed., The Future of Human Rights: U.S. Policy for a New Era (2008); Jerome J. Shestack, "An Unsteady Focus: The Vulnerabilities of the Reagan Administration's Human Rights Policy," 2 *Harvard Human Rights Yearbook* 25, 49–50 (1989) (listing several reasons that should "motivate an administration to afford human rights a central role in United States foreign policy as a matter of national interest").

[85] Richard B. Bilder, "Human Rights and U.S. Foreign Policy: Short-Term Prospects," 14 VIRGINIA J. INTERNATIONAL L. 597, 608 (1974).

Part II
First Principles

3
The Right to Moral Equality

As I said at the beginning of Chapter 1, liberal democracy is, as such – as *liberal* democracy – committed, first, to the proposition that each and every human being has equal inherent dignity and is inviolable and, second, to certain human rights. The right to moral equality, which I discuss in this chapter, is one of the human rights to which liberal democracy is (as such) committed. Liberal democracy's commitment to the right to moral equality follows naturally from its commitment to the equal inherent dignity and inviolability of every human being. Put another way, liberal democracy's commitment to the equal inherent dignity and inviolability of every human being entails its commitment to the right to moral equality.[1]

A democracy is committed to a human right, in the sense in which I mean, if in the legal system of the democracy the right is recognized and protected as a fundamental legal right. (That is, if the right is recognized and protected as a fundamental legal right against – *at least* against – government: lawmakers and other government officials.) Most liberal democracies recognize and protect, as *fundamental* legal rights, the human rights to which they are committed by entrenching

---

[1] Liberal democracy's commitment to the right to moral equality leads naturally to a further commitment: to the right to equal citizenship. The government of a liberal democracy may distinguish between citizens and noncitizens and treat the former more favorably than the latter in *some* respects (e.g., government may permit only citizens to vote). Under the right to equal citizenship, however, government may not treat any of its citizens less well than any of its other citizens on the basis of any trait (race, sex, religion, etc.) that is a prohibited basis of discrimination under the right to moral equality. For government to do *that* would be for it to treat some of its citizens as second-class citizens (or worse). The right to moral equality as it applies to citizens yields the right to equal citizenship. Because liberal democracy is (as such) committed to the right to moral equality, it is also committed to the right to equal citizenship.

those rights in their constitutions. And as it happens, the right to moral equality – in one or another version – is not only entrenched in the constitutional law of most liberal democracies; it is also recognized and protected by the international law of human rights.[2]

Understood as a right against government, the human right to moral equality is the right of every human being to be treated by lawmakers and other government officials as one who has equal inherent dignity and is inviolable:

> Government may not enact, maintain, or enforce a law (or other policy) based on the view that some human beings do not have equal inherent dignity, including the view that the well-being (eudaimonia, flourishing) of some human beings does not merit the same respect and concern as the well-being of some other human beings.

Let's call a view to that effect the view that some human beings are inferior human beings – second class, or worse. Enactment, maintenance, or enforcement of a law is based on such a view if but for the view – if in the absence of the view – there would not be, or have been, enactment, maintenance, or enforcement of the law.

Of course, the human right to moral equality does not require government to treat all human beings the same. For example, government may deny drivers' licenses to those who are not yet sixteen years old. But government must treat every human being as one who has equal inherent dignity and is inviolable; government may not treat any human being as an inferior human being – inferior in the specific sense just indicated.

---

[2] The International Covenant on Civil and Political Rights, in Article 26, bans "discrimination on any ground such as race, colour, sex, language, religion, political or other opinion, national or social origin, property, birth or other status." See Peter Berger, "On the Obsolescence of the Concept of Honor," in Stanley Hauerwas & Alasdair MacIntyre, eds., *Revisions: Changing Perspectives in Moral Philosophy* 172, 176 (1983): "Dignity... always relates to the intrinsic humanity divested of all socially imposed roles or norms. It pertains to the self as such, to the individual regardless of his position in society. This becomes very clear in the classic formulations of human rights, from the Preamble to the Declaration of Independence to the Universal Declaration of Human Rights of the United Nations." Cf. Charles E. Curran, *Catholic Social Teaching: A Historical and Ethical Analysis 1891–Present* 132 (2002): "Human dignity comes from God's free gift; it does not depend on human effort, work, or accomplishments. All human beings have a fundamental, equal dignity because all share the generous gift of creation and redemption from God.... Consequently, all human beings have the same fundamental dignity, whether they are brown, black, red, or white; rich or poor, young or old; male or female; healthy or sick."

Sometimes it is not open to serious question whether a law is based on the illicit view that some human beings are inferior human beings. Sometimes a law is *obviously* based on that view. For example, the laws struck down by the U.S. Supreme Court in *Brown v. Board of Education* (1954) (*de jure* racial segregation)[3] and the law struck down by the Court in *Loving v. Virginia* (1967)[4] (anti-miscegenation law) – laws that were aspects of a (dying) system of racial apartheid – were obviously based on that view.[5] Sometimes a law is obviously *not* based on that view (e.g., a law that denies driver's licenses to those who are not yet sixteen years old).

Sometimes, however, it is open to serious question whether a law is based on the illicit view – a law that by its terms singles out a particular group of persons (e.g., women) and treats them less well than other persons, for example, or a law that disproportionately disadvantages a particular group of persons (e.g., those of African ancestry). (One may have good reason to suspect that a particular law that disproportionately disadvantages a racial minority is based on racially selective sympathy and indifference, and therefore violates the right to moral equality, just as one may have good reason to suspect that a particular law that disproportionately disadvantages women is based on sexually selective sympathy and indifference.) And when it is open to serious question whether a law is based on the illicit view – when, in that sense, the law implicates the right to moral equality – two questions arise:

1. Does the law – that is, is the choice to single-out-and-treat-less-well, for example, if that is what is at issue, or the choice to adopt the

---

[3] 347 U.S. 483 (1954). For a compelling essay on the importance of the Supreme Court's decision in *Brown*, see Paul Finkelman, "Civil Rights in Historical Context: In Defense of *Brown*," 118 HARVARD L. REV. 973 (2005).

[4] 388 U.S. 1 (1967).

[5] Responding to "a now-discredited argument in defense of antimiscegenation laws" – namely, "that whites can marry only within their race; nonwhites can marry only within their race; therefore, antimiscegenation laws do not deny 'equal options'" – John Corvino has written:

> Putting aside the problematic assumption of two and only two racial groups – whites and nonwhites – the argument does have a kind of formal parity to it. The reason that we regard its conclusion as objectionable nevertheless is that we recognize that the very point of antimiscegenation laws is to signify and maintain the false and pernicious belief that nonwhites are morally inferior to whites (that is, unequal).

John Corvino, "Homosexuality and the PIB Argument," 115 ETHICS 501, 509 (2005).

policy that has the disproportionate impact rather than to forgo that policy in favor of a different policy, if that is what is at issue – serve a legitimate governmental interest, such as (what modern human rights instruments call) "public safety, order, health, or morals or the fundamental rights and freedoms of others"?[6] (I discuss "legitimate" governmental interests in the next two chapters, in the course of discussing the right to religious freedom and the right to moral freedom.)

2. If so, is that interest sufficiently weighty (important) to be proportionate to the cost the law imposes on those subject to the law?

If the law does not serve a legitimate governmental interest, or if the cost the law imposes on those subject to the law is so great, so disproportionate, relative to the benefit the law succeeds in achieving that there is no reasonable justification – no reasonable case to be made – for the law,[7] then we may fairly conclude that the law not only implicates the right to moral equality but violates it.

---

[6] See, e.g., Article 18 of the International Covenant on Civil and Political Rights.

[7] Cf. Wojciech Sadurski, "'Reasonableness' and Value Pluralism in Law and Politics" (2008), http://ssrn.com/abstract=1144284.

4
The Right to Religious Freedom

Again, liberal democracy is, as such, committed to certain human rights. No country is truly a *democracy* unless it is committed to – unless it recognizes and protects, as a fundamental legal right – the right to political freedom: the right, that is, to freedom to seek, receive, and share information and ideas; to vote, and to run for and hold office; and to petition the government for a redress of grievances. Similarly, no country is truly a *liberal* democracy unless it recognizes and protects, as a fundamental legal right, the right to religious freedom – the right, that is, to freedom of religious practice. Commitment to the right to religious freedom is a sine qua non of *liberal* democracy.[1] Nonetheless, the case for liberal democracy's commitment to the right to religious freedom is not self-evident.

As I explained in Chapter 1, we who affirm the morality of human rights, *because* we affirm it, should press our elected representatives not only not to violate human beings – *any* human beings – or otherwise cause them unwarranted suffering; *we should also press them to recognize and protect certain moral claims as fundamental legal claims: moral claims about what may not be done, or about what must be done, especially by government, given that every human being has inherent dignity and is inviolable.* The law of human rights is one way of trying to prevent governments – and others – from violating human beings or otherwise causing them unwarranted suffering.

In denying religious freedom to its citizens, is government violating its citizens? In doing *some* things to a human being – for example,

---

[1] Cf. Thomas F. Farr, "Religious Freedom and U.S. Foreign Policy," http://www.ssrc.org/blogs/immanent_frame/2008/10/27/religious-freedom-us-foreign-policy/: "The work of sociologists such as Pew Forum's Brian Grim and Penn State's Roger Finke strongly suggests that stable democracy requires a 'bundled commodity' of fundamental freedoms that cannot function properly without religious liberty. Absent that right, societies are highly vulnerable to democracy-killing religious conflict, persecution and extremism."

in torturing him prior to executing him – we may safely assume that government is violating him implicitly if not explicitly, by doing to him what one would not do to him if one genuinely perceived him to have inherent dignity. But as I am about to explain, through the medium of a fable about a country named Elysium, in denying religious freedom to its citizens, government is not necessarily violating its citizens even implicitly.

I. ELYSIUM

Elysium, like Saudi Arabia, has a population of about twenty-five million. Approximately 80 percent of Elysians belong to a religion known as The One True Faith (TOTF); the other five million belong to various other religions. TOTF vigorously affirms, and gives a theological ground in support of, the morality of human rights: According to one of TOTF's fundamental teachings, every human being has inherent dignity and is inviolable, because every human being is a beloved child of God and a sister/brother to oneself. Like many other religions, TOTF teaches that one cannot be coerced into accepting – truly accepting – a religion (religious beliefs) as her (or his) religion; and, indeed, the Elysian constitution, inspired in part by an argument John Locke makes in his *Letter Concerning Toleration*, forbids government to try to coerce anyone into accepting TOTF as her religion.[2] Relatedly, the Elysian constitution forbids government to prohibit

---

[2] See John Locke, *Letter Concerning Toleration* (1689), translated (from a less familiar to a more familiar English) by William Popple, http://www.constitution.org/tolerati.htm:
> No way whatsoever that I shall walk in against the dictates of my conscience will ever bring me to the mansions of the blessed. I may grow rich by an art that I take not delight in; I may be cured of some disease by remedies that I have not faith in; but I cannot be saved by a religion that I distrust and by a worship that I abhor.... [W]hatsoever may be doubtful in religion, yet this at least is certain, that no religion which I believe not to be true can be either true or profitable unto me. In vain, therefore, do princes compel their subjects to come to their Church communion, under pretence of saving their souls. If they believe, they will come of their own accord, if they believe not, their coming will nothing avail them. How great soever, in fine, may be the pretence of good-will and charity, and concern for the salvation of men's souls, men cannot be forced to be saved, whether they will or no. And therefore, when all is done, they must be left to their own consciences.

Locke wrote those words in 1689. Earlier in the seventeenth century, on a different continent, another prophet of religious toleration – Roger Williams – was pressing, with more passionate rhetoric, the same message. See Edward J. Eberle, "Roger Williams'

anyone from practicing her religion in private.³ Elysian statutory law specifies the "private" places where non-TOTFers may worship and otherwise practice their religion, including their own homes.

However, TOTF teaches that no human being can achieve eternal salvation who does not (freely) embrace TOTF as the one true faith. It is not surprising, therefore, that TOTF is the politically/legally favored religion – in that sense, the "established" religion – in Elysium.⁴ Accordingly, the Elysian constitution forbids the government to enact any law or adopt any policy that is inconsistent with the teachings of TOTF. Nonetheless, because Elysians have taken to heart James Madison's *Memorial and Remonstrance against Religious Assessments*, the Elysian constitution embraces a part of Thomas Jefferson's *Statute for Religious Freedom* and forbids the government to require any citizen to support, financially or otherwise, TOTF.⁵ So,

---

Gift: Religious Freedom in America," ROGER WILLIAMS UNIVERSITY L. REV. 425, 441–42, 443 (1999) (passages rearranged):

> [S]ince a religious conversion must involve an actual change of heart, [Roger] Williams denied that "the Arm of Flesh" or the "Sword of Steel" could ever "reach out to cut the darkness of the Mind, the hardness and unbelief of Heart, and kindly operate upon a Souls affections to forsake a long continued Fathers worship, and to embrace a new, though the best and truest." Persecution could only force worship, causing hypocrisy in belief.
>
> ...
>
> "I plead the cause of truth and innocency against the bloody doctrine of persecution for the cause of conscience" asserts Williams in *Bloody Tenent*, which best encapsulates his argument. "By "persecution for the cause of conscience," Williams means that it is "spiritual rape" to coerce people to faiths or beliefs they do not voluntarily subscribe to. It is, for example, "a spiritual rape [to] force the consciences of all to one worship," or "to batter down idolatry, false worship, [or] heresy, [with] . . . weapons [such as] . . . stocks, whips, prisons, [or] swords." Such "*Soule* or *Spiritual Rape*" is worse than "to force and ravish the Bodies of all the Women in the World."

³ Cf. id. at 444–45:
> [For Roger Williams, m]atters of conscience extend beyond questions of belief. "By persecution for cause of conscience, I . . . mean either for professing some point of doctrine which you believe in conscience to be the truth, or for practicing some work which you believe in conscience to be a religious duty." For Roger Williams, it is clear that conscience encompasses both belief ("professing some point you believe on concience to be the truth") and action ("practicing some work which you believe in conscience to be a religious duty").

⁴ See Chapter 6, n. 2.

⁵ In his *Memorial and Remonstrance against Religious Assessments*, which bears the date June 20, 1785, James Madison wrote:
> [W]e hold it for a fundamental and undeniable truth, "that religion or the duty which we owe to our Creator and the manner of discharging it, can be directed

the "establishment" of religion in Elysium is in some respects much less severe than it has been in other places at other times.[6] The establishment of religion in Elysium is certainly less severe than it is in Saudi Arabia today.[7]

We now come to the heart of the matter. John Locke wrote, in his *Letter Concerning Toleration*, that "the whole jurisdiction of the magistrate... neither can nor ought in any manner to be extended to the salvation of souls...."[8] The government of Elysium, however, disagrees with Locke. Elysian law bans any public practice of, and any proselytization on behalf of, any religion other than TOTF; it also bans any proselytization of positions, like atheism and agnosticism, that challenge theistic religion generally. The rationale for this policy is simple – and un-Lockean: By banning practices that will predictably cause some Elysians to abandon, and other Elysians not to embrace, TOTF, the policy is aimed at maximizing the number of Elysians who will achieve eternal salvation.[9]

> only by reason and conviction, not by force or violence." [Virginia Declaration of Rights, art. 16.] The Religion then of every man must be left to the conviction and conscience of every man; and it is the right of every man to exercise it as these may dictate.
>
> Thomas Jefferson drafted the *Virginia Statute for Religious Freedom*, but it was James Madison who secured its adoption by the Virginia legislature in 1786. The Statute remains a part of present-day Virginia's constitution. The part of the Statute embraced by the Elysian constitution states: "We the General Assembly of Virginia do enact that no man shall be compelled to frequent or support any religious worship, place, ministry whatsoever, nor shall be enforced, restrained, molested, or burdened in his body or goods, nor shall otherwise suffer, on account of his religious opinions or belief...."

[6] To establish a religion is not necessarily to violate the right to religious freedom. See Chapter 6, n. 26.

[7] See U.S. Department of State, *Country Reports on Human Rights Practices for the Year 2003*, http://www.state.gov/g/drl/rls/hrrpt/2003/27937pf.htm. For more on (the lack of) religious freedom in Saudi Arabia, see U.S. Department of State, *International Religious Freedom Report for 2003*, http://www.state.gov/g/drl/rls/irf/2003/24461.htm. For a report on (*inter alia*) the depressing state of intellectual life in Saudi Arabia, see Elizabeth Rubin, "The Jihadi Who Kept Asking Why," NEW YORK TIMES MAGAZINE, Mar. 7, 2004.

[8] Locke, n. 2.

[9] Cf. Steven D. Smith, "What Does Religion Have to Do with Freedom of Conscience?" 76 U. COLORADO L. REV. 911, 921 (2005):

> [S]uppression of heretical belief has typically been calculated not so much to induce genuine belief in the heretics themselves (though religious authorities have no doubt hoped for that result) as to prevent heretics from infecting others who if spared the exposure will continue to hold a sincere, untroubled belief rather than being led astray. These heretical beliefs have been compared to a

In denying to non-TOTFers freedom to practice their religion in public and to proselytize on behalf of their religion, are Elysian officials violating them, either explicitly or implicitly: explicitly, by explicitly denying that non-TOTFers have inherent dignity, or implicitly, by treating non-TOTFers in a way one would not treat them if one discerned their inherent dignity? To the contrary, it is *because* they insist that *all* Elysians, non-TOTFers no less than TOTFers, have inherent dignity – that *every* Elysian is a beloved child of God – that Elysian officials are trying maximize the number of Elysians who will achieve eternal salvation. In denying to non-TOTFers freedom to practice their religion in public and to proselytize, Elysian officials are acting out of a deep respect and concern for all Elysians; they are not violating non-TOTFers.

As the fable about Elysium illustrates, in denying religious freedom to its citizens, government is not necessarily violating its citizens even implicitly. But that fact has limited significance, because, as I am about to explain, the fundamental reason liberal democracy has for granting religious freedom to its citizens – in particular, for recognizing and protecting the right to religious freedom as a fundamental legal right – is not to prevent some human beings (government officials) from *violating* other human beings, but to prevent some human beings from *causing unwarranted suffering* to other human beings. To say that, however, is to presuppose that in denying religious freedom to its citizens, government is causing them *unwarranted* suffering. Is that presupposition correct?

We know why TOTFers believe that the suffering caused by Elysium's denial of that freedom to non-TOTFers is not unwarranted: Because of their exclusivist theology of salvation – their ridiculously narrow version of the doctrine *extra ecclesiam nulla salus* ("outside the church no salvation") – TOTFers believe that the denial of such freedom is justified, and the suffering it causes therefore warranted, as a loving effort to protect all Elysians, including non-TOTFers, from the worst fate, the most horrific fate, imaginable: the loss of eternal salvation. But we citizens of liberal democracy are not TOTFers. Even

> contagious disease, or to counterfeit currency, which the state ought to control and suppress. And there is no reason to suppose that coercion can achieve that end, at least under some conditions.

the Roman Catholic Church no longer subscribes to such a crabbed – literalist – reading of *extra ecclesiam nulla salus*. "For centuries it was the teaching of the Roman [Catholic] Church that the majority of human beings went to hell, and that only Catholics, and most likely only a minority of them, went to heaven.... Pope Boniface VIII concluded his Bull *Unam Sanctam*, 1302, with the words 'We declare, say, define, and proclaim to every human creature that if they are to be saved they must of necessity be subject to the Roman Pontiff'."[10] But in 1964, by contrast, Joseph Ratzinger, who is now Pope Benedict XVI, could proclaim in a sermon that "we are convinced that God is able [to save non-Christians] with or without our theories, with or without our perspicacity, and that we do not need to help [God] do it with our cognitions."[11]

II. LIBERAL DEMOCRACY AND RELIGIOUS FREEDOM

What is the right to religious freedom – and what is the case for liberal democracy's commitment to the right?

Religious liberty scholar Douglas Laycock has observed that "in history that was recent to the American Founders, governmental attempts to suppress disapproved religious views had caused vast human suffering in Europe and in England and similar suffering on a smaller scale in the colonies that became the United States."[12] It is easy enough to identify the kinds of serious human suffering that attend a war of any kind, including a war animated by religious differences – and the kinds of serious human suffering that attend the punishment government imposes on human beings, or threatens to impose on them, in consequence of their violating a criminal ban on one or more of their religious practices. But even in the absence of a religious war or other serious religious conflict, and even if no one violates the ban on one's religious practices, the ban nonetheless causes serious human suffering: the emotional (psychological) suffering, often traumatic, that attends one's being legally forbidden to live a

---

[10] Anthony Kenny, *What I Believe* 62–63 (2006).
[11] Joseph Ratzinger, "Are Non-Christians Saved," http://www.beliefnet.com/story/209/story_20936.html.
[12] Douglas Laycock, "Religious Liberty as Liberty," 7 J. CONTEMPORARY LEGAL ISSUES 313, 317 (1996).

life of integrity – legally forbidden, that is, to live one's life in harmony with the yield of one's religious conscience, in harmony with one's convictions and commitments. The kind of suffering human beings endure in consequence of being legally forbidden to practice their religion consists of the dis-integration of a central aspect of their lives.

Given the serious suffering it causes, government's denial to (some or all of) its citizens of the freedom to practice their religion is unjustified, and the serious suffering it causes is therefore unwarranted, unless government is warranted in doing so, unless it has good reason to do so. According to the international law of human rights to which the liberal democracies of the world are committed – in particular, according to the right to religious freedom to which they are committed – government has good reason to ban (or otherwise impede) a religious practice if, and only if, this condition is satisfied: The choice to enact the ban, rather than to forgo the ban in favor of a different policy, serves a governmental interest that is both legitimate and sufficiently weighty (important) to be proportionate to the weight of the burden imposed by the ban on those subject to the ban. Or, more simply: The ban is necessary to serve a legitimate and sufficiently weighty governmental interest. Article 18 of the ICCPR articulates what we may fairly take to be the canonical formulation of the right to religious freedom.[13] According to Article 18:

1. Everyone shall have the right to freedom of thought, conscience and religion. This right shall include freedom to have or to adopt a religion or belief of his choice, and freedom, either individually or in community with others and in public or private, to manifest his religion or belief in worship, observance, practice and teaching.
2. No one shall be subject to coercion which would impair his freedom to have or to adopt a religion or belief of his choice.
3. Freedom to manifest one's religion or belief may be subject only to such limitations as are prescribed by law and are necessary to

---

[13] The ICCPR, which is a treaty and as such is binding on the several state parties thereto, was adopted and opened for signature, ratification, and accession by the U.N. General Assembly on Dec. 16, 1966. The ICCPR entered into force on Mar. 23, 1976; as of January 2007, there were 160 state partiesto the ICCPR. The United States is a party to the ICCPR: In September 1992, with the support of President George H. W. Bush, the Senate ratified the ICCPR (subject to certain "reservations, understandings and declarations" that are not relevant here; see 138 Cong. Rec. S 4781–84 [daily ed. Apr. 2, 1992]).

protect public safety, order, health, or morals or the fundamental rights and freedoms of others.

4. The States Parties to the present Covenant undertake to have respect for the liberty of parents and, when applicable, legal guardians to assure the religious and moral education of their children in conformity with their own convictions.[14]

The Siracusa Principles – principles adopted by the United Nations for interpreting the "prescribed by law and are necessary to protect public safety, order, health, or morals or the fundamental rights and freedoms of others" language of Article 18 and similar language in other Articles of the ICCPR – state, in relevant part: "Whenever a limitation is required in the terms of the [ICCPR] to be 'necessary,' this term implies that the limitation: . . . (b) responds to a pressing public

---

[14] See also the European Convention on Human Rights and Fundamental Freedoms (Article 9) and the American Convention on Human Rights (Article 12).

Another international document deserves mention here: *The Declaration on the Elimination of All Forms of Intolerance and of Discrimination Based on Religion or Belief*, which was proclaimed by the U.N. General Assembly on Nov. 25, 1981. See Derek H. Davis, "The Evolution of Religious Freedom as a Universal Human Right: Examining the Role of the 1981 United Nations Declaration on the Elimination of All Forms of Intolerance and Discrimination Based on Religion or Belief," 2002 BRIGHAM YOUNG UNIVERSITY L. REV. 217. "[The] question, whether the Declaration should become a convention, is an especially difficult one. Even though the Declaration does not have binding status, it carries the weight of a solemn U.N. statement and a great degree of moral suasion." Id. at 230. See also Symposium, "The Foundations and Frontiers of Religious Liberty: A 25th Anniversary Celebration of the 1981 U.N. Declaration on Religious Tolerance," 21 EMORY INTERNATIONAL L. REV. 1–275 (2007).

Cf. John Witte, Jr., "Primer on the Rights and Wrongs of Proselytism," 31 CUMBERLAND L. REV. 619, 627 (2001):

The literal language of [Article 18 of the International Covenant on Civil and Political Rights] and its amplification in more recent instruments and cases certainly protect the general right to proselytize – understood as the right to "manifest," "teach," "express," and "impart" religious ideas for the sake, among other things, of seeking the conversion of another. . . . [T]he [ICCPR] regards the religious expression inherent in proselytism as no more suspect than political, economic, artistic, or other forms of expression and entitled to the same protection.

However, because it prohibits "coercion which would impair [one's] freedom to have or to adopt a religion or belief of his choice," section (2) of Article 18 not only "provides no protection for coercive proselytism. At a minimum, [it] bars physical or material manipulation of the would-be convert and in some contexts even more subtle forms of deception, enticement, and inducement to convert. [It] also casts serious suspicion on any proselytism among children or among adherents to minority religions." Id. at 627.

or social need, (c) pursues a legitimate aim, and (d) is proportionate to that aim."[15]

The religious practices protected by the right to freedom of religious practice include not just practices one believes oneself religiously obligated to engage in. Such a limitation would make little sense: A practice one believes oneself religiously obligated to engage in (e.g., forsaking meat on Lenten Fridays) may be relatively inconsequential next to a practice (e.g., receiving communion wine) that one does not believe oneself religiously obligated to engage in, but that one nonetheless has strong religious reason to engage in. As the Supreme Court of Canada put the point in a case involving religious freedom:

> [T]o frame the right either in terms of objective religious "obligation" or even as the sincere subjective belief that an obligation exists and that the practice is *required*... would disregard the value of non-obligatory religious experiences by excluding those experiences from protection. Jewish women, for example, strictly speaking, do not have a biblically mandated "obligation" to dwell in a succah during the Succot holiday. If a woman, however, nonetheless sincerely believes that sitting and eating in a succah brings her closer to her Maker, is that somehow less deserving of recognition simply because she has no strict "obligation" to do so? Is the Jewish yarmulke or Sikh turban worthy of less recognition simply because it may be borne out of religious custom, not obligation? Should an individual Jew, who may personally deny the modern relevance of literal biblical "obligation" or "commandment," be precluded from making a freedom of religion argument despite the fact that for some reason he or she sincerely derives a closeness to his or her God by sitting in a succah? Surely not.[16]

It bears emphasis that a practice one has religious reason to engage in should not be confused with a practice one does not have religious reason not to engage in. The right to religious freedom protects only practices of the former sort. A right that protected practices of the latter sort would protect a multitude of practices that cannot plausibly be described as religious in nature. Although I watch *Meet the Press* on Sunday mornings religiously, my doing so is not a religious practice.

---

[15] United Nations, Economic and Social Council, U.N. Sub-Commission on Prevention of Discrimination and Protection of Minorities, *Siracusa Principles on the Limitations and Derogation of Provisions in the International Covenant on Civil and Political Rights*, Annex, UN Doc E/CN.4/1984/4 (1984) at I.A.10.

[16] *Syndicat Northcrest v. Amselem*, [2004] 2 S.C.R. 551, 588.

First Principles

Understandably, the right to religious freedom is not unconditional (absolute).[17] If the condition just articulated – that the ban be necessary to serve a legitimate and sufficiently weighty governmental interest – is satisfied, government may ban a religious practice. (A right to religious freedom would provide little meaningful protection for freedom of religious practice if the consistency of a ban with the right was to be determined without regard to whether the weight of the interest served by the ban was relatively slight in relation to the weight of the burden imposed by the ban.) So for a country to reject the right to religious freedom is not for it to reject the claim that government should never ban or otherwise impede a religious practice. No country accepts that extreme, and extremely silly, claim. Rather, it is to reject the much more moderate claim that – it is to reject a discursive framework according to which – government should not ban a religious practice unless it can provide at least a plausible justification for doing so, a justification to the effect that the ban is

---

[17] The right to the free exercise of religion protected by the constitutional law of the United States is not absolute; it permits government to prohibit *some* religious practices. See, e.g., *Reynolds v. United States*, 98 U.S. 145, 166 (1879) (upholding the constitutionality of a law banning polygamy):

> Laws are made for the government of actions, and while they cannot interfere with mere religious belief and opinions, they may with practices. Suppose one believed that human sacrifices were a necessary part of religious worship, would it be seriously contended that the civil government under which he lived could not interfere to prevent a sacrifice? Or if a wife religiously believed it was her duty to burn herself upon the funeral pile of her dead husband, would it be beyond the power of the civil government to prevent her carrying her belief into practice?

By its very terms the free exercise right forbids government to prohibit, not the exercise of religion, but the "free" exercise of religion – that is, the freedom of religious exercise. Just as government may not abridge "the freedom of speech" or "the freedom of the press," so too it may not prohibit the freedom of religious exercise. The right to freedom of religious exercise is not an unconditional right to do, on the basis of religious belief or for religious reasons, whatever one wants. One need not concoct outdated hypotheticals about human sacrifice to dramatize the point. One need only point, for example, to the refusal of some Christian Science parents to seek readily available lifesaving medical care for their gravely ill child. See, e.g., *Lundman v. McKown*, 530 N.W.2d 807 (Minnesota 1995). See also Caroline Frasier, "Suffering Children and the Christian Science Church," ATLANTIC MONTHLY, April 1995, at 105. Just as the right to freedom of speech does not privilege one to say, and right to the freedom of the press does not privilege one to publish, whatever one wants wherever one wants whenever one wants, the right to freedom of religious exercise does not – because it cannot – privilege one to do, on the basis of religious belief or for religious reasons, whatever one wants wherever one wants whenever one wants.

necessary to serve a legitimate and sufficiently weighty governmental interest.[18]

Under the right to religious freedom, what counts as a legitimate governmental interest? Although no exhaustive list of such interests is possible, a ban that protects the lives, health, safety, liberty, property, or socioeconomic well-being of the citizenry undeniably serves a legitimate governmental interest, as does a ban on conduct that causes environmental degradation or that abuses animals. More to the point: There are certain imaginable governmental interests that cannot count as legitimate under the right to religious freedom, because to count them as legitimate would be to render the right, understood as a fundamental legal right, meaningless; it would be to take away with one's left hand what one had given with one's right. (As the Siracusa Principles state: "The scope of a limitation referred to in the Covenant shall not be interpreted so as to jeopardize the essence of the right concerned."[19]) To affirm the right as one the law should recognize and protect as a fundamental legal right is necessarily to reject, in particular, the following two govermental interests as illegitimate.

The first imaginable-but-illegitimate government interest is *protecting (what the powers-that-be regard as) religious truth*. We can easily imagine the powers-that-be declaring: "Certain religious teachings are true – for example, the teaching that one who embraces Christianity has a much better chance of being saved[20] – and no government

---

[18] Predictably, there will sometimes be disagreement about whether a particular ban is necessary to serve a legitimate governmental interest of sufficient weight to be proportionate to the burden imposed by the ban – and sometimes the disagreement will be reasonable, sometimes not. If a politically independent, religion-protective judicial or quasi-judicial body is not authorized to decide whether a particular ban is necessary to serve a legitimate and sufficiently weigthy governmental interest, then the right to religious freedom may not be much protected. Cf. Carolyn Evans, *Freedom of Religion Under the European Convention on Human Rights* (2001) (criticizing the decisions of the European Court of Human Rights in the area of religious freedom as insufficiently religion-protective); Benjamin D. Bleiberg, "Unveiling the Real Issue: Evaluating the European Court of Human Rights' Decision to Enforce the Turkish Headscarf Ban in *Leyla Sahin v. Turkey*," 91 CORNELL L. REV. 129 (2005) (critizing decision as insufficiently religion-protective).

[19] *Siracusa Principles*, n. 15, at I.A.2.

[20] See "Other Faiths Are Deficient, Pope Says," TABLET [London], Feb. 5, 2000, at 157: "The revelation of Christ is 'definitive and complete', Pope John Paul affirmed to the Congregation for the Doctrine of the Faith, on 28 January. He repeated the phrase twice in an address which went on to say that non-Christians live in 'a deficient situation,

should lack authority to ban practices, religious or not, that may lead some people to reject those teachings." We can also anticipate a secular version of the position: "Certain antireligious teachings are true – for example, the teaching that 'religion is unscientific, superstitious, and an enemy of progress'[21] – and no government should lack authority to ban practices, religious or not, that may lead some people to reject those teachings." Neither the religious nor the secular version of that position is persuasive to those of us who, after reflecting on historical experience, concur in John Locke's judgment that "[n]either the right nor the art of ruling does necessarily carry along with it the certain knowledge of other things, and least of all true religion."[22] (To Locke's "does necessarily carry" we may add "or has ever carried.") "The one only narrow way which leads to Heaven," said Locke, "is not better known to the Magistrate than to private persons, and therefore I cannot safely take him for my Guide, who may probably be as ignorant of the way as my self, and who certainly is less concerned for my Salvation than I my self am."[23] In our (Lockean) judgment, government is not to be trusted as an arbiter of religious (or anti-religious) truth. Or, because we are talking here specifically about government in a liberal democracy, we may say that a political majority is not to be trusted as an arbiter of religious truth. As Locke put it, "the business of

---

compared to those who have the fullness of salvific means in the Church'." Nonetheless, "[Pope John Paul II] recognised, following the Second Vatican Council, that non-Christians can reach eternal life if they seek God with a sincere heart. But in that 'sincere search' they are in fact 'ordered' towards Christ and his Church." Id.

[21] See Lawrie Breen, "A Chinese Puzzle," TABLET [London], Mar. 5, 2005 (reporting that "new regulations confirm that Beijing perceives religion as unscientific, superstitious and an enemy of progress"). "Last year a secret document, issued by the Central Committee's Propoganda Department, called for a new drive to promote Marxist atheism." Id.

[22] Locke, n. 2. Cf. John Perry, "John Locke's America: The Character of Liberal Democracy and Jeffrey Stout's Debate with the Christian Traditionalists," 27 J. SOCIETY OF CHRISTIAN ETHICS 227 (2007).

[23] Locke, n. 2. See James Madison, *Memorial and Remonstrance against Religious Assessments* (1785) (explaining why "We the subscribers, citizens of the said Commonwealth [Virginia]," reject the proposed "Bill establishing a provision for Teachers of the Christian Religion"):

> 5. Because the Bill implies either that the Civil Magistrate is a competent judge of Religious Truth; or that he may employ Religion as an engine of Civil policy. The first is an arrogant pretension falsified by the contradictory Rulers in all ages, and throughout the world; the second an unhallowed perversion of the means of salvation.

laws is not to provide for the truth of opinions, but for the safety and security of the commonwealth, and of every particular man's goods and persons."[24]

That is, government is not to be trusted as an arbiter of religious truth *beyond a certain point.*

- As noted at the beginning of Chapter 1, a *liberal* democracy is committed to the proposition that every human being has inherent dignity and is inviolable; in the political culture of a liberal democracy, that proposition is axiomatic. In a liberal democracy, government should act in accord with the proposition even if doing so government is implicitly rejecting the position of some (e.g., racist) religions and thereby, in that limited sense, acting as an arbiter of religious truth. ("The world is one in which every human being has inherent dignity and is inviolable; if God exists and created the world, then the world created by God is one in which every human being has inherent dignity and is inviolable.")
- Certain governmental interests are undeniably legitimate, and government must be legally free to serve such interests – for example, protecting the lives, health, and safety of the citizenry – even if in doing so government is sometimes implicitly rejecting the position of some religions and thereby, in that limited sense, acting as an arbiter of religious truth.

> A court orders a state to desegregate its schools, the country goes to war, educational funds are made available equally to men and women. The government has implicitly rejected religious notions that (1) God wishes rigid racial separation, (2) all killing in war violates God's commandments, (3) all women should occupy themselves with domestic tasks. A vast array of laws and policies similarly imply the incorrectness of particular religious views.[25]

But beyond that certain point, government is not to be trusted as an arbiter of religious truth. In particular, government need not act – and we are understandably and justifiably wary about its acting – as an arbiter of religious (theological) disagreements that do not implicate any legitimate governmental interest. We affirm, with Locke, that "the business of laws is not to provide for the truth of opinions, but [only] for the safety and security of the commonwealth, and of

---

[24] Locke, n. 2.
[25] Kent Greenawalt, "Five Questions about Religion Judges Are Afraid to Ask," in Nancy L. Rosenblum, ed., *Obligations of Citizenship and Demands of Faith* 196, 199 (2000).

every particular man's goods and persons."[26] Henceforth, when I say that government is not to be trusted as an arbiter of religious truth, I mean that government is not to be trusted as an arbiter of religious disagreements *that do not implicate a legitimate governmental interest*.

One can imagine the Roman Catholic Church of an earlier time replying to Locke that "so long as the state accepts *the Catholic Church* as the arbiter of religious truth, there is no problem, because the Catholic Church has 'certain knowledge' of religious truth." By the time of the Second Vatican Council (1962–65), however, the cardinals and bishops of the Catholic Church – a large majority of them – had come to accept that the era had ended in which the Church could realistically expect to wield the kind of influence over a state – *any* state – it had once wielded over some states, and that the Church too, therefore, should not trust any government, including any political majority in a liberal democracy, as an arbiter of religious truth. I discuss the post-Vatican II Church's embrace of the right to religious freedom in the next section of this chapter.

The second imaginable-but-illegitimate governmental interest is *protecting the religious unity of society*. We can easily imagine the powers-that-be declaring: "In the long run, religious unity, understood as a kind of 'glue', enhances the strength of a nation ('strength' as in 'united we stand, divided we fall'); therefore, no government should lack authority to ban practices, religious or not, that over time may diminish the nation's religious unity and thereby weaken the nation."[27] (In 1931, the fascist dictator of Italy, Benito Mussolini,

---

[26] Locke, n. 2.
[27] See Michael W. McConnell, "Establishment and Disestablishment at the Founding, Part I: Establishment of Religion," 44 WILLIAM & MARY L. REV. 2105, 2182 (2003): "Machiavelli, who called religion 'the instrument necessary above all others for the maintenance of a civilized state,' urged rulers to 'foster and encourage' religion 'even though they be convinced that is it quite fallacious.' Truth and social utility may, but need not, coincide." (Quoting Niccolo Machiavelli, *The Discourses* 139, 143 [Bernard R. Crick ed. & Leslie J. Walker trans., Penguin 1970] [1520].) Cf. "Atheist Defends Belief in God," TABLET [London], Mar. 24, 2007, at 33:
> A senior German ex-Communist has praised the Pope and defended belief in God as necessary for society.... "I'm convinced only the Churches are in a state to propagate moral norms and values," said Gregor Gysi, parliamentary chairman of Die Linke, a grouping of Germany's Democratic Left Party (PDS) and other

proclaimed that "religious unity is one of the great strengths of a people."[28]) But that position too is belied by historical experience – not least, the historical experience of religious freedom in the United States. Indeed, given the suffering it causes and the divisiveness it precipitates, the coercive imposition of religious uniformity – if not necessary to serve some other, important governmental interest, such as protecting the lives, health, or safety of the citizenry – is more likely to corrode than to nurture the strength of a democracy, especially if the democracy is, as liberal democracies typically and increasingly are, religiously pluralistic.[29]

This, then, is the fundamental warrant for liberal democracy's commitment to the right to religious freedom: Political majorities are not to be trusted (i.e., beyond a certain point) as arbiters of religious truth; moreover, the coercive imposition of religious uniformity is (beyond a certain point) more likely to corrode than to nurture the strength of a democracy. The warrant, which is rooted in historical experience, is fundamental in the sense that it is ecumenical: Both citizens who are religious believers and those who are not can affirm the warrant. And that the warrant is ecumenical is ideal: Liberal democracies are religiously pluralistic; the citizenry of a liberal democracy typically includes not only religious believers – indeed, religious believers of various stripes – but also nonbelievers. It is ideal that all citizens of liberal democracy – believers no less than nonbelievers – have the same basic reason to embrace the right to religious freedom.

This is not to say, of course, that every citizen embraces the right, or that every citzen who embraces the right does so for the same reason as every other citizen. In particular, to say that all citizens have the same basic reason to embrace the right to religious freedom is not to deny that some citizens may have an additional, religion-specific

---

left-wing groups. "I don't believe in God, but I accept that a society without God would be a society without values. This is why I don't oppose religious attitudes and convictions."

[28] Quoted in John T. Noonan, Jr., *A Church That Can and Cannot Change* 155–56 (2005).

[29] The *Declaration on the Elimination of All Forms of Intolerance and of Discrimination Based on Religion or Belief*, n. 14, declares: "[T]he disregard and infringement of . . . the right to freedom of thought, conscience, religion or whatever belief, have brought, directly or indirectly, wars and great suffering to mankind." Cf. Paul Cruickshank, "Covered Faces, Open Rebellion," NEW YORK TIMES, Oct. 21, 2006.

reason to embrace the right – for example, "It is God's will that everyone should enjoy the right to religious freedom." Nor is it to deny that a religion-specific reason may be, for some citizens, the dominant reason.

III. DIGNITATIS HUMANAE

The Roman Catholic Church was famously late to embrace the right to religious freedom. When at last the Church did embrace the right, in the 1960s, did it do so, as some have suggested, by abandoning certain of its fundamental theological beliefs – beliefs that had been eroded, or corroded, by the religiously and morally pluralistic culture of liberal democracy, with its live-and-let-live, let-a-thousand-flowers-bloom attitude toward religious and moral differences? The answer is no. We are now in a position to see that when the Church embraced the right, it did so *without* abandoning any of its fundamental theological beliefs.[30] The Church embraced the right to religious freedom on the basis of substantially the same, ecumenical rationale I have elaborated in this chapter. The story of the Church's conversion is worth recounting, if only briefly, because the story powerfully illustrates that all citizens – Catholics no less than non-Catholics, Christians no less than non-Christians, believers no less than nonbelievers – can, *consistently with their core theological or a-theological beliefs*, affirm the rationale.

In 1965, the cardinals and bishops at the Second Vatican Council (1962–65), by a vote of 2,308 to 70, adopted the Declaration on Religious Freedom, known by the first two words of the official – Latin – version: *Dignitatis Humanae*. Later that year, Pope Paul VI promulgated the Declaration as the teaching of the Roman Catholic Church. In *Dignitatis Humanae*, the Church finally came round to embracing the right to religious freedom as a right that, given the inherent dignity and inviolability of every human being, should be universally legislated.[31]

The pre-Vatican II Catholic Church, notwithstanding its vigorous affirmation of the inherent dignity and inviolability of every human

---

[30] It is implausible to claim that a literalist reading of *extra ecclesiam nulla salus* was one of the Church's fundamental theological beliefs. See nn. 10–11.
[31] See generally Leslie Griffin, "Commentary on *Dignitatis humanae* (*Declaration on Religious Freedom*), in Kenneth R. Himes, ed., MODERN CATHOLIC SOCIAL TEACHING: COMMENTARIES AND INTERPRETATIONS 244 (2004).

being, rejected the right to religious freedom as a right that should be universally legislated. Prior to 1965, the Church rejected the claim that non-Catholics should everywhere have the same legal freedom Catholics themselves should have to practice their religion in public and to proselytize. As Michael Walsh has explained:

> [In the 1940s,] Protestants had reason for their suspicion of Catholics. The "liberal" approach to the pluralism of religious practice found in the United States was certainly not replicated in Spain and some Latin American countries, or even, to some extent, in Italy. The Church had no problem with diversity of belief – it was accepted that no one could be coerced into Catholicism – but practice was a different matter. It was the duty of a Catholic state, the argument ran, to constrain public expression of religion other than Catholicism. Error, it was repeated mantra-like, has no right.[32]

Unlike the pre-Vatican II Catholic Church, the post-Vatican II Church accepts – indeed, celebrates – the right to religious freedom. Walsh's article provides a good summary of the fierce debate among the cardinals and bishops at the Second Vatican Council that preceded what Walsh calls the Council's "U-turn" with respect to the right to religious freedom, namely, its adoption of *Dignitatis Humanae*.[33]

Dignitatis Humanae's commitment to the right to religious freedom was – is – unmistakable and resounding. The human person is "not to be forced to act in a manner contrary to his conscience. Nor . . . is he to be restrained from acting in accordance with his conscience, especially in matters religion."[34] "This right of the human person to religious freedom is to be recognized in the constitutional law whereby society is governed and thus it is to become a civil right."[35] "Religious communities . . . have the right not to be hindered in their public teaching and witness to their faith, whether by the spoken or

---

[32] Michael Walsh, "U-turn on Human Rights," TABLET [London], Dec. 14, 2002. See also R. Scott Appleby, *The Ambivalence of the Sacred: Religion, Violence, and Reconciliation* 44 (1999) (quoting David Hollenbach's summary of the pre-Vatican II Church's rationale):
> The Roman Catholic faith is the true religion. It is good for people to believe what is true. The state is obliged to promote Catholic belief, and wherever possible to establish Catholicism as the religion of the state. Advocates of religious freedom are denying one of the cardinal premises of Roman Catholicism: they are rejecting the absolute truth of Catholic Christianity.

[33] See, in addition to Walsh's article (n. 32), John A. Coleman, SJ, "Religious Liberty: Unfinished Items from the Council," AMERICA, Nov. 28, 2005, at 9.

[34] *Dignitatis Humanae*, section 3.

[35] Section 2.

by the written word."³⁶ "[G]overnment is to assume the safeguard of the religious freedom of all its citizens, in an effective manner, by just laws and by other appropriate means."³⁷ Religious freedom "is to be recognized as the right of all men and communities and sanctioned by constitutional law."³⁸ In its final section, *Dignitatis Humanae* declares: "The fact is that men of the present day want to be able freely to profess their religion in private and in public. Indeed, religious freedom has already been declared to be a civil right in most constitutions, and it is solemnly recognized in international documents.... This council [Vatican II] greets with joy [this fact] as among the signs of the times."³⁹

In embracing the right to religious freedom, the Church, in *Dignitatis Humanae*, abandoned a theocratic conception of political authority. According to *Dignitatis Humanae*, "[n]o merely human power can either command [acts contrary to one's religious conscience] or prohibit [acts in accordance with one's religious conscience]."⁴⁰ "Government... would clearly transgress the limits set to its power, were it to presume to command or inhibit acts that are religious."⁴¹

Although *Dignitatis Humanae* succeeded in explaining, in clear terms consistent with earlier papal pronouncements, the Church's traditional support for the right to freedom of religious *belief*,⁴² it failed to explain in such terms – indeed, it was impossible to explain in such terms – the Church's U-turn with respect to the right to freedom of religious *practice*.⁴³ (Why didn't the authors of *Dignitatis Humanae*

---

³⁶ Section 4. *Dignitatis Humanae* goes on to say: "However, in spreading religious faith and in introducing religious practices everyone ought at all times to refrain from any manner of action which might seem to carry a hint of coercion or of a kind of persuasion that would be dishonorable or unworthy, especially when dealing with poor or uneducated people. Such a manner of action would have to be considered an abuse of one's right and a violation of the right of others." Id.
³⁷ Section 6.
³⁸ Section 13.
³⁹ Section 15.
⁴⁰ Id.
⁴¹ Id.
⁴² That is, the right to freedom of religious belief for "the nonbaptized." See John T. Noonan, Jr., *The Lustre of Our Country: The American Experience of Religious Freedom* 150 (1998): "As a review of history, [*Dignitatis Humanae*] failed badly.... It mentioned only the freedom traditionally accorded the nonbaptized. It never acknowledged the long record of coercing the baptized when they were considered to be in heresy."
⁴³ See generally Noonan, *A Church That Can and Cannot Change*, n. 28, at 145–58; Noonan, *The Lustre of Our Country*, n. 42, at 348–53.

forthrightly acknowledge in the text of the document the impossibility of such an explanation? "Reticence to reject the past by explicit reference to the rejected doctrine was, no doubt, the price paid for the unity finally achieved."[44]) One fierce critic of the Church's reversal has complained:

> The new year of 1995 marks thirty years since the close of the Second Vatican Council, and without a doubt the confusion, division and loss of faith within the Catholic Church can be directly attributed to some of the decrees and declarations of the Council, and the most destructive of the Catholic Faith after the Council, was the decree *Dignitatis Humanae* on Religious Liberty....
>
> The reason this decree was the most controversial and the most destructive is that it explicitly taught doctrines previously condemned by past Popes. And this was so blatant that many conservative Council Fathers opposed it to the very end; while even the liberal cardinals, bishops and theologians who promoted the teachings of *Dignitatis Humanae* had to confess their inability to reconcile this decree with the past condemnations of Popes.[45]

Nonetheless, the Catholic Church now embraces the right to religious freedom. "In a striking twentieth-century reversal," writes Catholic historian R. Scott Appleby of *Dignitatis Humanae*, "the Catholic Church abandoned its previous claims to political privilege, renounced the theocratic model of political order, and became a powerful proponent of religious liberty."[46] Appleby continues: "It is difficult to overstate the depth and scope of the ecclesial transformation that occurred over the course of the twentieth century."[47] What led to that "striking reversal"? (Again, much of what *Dignitatis Humanae* says

---

[44] Noonan, *A Church That Can and Cannot Change*, n. 28, at 158.

[45] Bishop Mark A. Pivarunas, CMRI, "The Doctrinal Errors of *Dignitatis Humanae*," http://www.cmri.org/95prog2.htm. For a taste of earlier papal condemnations of protestantism and the idea of religious freedom, see John Witte, Jr., "The Serpentine Wall of Separation," 101 MICHIGAN L. REV. 1869, 1899–900 (2003).

[46] Appleby, n. 32, at 42.

[47] Id. at 43. "Until 1965 Roman Catholicism had legitimated the denial of civil and other human rights to non-Catholics by teaching, in effect, that 'theological error has no rights' in a properly governed (i.e., Roman Catholic) state." Id.
   How far has the Church come? Consider this:
   In Italy, where there is an ongoing debate about the place of 900,000 Muslims in Italian society, reciprocity has become an issue. Should Muslim children be taught the Qur'an in Italian schools, as Catholic children are taught Christianity? Cardinal Renato Martino, head of the Pontifical Council for Justice and Peace, said this "sign of human respect" should not be regarded as something to barter, to improve the treatment of Christians in Muslim countries. He was right, for

First Principles

makes sense as an argument, not for the right to freedom of religious *practice*, but only for the right to freedom of religious *belief*.) What led the Church in 1965 to abandon its theocratic conception of political authority?

I suggested in the preceding section of this chapter that the fundamental warrant for liberal democracy's commitment to the right to religious freedom is rooted in historical experience. The same historical experience helps to explain *Dignitatis Humanae*; it helps to explain why in 1965 the Roman Catholic Church finally came round to embrace the very right to religious freedom to which liberal democracy is committed – and to embrace the right on substantially the same basis liberal democracy embraces it. An overwhelming majority of the cardinals and bishops at the council (2,308 to 70) accepted an argument the Church had long rejected: liberal democracy's argument for the right to religious freedom.

In particular, they accepted liberal democracy's claim that government is not to be trusted as an arbiter of religious (or anti-religious) truth. By the time of the Second Vatican Council, the era had largely ended in which the Church could realistically expect to wield the kind of influence over a state – *any* state – that it had once wielded over some states.[48] Moreover, a new era was well under way, one in which Catholicism and other religions rightly feared for their freedom at

> respect for the religious rights of Muslims is required by Catholic teaching. He presumably has the Pope's ear on this matter.

Editorial, "Religious Freedom Is Universal," TABLET [London], Mar. 15, 2006.

[48] See Griffin, n. 31, at 249: "According to [Jacques] Maritain, the sacral state was a thing of the past. In the modern world, both Church and state were autonomous." Cf. John L. Allen, Jr., "All Things Catholic," NCRonline.org, July 7, 2006 (quoting Mary Vincent, an expert on Spanish history at the University of Sheffield in England, responding to the question "Are the clashes between [Socialist Prime Minister Zapatero] and the [Catholic Church in Spain] the continuation of tensions that go back to the [Spanish] Civil War"):

> They're in continuity with conflicts surrounding the emergence of democracy in Spain in the 1970s... [T]he church was hugely important in creating a new model of Spanish society. Lay Catholics had been active leading up to the transition, inspired by the Second Vatican Council (1962–65). The days of the confessional state were over.
>
> ...
>
> For the left and for many secular commentators, this meant the church would exercise strict political neutrality, and concentrate on saving souls. For Catholics, their understanding was that the church would always have a public role, but the

the hands of militantly atheistic, totalitarian governments. *Dignitatis Humanae* notes and then denounces, "as only to be deplored," the fact "that forms of government still exist under which, even though freedom of religious worship receives constitutional recognition, the powers of government are engaged in the effort to deter citizens from the profession of religion and to make life very difficult and dangerous for religious communities."[49] Clearly, the claim that government is not to be trusted as an arbiter of religious truth was reinforced, for the cardinals and bishops at the Second Vatican Council, by "the negative experience of terrible totalitarian regimes."[50]

Moreover, "the positive experience of religious freedom under the American constitution"[51] made it much easier for the cardinals and bishops to accept the claim that government is not to be trusted as an arbiter of religious truth. The American experience demonstrated just how well religion – not least, Catholicism itself – can flourish where government is not trusted as an arbiter of religious truth – where, that is, religious freedom thrives. As John Noonan has recounted:

> Above all, there were the example and influence of the United States. Where else had Christianity thrived so well as in this nation where freedom of religion and the separation of Church and State were enshrined in the constitution of the country? For the bishops of the United States, freedom of religion was their issue. A bloc, powerful in their resources, the bishops had an articulate advisor and draftsman in John Courtney Murray,

> country was no longer a confessional state, and Spanish law would not necessarily be formed by Catholic morals.
>
> I would be hesitant to trace the conflict back before that, to the Civil War or the Second Republic (1931–39), because the church changed so fundamentally in the 1960s and 1970s. They realized that the confessional state under Franco did not accomplish what it was supposed to accomplish. It didn't manage to get people back to church; it didn't evangelize the working classes and other disaffected groups that had been lost in the early 20th century. All that became apparent, and it triggered an extraordinary examination of conscience within the Spanish church.

[49] Section 15.
[50] Noonan, *A Church That Can and Cannot Change*, n. 28, at 158. Cf. Abduh An-Na'im, in his new book: "The fundamental defect of the idea of the Islamic state is that the logic of the invocation of religious or moral authority can very easily be inverted, so that instead of regulating political power by religious authority, religion itself become subordinated to power."
[51] Noonan, *A Church That Can and Cannot Change*, n. 28, at 158.

a leading American jesuit, silenced in the years preceding the council, then shoehorned into its advisors by Cardinal Francis Spellman, archbishop of New York. The lustre of the American experience was not lost upon the Fathers of Vatican II.[52]

The cardinals and bishops at Vatican II brought to bear the lessons of historical experience, both negative and positive; they – and, ultimately, Pope Paul VI – concluded that there was much to be gained and little if anything to be lost by joining the growing movement for universal religious freedom. (John Courtney Murray said that "[t]he Church came late to a war that was already won."[53]) The small minority of cardinals and bishops at the council who refused to bow to the lessons of historical experience – who continued to reject liberal democracy's twofold argument for the right to religious freedom – "appear[ed] to be creatures from a cave where sunlight had never penetrated."[54]

Dignitatis Humanae demonstrates just how powerfully subversive a teacher historical experience can be: What "had [been] taught as the doctrine of the Church was now gone beyond recall. What had been folly for [earlier popes] now earned the praise of pope and council in 1965."[55]

The principal reason the magisterium of the Roman Catholic Church finally embraced, at the Second Vatican Council, the right to religious freedom – embraced it, that is, as a right to be universally legislated – was not specifically Christian, much less Catholic. That is not surprising because, again, all citizens of liberal democracy – Catholics no less than non-Catholics, Christians no less than non-Christians, believers no less than nonbelievers – have the same basic reason to embrace

---

[52] Id. at 155. See also Francis Campbell, "No Future in the Ghetto," TABLET [London], Feb. 1, 2008: "At the start of the twentieth century, Catholicism had a very ambivalent attitude to democracy.... Experience changed the stance of the Catholic Church towards democracy and religious freedom – the positive experience of Catholic minorities living in countries like the United States and other English-speaking countries, coupled with the negative experince of Catholics in Nazi Germany and Fascist Italy."

[53] Quoted in Coleman, n. 33, at 10.

[54] Noonan, *A Church That Can and Cannot Change*, n. 28, at 158.

[55] Id. Cf. Editorial, "The Challenge for Islam," TABLET [London], July 8, 2006, at 2: "A hundred years ago, convinced that the modern world was a threat, the [Catholic] Church then – like fundamentalist Muslims now – was implacably opposed to democracy, religious tolerance, and human rights. Now, thanks to the teachings of the Second Vatican Council and Pope John XXIII, it has no hesitation in standing up for them."

the right to religious freedom: *Government – a political majority – is not to be trusted (beyond a certain point) as an arbiter of religious truth; moreover, the coercive imposition of religious uniformity is (beyond a certain point) more likely to corrode than to nurture the strength of a democracy.* Religious believers do not have less reason than nonbelievers – instead, *religious believers and nonbelievers have the same basic reason* – to insist that government not ban (or otherwise impede) a religious practice unless the ban is necessary to serve a legitimate governmental interest, the weight of which is proportionate to the weight of the burden imposed by the ban.

5

Beyond Religious Freedom: The Right to Moral Freedom

At the Second Vatican Council (1962–65), the celebrated American Jesuit John Courtney Murray played a leading role, as is well known, in persuading the magisterium of the Roman Catholic Church – the bishops and, ultimately, the pope – to embrace the right to religious freedom.[1] (I discussed the fruit of Murray's labors, *Dignitatis Humanae*, in Chapter 4.) Murray was concerned with more than just religious freedom, however; he was also concerned with what we may call moral freedom. In 1960, the year in which the first and, so far, only Catholic was elected to the presidency of the United States, Murray published *We Hold These Truths: Catholic Reflections on the American Proposition*. Murray wrote, in that now-famous book, that "the moral aspirations of the law are minimal. Laws seek to establish and maintain only that minimum of actualized morality that is necessary for the healthy functioning of the social order."[2] According to Murray, the law should "not look to what is morally desirable, or attempt to remove every moral taint from the atmosphere of society. It [should] enforce only what is minimally acceptable, and in this sense socially necessary."[3]

"But *why* should 'the moral aspirations of the law' be only 'minimal'," we may fairly ask. "*Why* should 'laws seek to establish and maintain only that minimum of actualized morality that is necessary for the healthy functioning of the social order'? *Why* should the law 'enforce only what is minimally acceptable, and in this sense socially necessary'?" I provide an answer in this chapter, in the course of

---

[1] See Leslie Griffin, "Commentary on *Dignitatis humanae* (Declaration on Religious Freedom)," in Kenneth R. Himes, ed., MODERN CATHOLIC SOCIAL TEACHING: COMMENTARIES AND INTERPRETATIONS 244 (2004).
[2] John Courtney Murray, SJ, We *Hold These Truths: Catholic Reflections on the American Proposition* 166 (1960).
[3] Id.

defending this claim: The case for liberal democracy's commitment to the right to moral freedom is analogous to and no less compelling than the case for its commitment to the right to religious freedom; therefore, liberal democracy should be committed to the former right as well as to the latter; it should be committed to *moral* freedom as well as to *religious* freedom.

The right to moral freedom (as I conceive it) is analogous to the right to religious freedom: It is the right to freedom to live one's life in harmony with one's moral convictions and commitments. Like the right to religious freedom, the right to moral freedom is broad rather than narrow. The former right is broad in that it presupposes a broad account of "religion": Buddhism, for example, no less than Christianity, counts as a religion for purposes of the right, notwithstanding that Buddhism is, in the main, nontheistic. Similarly, the right to moral freedom is broad in that it presupposes a broad account – an ecumenical rather than sectarian account – of "morality": "Moral" convictions and commitments are the yield of one's conscientious effort to discern what choices – what voluntary, deliberate choices – are, *all things considered,* right rather than wrong, just rather than unjust, good rather than bad, or the like.

The "all things considered" in the preceding sentence is crucial. Let me repeat here something I said in Chapter 2:[4]

> In the real world, if not in every academic moralist's study, fundamental moral questions are intimately related to religious (or metaphysical) questions; there is no way to address fundamental moral questions without also addressing, if only implicitly, religious questions. (That is *not* to say that one must give a religious answer to a religious question, like the question, for example, Does God exist? Obviously many people do not give religious answers to religious questions.) In the real world, one's response to fundamental moral questions has long been intimately bound up with one's response – one's answers – to certain other fundamental questions: Who are we? Where did we come from; what is our origin, our beginning? Where are we going; what is our destiny, our end? What is the meaning of suffering? Of evil? Of death? And there is the cardinal question, the question that comprises many of the others: Is human life ultimately meaningful or, instead, ultimately bereft of meaning, meaning-less, absurd? If any questions are fundamental, *these* questions – "religious or limit questions" – are fundamental. Such questions – "naive" questions, "questions with no answers," "barriers that cannot be breached" – are "the most serious and

---

[4] See Chapter 2, nn. 40–47 and accompanying text.

difficult ... that any human being or society must face." John Paul II was surely right in his encyclical, *Fides et Ratio*, that such questions "have their common source in the quest for meaning which has always compelled the human heart" and that "the answer given to these questions decides the direction which people seek to give to their lives."

It is noteworthy that the Canadian Constitution seems to establish and protect a right substantially like the right to moral freedom. Section 2 of the Charter of Rights and Freedoms (1982), which is part of Canada's Constitution, states: "Everyone has the following fundamental freedoms: a) freedom of conscience and religion." The Supreme Court of Canada has written that "[t]he purpose of s. 2(a) is to ensure that society does not interfere with profoundly personal beliefs that govern one's perception of oneself, humankind, nature, and, in some cases, a higher or different order of being. These beliefs, in turn, govern one's practices."[5] According to the Canadian Supreme Court, the freedom established and protected by s. 2(a) "means that, subject to [certain limitations], no one is to be forced to act in a way contrary to his beliefs or his conscience."[6]

Recall from Chapter 4 that the right to religious freedom does not protect just choices (practices) one believes oneself religiously obligated to make. Such a limitation, as I explained, would make little sense: A choice one believes oneself religiously obligated to make (e.g., forsaking meat on Lenten Fridays) may be relatively inconsequential next to a choice (e.g., receiving communion wine) one does not believe oneself obligated to make but that, nonetheless, one has strong religious reason to make. Similarly, the right to moral freedom does not protect just choices one believes oneself morally obligated to make. A choice one believes oneself morally obligated to make may be relatively inconsequential next to a choice (e.g., working as a doctor in a desperately poor country, such as Haiti, rather than in the U.S. Army) one does not believe oneself morally obligated to make but that, nonetheless, one has strong moral reason to make.

(Just as a choice one has religious reason to make should not be confused with a choice one does not have religious reason not to make, so too a choice one has moral reason to make should not be confused with a choice one does not have moral reason not to make. The right to moral freedom protects only choices of the former sort.

---

[5] *R. v. Edwards Books and Art Ltd.*, [1986] 2 S.C.R. 713, 759.
[6] *R. v. Big M Drug Mart Ltd.*, [1985] 1 S.C.R. 295, 337.

A right that protected choices of the latter sort would protect a multitude of choices that cannot plausibly be described as moral in nature. My decision to run rather than bike this morning was not a moral choice.)

Consider the serious suffering human beings endure in consequence of being legally forbidden to live a life of moral integrity – legally forbidden, that is, to live one's life in harmony with the yield of one's moral conscience, in harmony with one's moral convictions and commitments. Being legally forbidden to practice – to put into practice – one's religion and being legally forbidden to practice one's morality lead to similar suffering, namely, the dis-integration of a central aspect of one's life.[7]

Given the serious suffering it causes, government's denial to (some or all of) its citizens of the freedom to practice their morality is unjustified, and the serious suffering it causes is therefore unwarranted, unless government has good reason to do so. According to the right to moral freedom, understood as analogous to the right to religious freedom, government has good reason to ban (or otherwise impede) a moral practice if, and only if, this condition is satisfied: The choice to enact the ban, rather than to forgo the ban in favor of a different policy, serves a governmental interest that is both legitimate and sufficiently weighty to be proportionate to the weight of the burden imposed by the ban on those subject to the ban. Or, more simply: The ban is necessary to serve a legitimate and sufficiently weighty governmental interest. What I said in the preceding chapter with respect to the right to religious freedom is no less true with respect to the right to moral freedom: A right to moral freedom would provide little meaningful protection for moral freedom if the consistency of the ban with the right was to be determined without regard to whether the weight of the interest served by the ban was relatively slight in relation to the weight of the burden imposed by the ban.

Under the right to moral freedom, what counts as a "legitimate" governmental interest? Although, again, no exhaustive list of such interests is possible, there are certain imaginable governmental interests that cannot count as legitimate under the right to moral freedom, because to count them as legitimate would be to render the right

---

[7] See Steven D. Smith, 'What Does Religion Have to Do with Freedom of Conscience?' 76 U. COLORADO L. REV. 911 (2005). Cf. id. at 932: "[H]aving and acting on core beliefs is central to what makes us 'persons'."

meaningless; it would be to take away with one's left hand what one has given with one's right. (Again, the Siracusa Principles state: "The scope of a limitation referred to in the Covenant shall not be interpreted so as to jeopardize the essence of the right concerned."[8]) To affirm the right as one the law should establish and protect is necessarily to reject, in particular, the following three imaginable govermental interests as illegitimate.

The first imaginable-but-illegitimate governmental interest is *protecting (what the powers-that-be regard as) moral truth.* We can easily imagine the powers-that-be declaring: "Certain moral teachings are true – for example, the teaching that homosexual sexual activity is immoral – and no government should lack authority to ban practices that may lead some people to reject those teachings." That position is not persuasive to those of us who, after reflecting on historical experience, are skeptical about government's ability – including, in a liberal democracy, a political majority's ability – to discern not just religious truth but also moral truth. We are understandably and justifiably wary not just about government's acting as an arbiter of religious truth but also about its acting as an arbiter of moral truth.[9]

That is, we are wary about government's acting as an arbiter of moral truth *beyond a certain point.*

- Again, a *liberal* democracy is committed to the proposition that every human being has inherent dignity and is inviolable; in the political culture of a liberal democracy, that proposition is axiomatic. In a liberal democracy, government should act in accord with the proposition even if some moralities reject the proposition.
- Certain govermental interests are undeniably legitimate, and government must be legally free to serve such interests: for example, protecting the lives, health, and safety of the citizenry. Decisions about whether in a particular context to serve such an interest, decisions about the extent to which to do so, decisions about how to do so – these are all, whatever else they are, moral decisions. So government must act as an arbiter of moral disagreements that implicate one or more legitimate governmental interests.

---

[8] United Nations, Economic and Social Council, U.N. Sub-Commission on Prevention of Discrimination and Protection of Minorities, *Siracusa Principles on the Limitations and Derogation of Provisions in the International Covenant on Civil and Political Rights,* Annex, UN Doc E/CN.4/1984/4 (1984) at I.A.2.

[9] See n. 14 and accompanying text.

But beyond that certain point, government should not be trusted as an arbiter of moral truth. In particular, government need not act – and we should be wary about its acting – as an arbiter of moral disagreements that do not implicate any legitimate governmental interest. We should affirm, with Locke, that "the business of laws is not to provide for the truth of opinions, but [only] for the safety and security of the commonwealth, and of every particular man's goods and persons."[10] Henceforth, when I say we should not trust government as an arbiter of moral truth, I mean that we should not trust government as an arbiter of moral disagreements *that do not implicate a legitimate governmental interest.*

Notice, then, the right to moral freedom does not remove – nor is it aimed at removing – moral controversies from the politics of a liberal democracy. (What a quixotic ambition that would be!) Even in a liberal democracy that takes seriously the right to moral freedom, politics will provide many occasions for serious moral controversy. Something Robin Lovin wrote, in commenting on my argument, is relevant here:

> If we adopt Michael's proposal about moral tolerance and the purposes of government, we will need to be candid that we are not proposing it as an end to social conflict over moral issues. We are proposing that if we are going to make morality the subject of political discussion, the questions at issue must concern things with which government is necessarily involved, not simply those issues in which some of us want to use the coercive powers of government to keep other people from doing things we think they ought not to do. I, for one, would welcome that shift in the terms of the public moral argument, but I wouldn't expect it to be any less contentious than the arguments we are having now.[11]

The second imaginable-but-illegitimate governmental interest is *protecting the moral unity of society.* We can easily imagine the

---

[10] John Locke, *Letter Concerning Toleration* (1689), translated (from a less familiar to a more familiar English) by William Popple, http://www.constitution.org/j1/tolerati.htm.

[11] Lovin also said:
> It is important to recognize that freedom of moral practice is a moral commitment, because although the moral arguments for it are the same as the moral arguments for religious freedom, we cannot offer the same practical or prudential incentives for moral tolerance that Locke, for example, could offer his contemporaries for accepting religious tolerance. He could suggest, plausibly, that that toleration would reduce the social friction of religious conflict, and for a nation that still had a wary eye to the recent history of religious warfare, that was often a good enough reason to try it. Freedom of moral practice, I think, is not likely to reduce conflict, but to shift its terms.

powers-that-be declaring: "In the long run, moral unity, understood as a kind of 'glue', enhances the strength of a nation; therefore, no government should lack authority to ban practices that over time may diminish the nation's moral unity and thereby weaken the nation." But that position is farfetched: If it is not necessary to serve some other governmental interest – for example, protecting the lives, health, or safety of the citizenry – the coercive imposition of moral uniformity, like the coercive imposition of religious uniformity, is more likely to corrode than to nurture the strength of a democracy, especially if the democracy is, as liberal democracies typically and increasingly are, morally as well as religiously pluralistic.

The final imaginable-but-illegitimate interest is *protecting the moral "health" of the citizenry*. Health includes, of course, psychological as well as physical health; indeed, we have learned – and are still learning – that with respect to many illnesses, such as clinical ("major") depression, the line between the "physical" (e.g., genetic) and the "psychological" is far from clear. In any event, one's psychological health, no less than one's physical health, is a legitimate governmental concern. (Bans on the use of some addictive substances, such as heroin, are best understood, I think, as aimed at least partly at protecting psychological health.) But does health also include what one may call "moral" health, so that protecting the moral health of the citizenry is a legitimate governmental interest?

In the context of religion and morality, we must be wary about using the term *health* metaphorically.[12] To affirm the right to religious freedom is to reject the proposition that protecting the religious (or spiritual) health of the citizenry is a legitimate governmental interest, because if protecting the citizenry's religious health were a legitimate governmental interest, the right to religious freedom would be largely meaningless: A political majority could ban a religious practice whenever it judged the practice, and the religious belief that animates the practice, to be seriously detrimental to the religious health – the religious well-being – not only of those who engage in the practice, but also of those who might be influenced to do likewise. ("Practicing

---

[12] Moreover, we must be alert to the possibility that a conception of moral health is distorting a conception of psychological health. The most prominent recent example of that phenomenon: The traditional moral condemnation of homosexuality is one of the main factors that led psychiatrists to understand homosexuality as a psychopathology. See Ronald Bayer, *Homosexuality and American Psychiatry: The Politics of Diagnosis* (1981).

a false religion – say, one according to which Jesus Christ is *not* the Son of God and the Lord and Saviour of all – is profoundly detrimental to one's religious health.") Similarly, to affirm the right to moral freedom is to reject the proposition that protecting the moral health of the citizenry is a legitimate governmental interest, because if protecting the citizenry's moral health were a legitimate governmental interest, the right to moral freedom would be largely meaningless: A political majority could ban a moral practice whenever it judged the practice, and the moral belief that animates the practice, to be seriously detrimental to the moral health – the moral well-being – not only of those who engage in the practice, but also of those who might be influenced to do likewise. ("Practicing a false morality – say, one according to which same-sex sexual intimacy can be a great human good – is profoundly detrimental to one's moral health.") Protecting one's physical and/or psychological health is undeniably a legitimate governmental interest, but protecting one's moral health cannot be, consistently with the right to moral freedom, a legitimate governmental interest, any more than protecting one's religious health can be, consistently with the right to religious freedom, a legitimate governmental interest.

So, if one thinks that in a liberal democracy there is no good reason for us not to trust political majorities as arbiters of religious truth, and that protecting the religious health of the citizenry should therefore be deemed a legitimate governmental interest, one should – like the pre-Vatican II Catholic Church – oppose the right to religious freedom. Similarly, if one thinks that there is no good reason for us not to trust political majorities as arbiters of moral truth, and if, like Catholic moralist Robert George, one thinks that protecting the moral health of the citizenry – and, relatedly, the moral "ecology" of the community, as George puts it – should therefore be deemed a legitimate governmental interest,[13] one should, and no doubt will, oppose the proposed right to moral freedom. *Pace* evangelical-Christian scholar (and federal judge) Michael McConnell, we may ask Robert George: "Is the Civil Magistrate about whom John Locke wrote more 'competent a judge' of the 'Truth' about, for example, human sexuality than about religion?"[14]

---

[13] See Robert P. George, "Law and Moral Purpose," FIRST THINGS, January 2008, at 22.
[14] Michael W. McConnell, "The Problem of Singling Out Religion," 50 DEPAUL L. REV. 1, 44 (2000).

First Principles

For those of us who think that there is good reason – that our historical experience provides us with good reason – not to trust political majorities as arbiters of moral truth (or moral health), and who support the proposed right to moral freedom, the trajectory of American law over the course of the last century is heartening. In practice if not in principle, American law has been moving in the direction of moral freedom. As legal historian William Novak has noted, "[b]y the standards of late twentieth-century law, the public regulation of morality is increasingly suspect."[15] Novak explains:

> The burgeoning public/private distinction, the jurisprudential separation of law and morality, and the expansion of constitutionally protected rights of expression and privacy have yielded a polity whose legitimacy theoretically rests on its ability to keep out of the private moral affairs of its citizens. As the American Law Institute declared in the 1955 Model Penal Code, "We deem it inappropriate for the government to attempt to control behavior that has no substantial significance except as to the morality of the actor." "Public morality" may soon become an oxymoron.[16]

In my judgment, the right to *moral* freedom is a compelling extension of the right to *religious* freedom – an extension animated by the logic, so to speak, of the fundamental warrant for liberal democracy's commitment to the right to religious freedom.[17]

---

[15] William J. Novak, *The People's Welfare: Law and Regulation in Nineteenth-Century America* 149 (1996).

[16] Id. Novak goes on to illustrate that "[t]he relationship between laws and morals in the nineteenth century could not have been more different. Of all the contests over public power in that period, morals regulation was the easy case." Id. at 149. See id. at 149–89. For a constitutional decision that tends to confirm Novak's prediction about public morality's becoming an oxymoron, see *Lawrence v. Texas*, 539 U.S. 558 (2003).

[17] According to Greg Kalscheur, the logic of *Dignitatis Humanae* supports the right to moral freedom no less than the right to religious freedom. See Gregory A. Kalscheur, SJ, "Moral Limits on Morals Legislation: Lessons for U.S. Constitutional Law from the Declaration on Religious Freedom," 16 SOUTHERN CALIFORNIA INTERDISCIPLINARY L. J. 1 (2006).

For an argument that the free exercise clause of the U.S. Constitution *can* be interpreted broadly to protect (some) nonreligious moral practice as well as (some) religious practice, see Smith, n. 7, at 911–13. For arguments that the free exercise clause *should* be interpreted broadly to protect nonreligious moral practice, see Douglas Laycock, "Regulatory Exemptions of Religious Behavior and the Original Understanding of the Establishment Clause," 81 NOTRE DAME L. REV. 1793, 1838–39 (2006); Chad Flanders, "The Possibility of a Secular First Amendment," 26 QUEEN'S L. REV. 257, 288–303 (2008). Cf. Benjamin M. Eidelson, "A Penumbra Overlooked: The Free Exercise Clause and *Lawrence v. Texas*," 30 HARVARD J. L. & GENDER 203 (2007).

It is fitting, therefore, that Article 18 of the ICCPR, which recognizes and protects the right to religious freedom, also recognizes and protects – or certainly seems to – the right to moral freedom. Article 18 states that "[e]veryone shall have the right to freedom of . . . conscience" as well as to freedom of religion, and states further that "[t]his right shall include freedom to have or adopt a religion *or belief* of his choice, and freedom, either individually or in community with others and in public or private, to manifest his religion *or belief* in worship, observance, practice and teaching" (emphasis added). Article 18 explicitly affirms the close connection between religious freedom and moral freedom when it states that "[t]he State parties to the [ICCPR] undertake to have respect for the liberty of parents and, when applicable, legal guardians to assure the religious *and moral* education of their children in conformity with their own convictions." According to Article 18, "[f]reedom to manifest one's religion *or belief* may be subject only to such limitations as are prescribed by law and are necessary to protect public safety, order, health, or morals or the fundamental rights and freedoms of others" (emphasis added). Again, the Siracusa Principles state, in relevant part: "Whenever a limitation is required in the terms of the [ICCPR] to be 'necessary,' this term implies that the limitation: . . . (b) responds to a pressing public or social need, (c) pursues a legitimate aim, and (d) is proportionate to that aim."[18]

As with the right to religious freedom, so too with the right to moral freedom: All citizens of liberal democracy – Christians of every stripe, Catholics included, no less than non-Christians and nonbelievers – have the same basic reason to embrace the right to moral freedom: *Government – a political majority – is not to be trusted (i.e., beyond a certain point) as an arbiter of moral truth; moreover, the coercive imposition of moral uniformity is (beyond a certain point) more likely to corrode than to nurture the strength of a democracy.* Religious believers do not have less reason than nonbelievers – instead, *religious believers and nonbelievers have the same basic reason* – to insist that government not ban (or otherwise impede) a moral practice unless the ban is necessary to serve a legitimate governmental interest, the weight of which is proportionate to

---

[18] United Nations, Economic and Social Council, U.N. sub-Commission on Prevention of Discrimination and Protection of Minorities, *Siracusa Principles on the Limitations and Derogration of Provisions in the International Covenant on Civil and Political Rights*, Annex, UN Doc E/CN.4/1984/4 (1984) at I.A.10.

the weight of the burden imposed by the ban. Christians and other believers no less than nonbelievers – all of them have good reason, *the same good reason*, to affirm, with John Courtney Murray, that "the moral aspirations of the law [should be] minimal. Laws [should] seek to establish and maintain only that minimum of actualized morality that is necessary for the healthy functioning of the social order."[19]

If, as I have argued in this chapter, the right to *moral* freedom is a compelling extension of the right to *religious* freedom – an extension animated, as I said, by the logic of the fundamental warrant for liberal democracy's commitment to the right to religious freedom – then liberal democracy should recognize and protect the right to moral freedom as a fundamental legal right, just as it recognizes and protects the right to religious freedom as a fundamental legal right.

In the United States and in most other liberal democracies, the courts are empowered to enforce fundamental legal rights. The question arises, therefore, how deferential or nondeferential should the courts be, to the country's lawmakers and other policymakers, in enforcing the right to moral freedom. I address that question, with particular reference to the U.S. Supreme Court, in Chapter 9.[20]

Let's assume, however, for the sake of discussion, that in a particular liberal democracy, for one reason or another reason, the courts are not empowered to enforce fundamental legal rights;[21] or, at least, that they are not empowered to enforce the right to moral freedom, perhaps because the right to moral freedom is not, in that democracy,

---

[19] See n. 1.

There are many well-rehearsed *practical* problems with using the criminal law to regulate morality – problems that lead even some who would reject the right to moral freedom to oppose some instances of so-called morals legislation. See, e.g., Robert P. George, *Making Men Moral* 41–42 (1993). See also David Skeel & William J. Stuntz, "Christianity and the (Modest) Rule of Law" (arguing that in part because of such practical problems, Christians should be wary about using the criminal law to regulate morality); Joseph Boyle, "Positivism, Natural Law, and Disestablishment," 20 VALPARAISO L. REV. 55, 59 (1985): "Thomas Aquinas, a natural lawyer if ever there was one, ... argues that the law should not seek to prohibit all vices, but only the more serious ones, and 'especially those which involve *harm to others*, without whose prohibition human society could not be preserved.'" (Quoting Thomas Aquinas, *summa theologiae* at First Part of the Second Part, Question 96, Article 2; emphasis added.)

[20] See also Michael J. Perry, *Constitutional Rights, Moral Controversy, and the Supreme Court* (2009).

[21] Cf. Jeremy Waldron, "The Core of the Case Against Judicial Review," 115 YALE L. J. 1346 (2006).

a fundamental legal right. Even so, the right to moral freedom can serve, in the political culture of a liberal democracy, as a fundamental political-moral norm.[22] And, for the reasons I have given in this chapter, the right should serve, in the political culture of every liberal democracy, as a fundamental political-moral norm.

In Chapters 7 and 8, I illustrate the important role the right to moral freedom can play – that is, the right understood (only) as a fundamental political-moral norm – *in shaping a liberal democracy's discourse about vexing, divisive political-moral controversies*, such as those in the United States over abortion (may government ban it?) and same-sex unions (may government refuse to extend the benefit of law to them?).

---

[22] Cf. James B. Thayer, "The Origin and Scope of the American Doctrine of Constitutional Law," 7 HARVARD L. REV. 129, 130 (1893) (quoting Albert Venn Dicey, *An Introduction to the Study of the Law of the Constitution* [1885]): "The restrictions placed on the action of the legislature under the French constitution are not in reality laws, since they are not rules which in the last resort will be enforced by the courts. Their true character is that of maxims of political morality, which derive whatever strength they possess from being formally inscribed in the constitution, and from the resulting support of public opinion."

6
Religion as a Basis of Lawmaking

A law that *implicates* either the right to religious freedom or the right to moral freedom (or both) *violates* the right unless the law serves a governmental interest that is both legitimate and sufficiently weighty to be proportionate to the weight of the burden imposed by the ban on those subject to the ban. Assume that the only reason for concluding that a law serves a legitimate and sufficiently weighty governmental interest – the only reason, that is, other than an implausible secular reason – is a religious reason. ("God will punish us, in the here-and-now – God will visit a plague or pestilence on us – unless we ban behavior X!") Is such a rationale – a *religious* rationale – a legitimate basis of lawmaking in the United States? Is such a rationale a legitimate basis of lawmaking in any liberal democracy?

I. RELIGION AS A BASIS OF LAWMAKING IN THE UNITED STATES

Like other liberal democracies, the United States is committed to the right to religious freedom. Unlike most other liberal democracies, however, the United States is also committed to the nonestablishment of religion.[1] According to the constitutional law of the United States, government – that is, lawmakers and other government officials – may

---

[1] Like the United States, France is constitutionally committed to the nonestablishment of religion, which in France is called "laïcité." See Cécile Laborde, "Secular Philosophy and Muslim Headscarves in Schools," 13 J. POLITICAL PHILOSOPHY 305, 308 (2005):
> On 11 December 1905, republicans in power [in France] abolished the *Concordat* which, since 1801, had regulated the relationships between the French state and "recognized religions" and had, in practice, entrenched the political and social power of the dominant Catholic Church. The first two articles of the 1905 Law of Separation between Church and State read:
>> Article 1. The Republic ensures freedom of conscience. It guarantees the free exercise of religions.
>> Article 2. It neither recognises nor subsidises any religion.

Religion as a Basis of Lawmaking

neither prohibit the "free exercise" of religion nor "establish" religion.[2] Does the nonestablishment norm (as I like to call it) ban religion as a basis of lawmaking? More precisely, should the nonestablishment norm be understood to ban laws (and other policies) for which the only discernible rationale – other than, perhaps, an implausible secular rationale – is religious?[3]

A. May Government Affirm Religion?

The idea of an "established" church is familiar.[4] For Americans, the best-known and most relevant example is the Church of England,

> The principle of separation between church and state has since been recognized as a quasi constitutional principle, and is implicitly referred to in Article 1 of the 1946 Constitution, according to which "France is an indivisible, *laïque*, democratic and social republic."

[2] The First Amendment to the U.S. Constitution states, in relevant part: "Congress shall make no law respecting an establishment of religion, or prohibiting the free exercise thereof." I concur in Kent Greenawalt's judgment that "[b]y far the most plausible reading of the original religion clauses – based on their text, the history leading up to their enactment, and legislation enacted by Congress is that Congress could protect but not impair free exercise in carrying out its delegated powers for the entire country and within exclusively federal domains, that Congress could neither establish a religion within the states nor interfere with state establishments [of religion], and that Congress could not establish religion within exclusively federal domains." Kent Greenawalt, "Common Sense about Original and Subsequent Understandings of the Religion Clauses," 8 J. CONSTITUTIONAL LAW 479, 511 (2005). See also id. at 491; Kent Greenawalt, 2 *Religion and the Constitution: Establishment and Fairness* 38 (2008).

The religion clauses have long been held to apply not just to Congress but to the entire national government, and not just to the national government but to state government as well. In effect, then, the clauses provide that government may neither establish religion nor prohibit the free exercise thereof. See Michael W. McConnell, "Accommodation of Religion: An Update and Response to the Critics," 60 GEORGE WASHINGTON L. REV. 685, 690 (1992): "The government may not 'establish' religion and it may not 'prohibit' religion." McConnell explains, in a footnote attached to the word "establish," that "[t]he text [of the First Amendment] states the 'Congress' may make no law 'respecting an establishment' of religion, which meant that Congress could neither establish a national church nor interfere with the establishment of state churches as they then existed in the various states. After the last disestablishment in 1833 and the incorporation of the First Amendment against the states through the Fourteenth Amendment, this 'federalism' aspect of the Amendment has lost its significance, and the Clause can be read as forbidding the government to establish religion." Id. at 690 n. 19.

[3] R is the only discernible rationale for a law if but for R – if in the absence of R – the law would not have been enacted.

[4] If the idea is insufficiently familiar, see Michael W. McConnell, "Establishment and Disestablishment at the Founding, Part I: The Establishment of Religion," 44 WM. & MARY L. REV. 2105 (2003). For a sketch of different kinds of religious establishment,

which from before the time of the American founding to the present has been the established church in England.[5] (The Church of England was much more strongly established in the past than it is today.[6]) In the United States, however, unlike in England, there may be no established church. The imperative that government not establish religion means that government may not treat any church as the official church of the political community. (When I say "any church," I mean to include any range of theologically kindred churches – for example, Christian churches, which, although denominationally diverse, are sometimes referred to in the singular, as "the Christian church.") More precisely, government may not privilege any church in relation to any other church on the basis of the view that the favored church is, as a church, as a community of faith, better along one or another dimension of value – truer, for example, or more efficacious spiritually or politically,[7] or more authentically American.[8] In particular, government may not privilege, in law or policy, membership in any church – in the Fifth Avenue Baptist Church, for example, or in

---

from strong to weak, see W. Cole Durham, Jr., "Perspectives on Religious Liberty: A Comparative Framework," in Johan D. van der Vyver & John Witte, Jr., eds., *Religious Human Rights in Global Perspective: Legal Perspectives* 1, 19 et seq. (1996).

[5] Cf. Akhil Reed Amar, "Foreword: The Document and the Doctrine," 114 HARVARD L. REV. 26, 119 (2000): "Let us recall the world the Founders aimed to repudiate, a world where a powerful church hierarchy was anointed as the official government religion, where clerics ex officio held offices in the government, and where members of other religions were often barred from holding government posts."

[6] See Cheryl Saunders, "Comment: Religion and the State," 21 CARDOZO L. REV. 1295, 1295–96 (2000). Nonetheless, that England *still* has an established church remains controversial. See, e.g., Kenneth Leech, ed., *Setting the Church of England Free: The Case for Disestablishment* (2001); Clifford Longley, "Establishment – It's Got to Go," TABLET [London], May 11, 2002, at 2; Paul Weller, *Time for a Change: Reconfiguring Religion, State and Society* (2005). Cf. "The Act of Settlement Debate," TABLET [London], Aug. 11, 2007, at 4; Tim Hames, "'It would have been more honest to have called it the Dangerous Catholics Act,'" TABLET [London], Aug. 11, 2007, at 5 (the "it" in the title is the 1701 Act of Settlement).

[7] More efficacious politically? Imagine: A machiavellian advisor counsels the powers-that-be – who, let us assume, are atheists – that it would be better for social harmony if there were an established church, and that because the vast majority of the citizens are members of Church A, it makes more sense to establish Church A than Church B or Church C (etc.).

[8] As Justice William Brennan once put it: "It may be true that individuals cannot be 'neutral' on the question of religion. But the judgment of the Establishment Clause is that neutrality by the organs of *government* on questions of religion is both possible and imperative." *Marsh v. Chambers*, 463 U.S. 783, 821 (1983) (Brennan, J., joined by Marshall, J., dissenting).

Religion as a Basis of Lawmaking

the Roman Catholic Church, or in the Christian church generally;[9] nor may it privilege a worship practice – a prayer, liturgical rite, or religious observance[10] – or a theological doctrine peculiar to any church.[11]

Is it also the case that under the nonestablishment norm, government may not affirm any religious (theological) premises?

There are many different ways in which government in the United States affirms, or has affirmed, one or more religious premises. Here are some prominent examples: In 1954, the U.S. Congress added the words "under God" to the Pledge of Allegiance ("one nation under God").[12] Also in 1954, "Congress requested that all U.S. coins and paper currency bear the slogan, 'In God We Trust.' On July 11, 1955, President Eisenhower made this slogan mandatory on all currency. In 1956 the national motto was changed from 'E Pluribus Unum' to 'In God We Trust.'"[13] The proceedings of many American courts, including the U.S. Supreme Court, begin with a court official intoning "God

---

[9] For an example of a position that privileges the Christian church generally, see "Other Faiths Are Deficient, Pope Says," TABLET [London], Feb. 5, 2000, at 157: "The revelation of Christ is 'definitive and complete,' Pope John Paul affirmed to the Congregation for the Doctrine of the Faith, on 28 January. He repeated the phrase twice in an address which went on to say that non-Christians live in 'a deficient situation, compared to those who have the fullness of salvific means in the Church'." Nonetheless, "[Pope John Paul II] recognised, following the Second Vatican Council, that non-Christians can reach eternal life if they seek God with a sincere heart. But in that 'sincere search' they are in fact 'ordered' towards Christ and his Church." Id.

[10] Cf. Douglas Laycock, "Freedom of Speech That Is Both Religious and Political," 29 U. CALIFORNIA, DAVIS L. REV. 793, 812–13 (1996) (arguing that "[a]t the core of the Establishment Clause should be the principle that government cannot engage in a religious observance or compel or persuade citizens to do so").

[11] I don't discuss in this chapter the nonestablishment case law fashioned by the justices of the U.S. Supreme Court. It bears mention, however, that if Justice Clarence Thomas is right, that caselaw "is in hopeless disarray...." *Rosenberger v. Rector and Visitors of University of Virginia*, 515 U.S. 819, 861 (1995) (Thomas, J., concurring). Many constitutional scholars have said much the same thing. See, e.g., Jesse H. Choper, *Securing Religious Liberty: Principles for Judicial Interpretation of the Religion Clauses* 174–76 (1995); William Van Alstyne, "Ten Commandments, Nine Justices, and Five Versions of One Amendment – The First. ('Now What?')," 14 WM. & MARY BILL RTS. J. 17 (2005). Akhil Amar has referred to "the many outlandish (and contradictory) things that have been said about [the nonestablishment norm] in the *United States Reports*." Amar, n. 5, at 119.

[12] For a history of the Pledge of Allegiance, which makes its first appearance in 1892, see John W. Baer, *The Pledge of Allegiance: A Centennial History, 1892–1992* (1992). The story of adding "under God" to the Pledge involves both the Knights of Columbus (a Roman Catholic organization) and post-World War II anti-communism. See id. at 62–63.

[13] Id. at 63.

First Principles

save the United States and this Honorable Court."[14] Some states provided that their public schools should begin the day with Bible reading or prayer.[15] Some state officials, including some state judges, posted the Ten Commandments on government property, such as a public school classroom or hallway, a courtroom wall, or a courthouse lawn.[16] In at least some such instances, government was affirming one or more religious premises. Is the nonestablishment norm best understood to forbid government to affirm any religious premise whatsoever, no matter what the premise?

I am about to sketch two different understandings of what the nonestablishment norm forbids. But it bears emphasis that no sensible understanding of what the norm forbids denies either of these two propositions:

1. The nonestablishment norm forbids government to affirm any religious premise whose affirmation by government would violate the central meaning of the norm. For example, government may not affirm – explicitly or implicitly, directly or indirectly – that Jesus is Lord, or that the Roman Catholic Church is the one true church.
2. *If* there are one or more religious premises government may affirm – one or more premises, that is, whose affirmation by government would not violate the central meaning of the nonestablishment norm – government, in affirming such a premise, may not coerce anyone to affirm the premise or disadvantage anyone who refuses to do so.[17]

Given the central meaning of the nonestablishment norm, the first proposition follows as night follows day. We don't need the nonestablishment norm to warrant the second proposition; the free exercise norm – the right to the free exercise of religion – is sufficient. The

---

[14] See *Marsh v. Chambers*, 463 U.S. 783, 786 (1983): "In the very courtrooms in which the United States District Judge and later three Circuit Judges heard and decided this case, the proceedings opened with an announcement that concluded, 'God save the United States and this Honorable Court.' The same invocation occurs at all sessions of this Court."

[15] See, e.g., *Engel v. Vitale*, 370 U.S. 421 (1962); *School District of Abington Township v. Schempp and Murray v. Curlett*, 374 U.S. 203 (1963).

[16] See, e.g., *Stone v. Graham*, 449 U.S. 39 (1980); *McCreary County v. ACLU of Ky.*, 545 U.S. 844 (2005); *Van Orden v. Perry*, 545 U.S. 677 (2005).

[17] Sharp disagreement about whether government is in fact coercing anyone – or, more generally, about what, at the margin, "coerce" should be understood to mean – is not uncommon. See, e.g., *Lee v. Weisman*, 505 U.S. 577 (1992).

free exercise norm protects not only one's freedom to practice one's own religion, but also one's freedom *not* to practice, *not* to participate in, someone else's religion or indeed any religion at all. That "negative" freedom – that freedom not to practice a religion one rejects – includes the freedom not to affirm a religious premise one rejects.

Now, imagine two different understandings of what, in the context at hand, the nonestablishment norm forbids. According to the first, and more restrictive, understanding, government may not affirm any religious premise whatsoever. According to the second, and less restrictive, understanding, government may affirm any religious premise whatsoever whose affirmation by government would not violate the central meaning of the norm. The more restrictive understanding would be compelling if there were *no* religious premise whose affirmation by government would not violate the central meaning of the nonestablishment norm. But there are *some* religious premises whose affirmation by government does not violate the central meaning of the norm. A single example will suffice. Since 1954, the Pledge of Allegiance has echoed Abraham Lincoln's Gettysburg Address in declaring that we are "one nation under God." (At Gettysburg, Lincoln resolved that "this nation, under God, shall have a new birth of freedom.") In affirming, with Lincoln, that ours is a nation that stands under the judgment of a righteous God,[18]

---

[18] The Declaration of Independence, which marks the first formative moment in the emergence of the United States of America, famously relies – explicitly so – on belief in God: "We hold these truths to be self-evident, that all men are *created* equal, that they are endowed *by their Creator* with certain inalienable rights..." (emphasis added). If the Declaration marks a formative moment in the birth of the United States, two texts of Abraham Lincoln mark formative moments in the nation's rebirth: the Gettysburg Address and the Second Inaugural Address, which is surely one of the most theologically intense political speeches in American history. "The Almighty," said Lincoln in his Second Inaugural, "has his own purposes. 'Woe unto the world because of offences! for it must needs be that offences come; but woe to that man by whom the offence cometh!'" Lincoln continued:

> If we shall suppose that American Slavery is one of those offenses which, in the providence of God, must needs come, but which, having continued through his appointed time, He now wills to remove, and that He gives to both North and South, this terrible war, as the woe due to those by whom the offence came, shall we discern there any departure from those divine attributes which the believers in a Living God always ascribe to Him? Fondly do we hope – fervently do we pray – that this mighty scourge of war may speedily pass away. Yet, if God wills that it continue, until all the wealth piled by the bond-man's two hundred and fifty years of unrequited toil shall be sunk, and until every drop of blood drawn with the lash, shall be paid by another drawn by the sword, as was said three

First Principles

government is not treating any church – including the denominationally diverse Christian church – as the official church of the political community; government is not favoring any church in relation to any other church on the basis of the view that the favored church is, as a church, as a community of faith, better along one or another dimension of value; government is not privileging membership in, a worship practice of, or a theological doctrine peculiar to any church. The less restrictive understanding of what the nonestablishment norm forbids makes more sense than the more restrictive understanding, because there are *some* religious premises whose affirmation by government does not, or would not, violate the central meaning of the nonestablishment norm.[19]

Let's look more closely at the less restrictive understanding, according to which, again, having "under God" in the Pledge, or the like, does not violate the nonestablishment norm. Would it violate the nonestablishment norm, according to the less restrictive understanding,

> thousand years ago, so still it must be said "the judgments of the Lord, are true and righteous altogether." With malice toward none; with charity for all; with firmness in the right, as God gives us to see the right, let us strive on to finish the work we are in....
>
> Although U.S. citizens don't recite the Declaration, the Gettysburg Address, or Lincoln's Second Inaugural, we *do* recite, frequently, the Pledge of Allegiance. According to the Pledge, the United States of America is a nation "under God": a nation that, as Lincoln insisted in his Second Inaugural, stands under the judgment of a righteous God. Politicians and others are fond of asking God to "bless" America. Lincoln understood that the God who can, in judgment, bless America can also, in judgment, damn her: "He gives to both North and South, this terrible war, as the woe due to those by whom the offence came.... [A]s was said three thousand years ago, so still it must be said 'the judgments of the Lord, are true and righteous altogether.'"

[19] I am admittedly swimming against the tide of much scholarly opinion in contending for the less restrictive understanding of the nonestablishment norm. For a sampling of that opinion, see Kent Greenawalt, "Five Questions about Religion Judges Are Afraid to Ask," in Nancy L. Rosenblum, ed., *Obligations of Citizenship and Demands of Faith* 196, 197 (2000) (declaring that "[t]he core idea that government may not make determinations of religious truth is firmly entrenched"); Andrew Koppelman, "Secular Purpose," 88 VIRGINIA L. REV. 87, 108 (2002) (stating that is it an "axiom" that the "Establishment Clause forbids the state from declaring religious truth"); Douglas Laycock, "Equal Access and Moments of Silence: The Equal Status of Religious Speech by Private Speakers," 81 NORTHWESTERN U. L. REV. 1, 7 (1986) ("In my view, the establishment clause absolutely disables the government from taking a position for or against religion.... The government must have no opinion because it is not the government's role to have an opinion."). But see Steven H. Shiffrin, "The Pluralistic Foundations of the Religion Clauses," 90 CORNELL L. REV. 9, 72 (2004): "[T]he United States Constitution is best interpreted to be consistent with monotheistic ceremonial prayers that do not involve coercion."

to have "under Christ" in the Pledge ("one nation under Christ") or "In Christ We Trust" (or "Jesus Is Lord") as the national motto, or to begin a session of court with "Christ save the United States and this Honorable Court"? To answer the question, we must inquire: In adding "under Christ" to the Pledge, is government treating any church as the official church of the political community? Is it favoring any church in relation to any other church on the basis of the view that the favored church is, as a church, as a community of faith, better along one or another dimension of value? In adding "under Christ" to the Pledge, government is treating the Christian church – the Christian church *as a whole*, although not any particular denomination of it – as the official church of the political community; government is favoring the Christian church in relation to other churches and communities of faith on the basis of the view that the Christian church is, as a church, as a community of faith, better along one or another dimension of value. So, according to the less restrictive understanding of what the nonestablishment norm forbids, having "under Christ" in the Pledge *would* violate the norm.[20]

But for government to affirm any religious premise (or premises) that is ecumenical (nonsectarian) as among the three great monotheistic faiths – Judaism, Christianity, and Islam – would not be for it to violate the nonestablishment norm (according to the less restrictive understanding of the norm). However, for government to affirm any religious premise that is sectarian as among the monotheistic faiths would be for it to violate the norm. In affirming any religious premise that is not ecumenical as among Christians, religious Jews, and Muslims – for example, the premise that Jesus is Lord – government is violating the nonestablishment norm, even according to the less restrictive understanding of what the norm forbids. Indeed, for government to affirm any religious premise that is sectarian as among the denominations within one of the three monotheistic faiths – for example, the Catholic premise that the pope is the Vicar of Christ on earth – would be for government to violate the nonestablishment norm.

---

[20] According to the less restrictive understanding of what the nonestabishment norm forbids, affirming one or another version of the Decalogue also violates the norm. See Paul Finkelman, "The Ten Commandments on the Courthouse Lawn and Elsewhere," 73 FORDHAM L. REV. 1477, 1480–98 (2005). Cf. Frederick Mark Gedicks & Roger Hendrix, "Uncivil Religion: Judeo-Christianity and the Ten Commandments," 110 WEST VIRGINIA L. REV. 275 (2007).

First Principles

Why shouldn't we go further and embrace an understanding of the nonestablishment norm according to which government may not affirm any religious premise whatsoever? Again, the central meaning of the nonestablishment norm does not require such an understanding. Moreover, no historically grounded reading of the norm – no reading grounded in *American* history – supports that understanding, and it is, after all, the *American* Constitution we are expounding. "[The establishment clause] was not... understood to be a prohibition against employing generalized religious language in official discourse. The notion that the First Amendment was designed to impose a secular political culture on the nation would have struck most 19th Century judges as absurd."[21] Consider, for example, these data:

> Fully twenty-seven, or two-thirds, of [the] 1868 state constitutions contained an explicit reference to God in the preamble. A typical such reference stated that "We, the people of the State of Indiana, grateful to Almighty God for the free exercise of the right to choose our own form of government, do ordain this Constitution.'"...
>
> In addition to these references to God in the preambles of state constitutions, thirty state constitutions in 1868, or more than three-fourths of the total, contained reference to God.... Examples... include the use in constitutional texts of such phrases as "Almighty God," "Supreme Being and Great Creator and Preserver of the Universe," "Author of the universe," "Author of all good government," "Sovereign Ruler of the

---

[21] *ACLU of Ohio v. Capitol Square Review & Advisory Board*, 243 F.3d 289, 297 (6th Cir. 2001). Earlier in its opinion, the court quoted the following passage from an article by Steve Smith:

> In approving the establishment clause, the framers had adopted a principle of institutional separation, but they had undertaken neither to impose a secular political culture on the nation nor consented to abandon their own religious values or culture when serving as public officials. Indeed, any such undertaking would have required a seemingly impossible intellectual and psychological surgery. Proclaiming a national day of thanksgiving, or inviting a chaplain to offer a prayer before congressional sessions, were actions of undeniable religious import. But through these actions the government did not intrude into the internal affairs of any church. Nor did these actions confer governmental authority upon churches; Congress did not endow the chaplain with authority to debate, vote, or directly influence governmental decisions. Hence thanksgiving proclamations and legislative prayers were simply not inconsistent with the decision reflected in the establishment clause.

Id. at 297 (quoting Steven D. Smith, "Separation and the 'Secular': Reconstructing the Disestablishment Decision," 67 TEXAS L. REV. 955, 973 [1989]).

Universe," "Divine Being," "Great Legislator of the Universe," and "our Creator."[22]

I can discern no good reason either for expecting the Supreme Court to accept and enforce an understanding of the nonestablishment norm that is not historically grounded or for thinking that the Court should accept and enforce such an understanding.[23] It is surely at least a minor virtue of the understanding of the nonestablishment norm I am defending here – the less restrictive understanding – that it does not entail a conclusion – namely, that having "under God" in the Pledge or "In God We Trust" as the national motto, or beginning a session of court with "God save the United States and this Honorable Court," violates the constitutional imperative that government not establish religion – that most U.S. citizens, present as well as past, would greet, or would have greeted, as ridiculously extreme.[24]

---

[22] Steven G. Calabresi & Sarah E. Agudo, "Individual Rights Under State Constitutions When the Fourteenth Amendment Was Ratified in 1868: What Rights Are Deeply Rooted in American History and Tradition?," 87 TEXAS L. REV. 7, 37 (2008).

[23] I began the paragraph accompanying this note by asking why shouldn't we go further and embrace an understanding of the nonestablishment norm according to which government may not affirm any religious premise whatsoever. However, someone may want to ask a question that pushes in the opposite direction: Why shouldn't we embrace an understanding according to which government may affirm a specifically Christian premise if the premise is nonsectarian as among Christians? As Antonin Scalia has observed, "our constitutional tradition...ruled out of order government-sponsored endorsement of religion...where the endorsement is sectarian, in the sense of specifying details upon which men and women who believe in a benevolent, omnipotent Creator and Ruler of the world are known to differ (e.g., the divinity of Christ)." *Lee v. Weisman*, 505 U.S. 577, 641 (1992) (Scalia, J., dissenting).

A bit of American history is interesting here. The National Association to Secure the Religious Amendment to the Constitution was formed in 1864 "to propose the following change to the preamble to the Constitution (in brackets): 'We, the People of the United States, [recognizing the being and attributes of Almighty God, the Divine Authority of the Holy Scriptures, the Law of God as the paramount rule, and Jesus, the Messiah, the Savior and Lord of all,] in order to form a more perfect union, establish justice, ensure domestic tranquility, provide for the common defense, promote the general welfare, and secure the blessings of liberty to ourselves and our posterity, do ordain and establish this Constitution for the United States of America.'" Jay Alan Sekulow, *Witnessing Their Faith: Religious Influence on Supreme Court Justices and Their Opinions* 125 (2006). The Christian Amendment, as it was called, "was considered twice by Congress: once in 1874 and again in 1894. The House Judiciary Committee rejected the amendment on both occasions." Id. at 126. Other interesting bits of American history are recounted in this op-ed by Jon Meacham, the editor of *Newsweek*: "A Nation of Christians Is Not a Christian Nation," NEW YORK TIMES, Oct. 7, 2007.

[24] As even those who reject the less restrictive understanding of the nonestablishment norm will likely agree, the Supreme Court will not, in any remotely foreseeable future,

First Principles

True, having "under God" in the Pledge, "In God We Trust" as the national motto, and the like, offends some U.S. citizens. But as long as government fully respects one's right to the free exercise of religion, government's affirmation of one or more religious premises does not violate anyone's human rights.[25] For example, that the Constitution of the Republic of Ireland makes a number of theological affirmations – while also vigorously protecting every Irish citizen's right to freedom of religious practice – does not violate anyone's human rights.[26] More generally, the international law of human rights features the right to

rule that having "under God" in the Pledge (or "In God We Trust" as the national motto, or the like) is unconstitutional. If the Supreme Court, in a science-fiction scenario, were to so rule, the citizenry of the United States would rush to amend the Constitution to overrule the Court. Cf. Steven G. Gey, "'Under God,' the Pledge of Allegiance, and Other Constitutional Trivia," 81 NORTH CAROLINA L. REV. 1865, 1866–69 (2003) (reporting on the virtually unanimous negative response to the federal court's (subsequently amended) decision in *Newdow v. U.S. Congress*, 292 F.3d 597 [9th Cir. 2002]); Evelyn Nieves, "Judges Ban Pledge of Allegiance from Schools, Citing 'Under God'," NEW YORK TIMES, June 27, 2002; Howard Fineman, "One Nation, Under...Who?," NEWSWEEK, July 8, 2002, at 20. Religious liberty scholar Steven Shiffrin has argued that the United States has evolved from a country that is historically Christian into a country that is "officially monotheistic." See Steven H. Shiffrin, "Liberalism and the Establishment Clause," 78 CHICAGO-KENT L. REV. 717, 727 (2003). See also Shiffrin, "The Pluralistic Foundations of the Religion Clauses," n. 19, at 70–73.

[25] Cf. Steven D. Smith, *Foreordained Failure: The Quest for a Constitutional Principle of Religious Freedom* 164–65 n. 66 (1995):

[T]he very concept of "alienation," or symbolic exclusion, is difficult to grasp. How, if at all, does "alienation" differ from "anger," "annoyance," "frustration," or "disappointment" that every person who finds himself in a political minority is likely to feel? "Alienation" might refer to nothing more than an awareness by an individual that she belongs to a religious minority, accompanied by a realization that at least on some issues she is unlikely to be able to prevail in the political process.... That awareness may be discomforting. But is it the sort of phenomenon for which constitutional law can provide an efficacious remedy? Constitutional doctrine that stifles the message will not likely alter the reality – or a minority's awareness of that reality.

[26] In its Preamble, the Irish Constitution affirms a nonsectarian Christianity: "In the name of the Most Holy Trinity, from Whom is all authority and to Whom, as our final end, all actions both of men and States must be referred, we, the people of Eire, humbly acknowledging all our obligations to our Divine Lord, Jesus Christ, Who sustained our fathers through centuries of trial, ... do hereby adopt, enact, and give to ourselves this Constitution." Moreover, Article 6 states, in relevant part: "All powers of government, legislative, executive, and judicial, derive, *under God*, from the people, whose right it is to designate the rulers of the State and, in the final appeal, to decide all questions of national policy, according to the requirements of the common good" (emphasis added). And Article 44 of the Constitution states, in relevant part: "The State acknowledges that the homage of public worship is due to Almighty God. It shall hold His Name in

freedom of religious practice but does not include anything like a nonestablishment norm; in particular, the Declaration on the Elimination of All Forms of Intolerance and of Discrimination Based on

> reverence, and shall respect and honor religion." On "religion in the Preamble," see Gerard Hogan & G. F. Whyte, *J.M. Kelly's The Irish Constitution* 6–7 (3d ed., 1994). (Although it affirms Christianity, the Irish Constitution explicitly disallows the "endowing" of any religion. Article 44.2.1 states: "The State guarantees not to endow any religion.")
>
> Given the religious commitments of the vast majority of the people of Ireland, it is not at all surprising that the Irish Constitution affirms Christianity. In so doing, the Irish Constitution violates no human right. Three things are significant here. First, the religious convictions implicit in the Irish Constitution's affirmation of Christianity in no way deny – indeed, they affirm – the idea that *every* human being, *Christian or not*, is inviolable; they affirm, that is, the idea of human rights. Second, the Irish Constitution's affirmation of Christianity is not meant to insult or demean anyone; it is meant only to express the most fundamental convictions of the vast majority of the people of Ireland. Third, and most importantly, the Irish Constitution protects the right, which is a human right, to freedom of religious practice; moreover, it protects this right not just for Christians, who are the vast majority in Ireland, but for all citizens. Article 44 states, in relevant part: "Freedom of conscience and the free profession and practice of religion are... guaranteed to every citizen.... The State shall not impose any disabilities or make any discrimination on the ground of religious profession, belief or status." Article 44 also states that "[l]egislation providing State aid for schools shall not discriminate between schools under the management of different religious denominations, *nor be such as to effect prejudicially the right of any child to attend a school receiving public money without attending religious instruction at that school*" (emphasis added). Therefore, the conclusion that in affirming Christianity the Irish Constitution violates a human right – or that in consequence of the affirmation Ireland falls short of being a full fledged liberal democracy – is, in a word, extreme. For an excellent essay on religious liberty in Ireland, see G. F. Whyte, "The Frontiers of Religious Liberty: A Commonwealth Celebration of the 25th Anniversary of the U.N. Declaration on Religious Tolerance – Ireland," 21 EMORY INTERNATIONAL L. REV. 43 (2007).
>
> If what Brian Barry says in the following passage is true with respect to England, which has an established church, then it is even more true – it is true in spades – with respect to the United States, which has no established church but only such comparatively minor things as "under God" in the Pledge and "In God We Trust" as the national motto:
>> We must, of course, keep a sense of proportion. The advantages of establishment enjoyed by the Church of England or by the Lutheran Church in Sweden are scarcely on a scale to lead anyone to feel seriously discriminated against. In contrast, denying the vote to Roman Catholics or requiring subscription to the Church of England as a condition of entry to Oxford or Cambridge did constitute a serious source of grievance. Strict adherence to justice as impartiality would, no doubt, be incompatible with the existence of an established church at all. But departures from it are venial so long as nobody is put at a significant disadvantage, either by having barriers put in the way of worshipping according to the tenets of his faith or by having his rights and opportunities in other matters (politics, education, occupation, for example) materially limited on the basis of his religious beliefs.
>
> Brian Barry, *Justice as Impartiality* 165, n. *c* (1995).

First Principles

Religion or Belief, which is the principal international document concerning religious freedom, includes nothing like a nonestablishment requirement.

Is it really the case that the more restrictive understanding of what the nonestablishment norm forbids yields the conclusion that having "under God" in the Pledge or "In God We Trust" as the national motto, or beginning a session of court with "God save the United States and this Honorable Court," is unconstitutional? Is there a way for one who accepts the more restrictive understanding to avoid that conclusion, which, again, most citizens of the United States would greet as ridiculously extreme?

Consider the suggestion that having "under God" in the Pledge or "In God We Trust" as the national motto (or the like) is not unconstitutional because such statements do not really constitute an affirmation by government of a religious premise; instead, such statements are merely patriotic or ceremonial utterances devoid of authentically religious content. In 1983, Supreme Court Justice William Brennan, joined by Justice Thurgood Marshall, wrote:

> I frankly do not know what should be the proper disposition of features of our public life such as "God save the United States and this Honorable Court," "In God We Trust," "One Nation Under God," and the like. I might well adhere to the view... that such mottoes are consistent with the Establishment Clause... because they have lost any true religious significance.[27]

In 2004, Chief Justice William Rehnquist, joined by Justice Sandra Day O'Connor, said something similar: "The phrase 'under God' is in no sense a prayer, nor an endorsement of any religion.... Reciting the Pledge, or listening to others recite it, is a patriotic exercise, not a religious one; participants promise fidelity to our flag and our Nation, not to any particular God, faith, or church."[28]

---

[27] *Marsh v. Chambers*, 463 U.S. 783, 818 (1983) (dissenting).

[28] *Elk Grove Unified School District v. Newdow*, 542 U.S. 1, 31 (2004) (concurring in judgment). *Newdow* is the case in which it was claimed that just as having public school children recite a prayer violates the nonestablishment norm, so too having them recite the Pledge of Allegiance violates the nonestablishment norm, because the Pledge states that the United States is a nation "under God" and recitation of the Pledge is therefore a religious exercise. The U.S. Court of Appeals for the Ninth Circuit agreed, and the case ended up in the U.S. Supreme Court, where

Religion as a Basis of Lawmaking

Asserting that "one nation under God" or "In God We Trust" are merely patriotic or ceremonial utterances devoid of authentically religious content is obviously a convenient strategy for avoiding the conclusion that under the more restrictive understanding of the nonestablishment norm, having "under God" in the Pledge or "In God We Trust" as our national motto is unconstitutional. It is also a palpably disingenuous strategy.[29] There are *some* citizens, no doubt, for whom the statements are merely ceremonial, religiously empty utterances; it is simply mistaken, however, to think that the statements are religiously empty for most, or even for many, citizens of the United States – or that they were religiously empty for the members of Congress who, in 1954, added "under God" to the Pledge.[30] For most Americans, the statements resonate, as indeed they were meant to, with an authentically and rich theological content: that there is a God; that God created us and sustains us; that every human being has a God-given dignity and inviolability; and that, as Lincoln proclaimed in his Second Inaugural, we stand under the judgment of that righteous God.[31]

There is no intellectually honest way for one who accepts the more restrictive understanding of the nonestablishment norm to avoid the conclusion that having "under God" in the Pledge or "In God We

> [s]ix Justices reversed on a procedural ground, arguing that Newdow did not have standing to bring the action. Three justices, however, namely, Chief Justice Rehnquist and Justices O'Connor and Thomas, disagreed with [the Ninth Circuit] on the merits.
>
> Analyzing [the Ninth Circuit's] opinion requires separation of two issues: First, is the Pledge a *religious* exercise, and, second, can a government actor constitutionally require that the Pledge be part of the official public school day? Chief Justice Rehnqyuist and Justice O'Connor both denied that the Pledge was a religious exercise and, therefore, concluded that it could be a part of the official public school day. Justice Thomas coinceded that the Pledge was religious but . . . argued it was constitutional nonetheless.
>
> Shiffrin, "The Pluralistic Foundations of the Religion Clauses," n. 19, at 65–66. Shiffrin argues "that the Pledge is religious and that it is constitutional for Congress to encourage its use, but that it should not be considered constitutionally permissible to use the Pledge in public school classrooms." Id. at 66.

[29] See Richard John Neuhaus, "Nasty and Nice in Politics and Religion in the Public Sqare: A Survey of Religion and Public Life," FIRST THINGS, March 2004, at 69, 70.

[30] See Gey, n. 24, at 1873–80.

[31] See n. 18. See also Douglas Laycock, "Theology Scholarships, the Pledge of Allegiance, and Religious Liberty: Avoiding the Extremes, Missing the Liberty," 118 HARVARD L. REV. 155, 224–27 (2004) (arguing that recitation of the Pledge of Allegiance is a profession of faith).

Trust" as the national motto, or beginning a session of court with "God save the United States and this Honorable Court," is unconstitutional. For one who is intellectually honest, to accept the more restrictive understanding is to accept that conclusion.[32]

B. May Government Rely on Religion as a Basis of Coercive and/or Discriminatory Lawmaking?

Now, the question-in-chief: Is religion (religious rationales) a legitimate – a *constitutionally* legitimate – basis of lawmaking in the United States? More precisely, should the nonestablishment norm be understood to ban laws (and other policies) for which the only discernible rationale (other than an implausible secular rationale) is religious?

Two clarifications:

1. The laws at issue are mainly – not exclusively, but mainly – either (a) those that are coercive (forbidding one to do what one wants to do or requiring one to do what one wants not to do) or (b) those that discriminate against some persons, that single out some persons and treat them less well than others.[33] If the only discernible rationale for such a law – a law that is either coercive or discriminatory (or both) – is religious, then the law constitutes a kind of religious imposition on those it coerces or against whom it discriminates. Kent Greenawalt is right: Laws "that enforce a purely religious morality...unacceptably impose religion on others."[34]

---

[32] See Shiffrin, "The Pluralistic Foundations of the Religion Clauses," n. 19, at 66–70 (explaining why the positions of Rehnquist and O'Connor in the *Newdow* case [see n. 28] are untenable).

[33] Why do I say that the laws at issue are mainly, *but not exclusively*, coercive and/or discriminatory laws? Consider, for example, a policy according to which embryonic stem cell research is not funded by government on the basis of the view that such research is contrary to the will of God. Although the policy is neither coercive nor discriminatory, the policy could have profoundly negative consequences for some people: those who would be the beneficiaries of such research if the research were successful. So it makes little if any sense to say that such a policy, simply because it is neither coercive nor discriminatiory, should not be subject to the nonestablishment ban I am about to articulate.

[34] Greenawalt gives, as an example, "laws against homosexual relations based on the view that the Bible considers such relations sinful...." Kent Greenawalt, "History as Ideology: Philip Hamburger's *Separation of Church and State*," 93 CALIFORNIA L. REV. 367, 390–91 (2005). See also Greenawalt, 2 *Religion and the Constitution*, n. 2, at 533: "[R]equiring people to comply with the moral code of a religion, absent any belief about ordinary

2. By a "religious" rationale I mean a rationale that depends, at least in part, on a religious premise; a "secular" rationale, by contrast, does not depend on any religious premise. By a "religious" premise I mean, in this book, a premise – a claim – about the existence,[35] nature, activity, or will of God, such as the premise that same-sex unions are contrary to the will of God.[36]

I argued in the preceding section that according to the most balanced understanding of what it forbids, the nonestablishment norm forbids government to affirm some, indeed most, religious premises.[37] It follows from that argument that the nonestablishment norm should be understood to ban laws for which the only discernible rationale is a religious rationale that depends on – and in that sense affirms – a religious premise government may not affirm.

A lawmaker supports a law – he or she votes to enact a law – "on the basis of" a religious rationale if but for the religious rationale – if in the absence of the religious rationale – the lawmaker would not vote to enact the law; put another way, a lawmaker votes to enact a law based on a religious rationale if there is no secular rationale that by itself would move him or her to enact the law.[38] However, the

---

harm to entities deserving protection, is a kind of imposition of that religious view on others."

[35] On nonexistence. Atheism is a religious position – a position on a religious question – for purposes of the nonestablishment norm. Cf. Derek H. Davis, "Is Atheism a Religion? Recent Judicial Perspectives on the Constitutional Meaning of 'Religion'," 47 J. CHURCH & STATE 707 (2005).

[36] Cf. Christopher J. Eberle, *Religious Conviction in Liberal Politics* 71 (2002):
> I shall understand a religious ground...as any ground that has *theistic content*. Paradigmatic religious grounds are, for example, a putative experience of God as affirming racial harmony, the claim that God has revealed in the Bible that homosexual relations are morally forbidden, the testimony of a religious authority that God abhors despoliation of the environment.

[37] Although under the nonestablishment norm there are some religious premises government may not affirm – for example, the premise that God created the universe not six thousand years ago, as some "young-earth creationists" claim, but billions of years ago – government may nonetheless affirm a premise that is consistent with a religious premise it may not affirm, so long as government's rationale for affirming the non-religious premise does not rely on a religious premise government may not affirm. So government may affirm the premise that the universe is billions of years old. See *McGowan v. Maryland*, 366 U.S. 420 (1961).

[38] Cf. Eberle, *Religious Conviction in Liberal Politics*, n. 36, at 73:
> Whether [one] supports a given law on the basis of his religious convictions alone depends on the answer to a conterfactual question: would [he] continue to regard moral claim C (on the basis of which he supports a proposed law) as

nonestablishment ban I defend here is indifferent to whether a lawmaker who voted to enact a law *actually* did so, either wholly or partly, on the basis of an "offending" religious rationale – a rationale that depends on a religious premise government may not affirm. There are several good reasons for that indifference:

- It is unrealistic to expect most lawmakers to have a confident answer to the question whether they would have voted to enact a law but for an offending religious rationale.
- The ban, *qua legal*, is meant to be judicially enforceable. If most lawmakers themselves don't have a confident answer to the question whether they would have voted to enact a law but for an offending religious rationale, how is a court supposed to know whether they would have done so?
- Moreover, if courts were in the business of speculating about whether the lawmakers would have voted to enact a law but for an offending religious rationale, some lawmakers would respond by engaging in strategic behavior aimed at making it appear that they would have voted to enact the law on the basis of a plausible secular rationale and/or a nonoffending religious rationale.
- Finally, consider this scenario: A court speculates that the lawmakers in State A would have voted to enact law L on the basis of a plausible secular rationale and therefore concludes that L is not unconstitutional, while a different court speculates that the lawmakers in State B would not have voted to enact the very same law on the basis of any plausible secular rationale and therefore concludes that L is unconstitutional. In State A, L is constitutional; in State B, L is unconstitutional. What an unseemly state of affairs that would be!

So the nonestablishment norm is better understood not to forbid a lawmaker to support a law on the basis of an offending religious rationale, but only to ban laws for which the only discernible rationale is an offending religious rationale.

As a practical matter, how significant is a ban on such laws? In the United States today there are, and in the foreseeable future there will be, almost no actual or proposed laws – at least, almost no proposed laws that have a realistic chance of becoming actual laws – that fit the

<blockquote>sufficient reason for that law if he didn't believe that theistic claim T constitutes adequate reason for C?</blockquote>

profile "laws for which the only discernible rationale is an offending religious rationale." For example, and as I explain in Chapter 7, there is a plausible secular rationale – a secular rationale that rational, well-informed, and thoughtful fellow citizens could affirm, and that many do affirm – for laws banning most abortions. There is one policy, however, with respect to which the ban may have bite: Many states refuse to recognize – they refuse to extend the benefit of law to – same-sex unions. Is there a plausible secular rationale that *could* account for that policy – that is, *a plausible secular rationale we can realistically assume the lawmakers accept, whether or not their support for the policy is actually based on that rationale?* Or are the only rationales that could account for the policy implausible secular rationales and/or a rationale that depends on the premise that same-sex sexual conduct is contrary to the will of God? If the latter, then this becomes the determinative question: May government affirm the premise that same-sex sexual conduct is contrary to the will of God? I address that question in Chapter 8, in the course of discussing the controversy over same-sex unions.

Should the nonestablishment norm be understood to ban laws for which the only discernible rationale is religious? Yes, if the rationale depends on a religious premise that under the nonestablishment norm government may not affirm. If, therefore, the only discernible rationale for concluding that a coercive and/or discriminatory law serves a legitimate governmental interest (of sufficient weight) is a religious rationale government may not affirm – if, in that sense, there is no constitutionally adequate rationale for concluding that a coercive and/or discriminatory law serves a legitmate governmental interest – then the law does not serve, *it should be deemed not to serve*, a legitimate governmental interest. Because it "enforce[s] a purely religious morality [and thereby] unacceptably impose[s] religion on others,"[39] such a law is in conflict with the constitutional imperative that government not establish religion.[40]

[39] See n. 34.
[40] Steve Shiffrin has espoused much the same position: Steven Shiffrin, "Religion and Democracy," 74 NOTRE DAME L. REV. 1631, 1652–56 (1999). So has Kent Greenawalt: Greenawalt, 2 *Religion and the Constitution*, n. 2, at 525–37.
> [A]s a matter of theoretical principle, I think enactment of a religious morality could violate the Establishment Clause, even if the religion, as a set of beliefs and religious practices, is not promoted or endorsed in the more straighforward sense.... A law violates the Establishment Clause if the ascertainable dominant

First Principles

We can anticipate the (understandable) complaint that the position I have articulated and defended here is unduly restrictive of religious believers. In the United States today, however, there are, and in the foreseeable future there will be, as I just remarked, few if indeed any actual or proposed laws that lack a plausible secular rationale. Moreover, the vast majority of religious believers in the United States today offer secular rationales for their political positions on controversial moral issues. Even "[m]ost religious conservatives do, frequently and loudly, make arguments for their positions *on nontheological grounds*.... [T]he evils of abortion, the value of heterosexual monogamy, the costs of promiscuity and pornography – all these issues are constantly being raised by social conservatives without appeals to the divine inspiration of the Bible."[41] The serious question, then, is not whether the nonestablishment ban on laws for which the only discernible rationale is an offending religious rationale is unduly restrictive, but whether as a practical matter the ban has much if any bite.

II. RELIGION AS A BASIS OF LAWMAKING IN A LIBERAL DEMOCRACY

Everything I said in the preceding section of this chapter is relevant to a particular liberal democracy, the United States, because the United States is constitutionally committed to "no 'establishment' of religion." But what about *other* liberal democracies, most of which, as noted at the beginning of this chapter, are not constitutionally committed to the nonestablishment of religion – the United Kingdom, for example. Is the United Kingdom free to enforce a coercive and/or discriminatory law for which the only rationale, other than an implausible secular rationale, is religious?

> reason for its passage was a view that acts are immoral, based on a religious point of view and detached from any perspective about harm in this life that would be sufficient to justify a prohibition or regulation.
>
> Id. at 533 & 535. Moreover, Greenawalt says about his position what I have said in this chapter about mine: that the position "will rarely, if ever, lead a court to invalidate a law.... [T]he limits on appropriate grounds for laws [entailed by the position] are too narrow to have much practical significance." Id. at 536 & 537.

[41] Ross Douthat, "Theocracy, Theocracy, Theocracy," FIRST THINGS, August/September 2006, at 23, 28 (emphasis added).

Religion as a Basis of Lawmaking

As I emphasized in Chapter 4, every liberal democracy is, as such, committed to the right to religious freedom. If the only rationale for concluding that a coercive and/or discriminatory law serves a legitimate and sufficiently weighty governmental interest – the only reason, that is, other than an implausible secular rationale – is a religious rationale, then the law violates the right to freedom of religion, which includes, after all, not only freedom *to* practice one's own religion (if one has a religion) but also freedom *not* to practice someone else's religion – or, indeed, any religion at all. Freedom not to practice someone else's religion includes, of course, freedom not to be punished or discriminated against based on one's refusal to practice someone else's religion. A coercive and/or discriminatory law for which the only rationale, other than an implausible secular rationale, is religious imposes religion on those the law coerces or against whom it discriminates; such a law, in the words of Kent Greenawalt, "enforce[s] a purely religious morality [and thereby] unacceptably impose[s] religion on others."[42]

The United Kingdom, therefore, is not free to enforce a coercive and/or discriminatory law that is bereft of a plausible secular rationale. Indeed, even if it were not constitutionally committed to the nonestablishment of religion, the United States would not be free to enforce such a law. (Thus, even if one rejects my construal of the nonestablishment norm, the United States is not free to enforce such a law.) Given the constitutive commitment of liberal democracy to the right to religious freedom, no liberal democracy is free to enforce a coercive and/or discriminatory law *if the only rationale for concluding that the law serves a legitimate and sufficiently weighty governmental interest, other than an implausible secular rationale, is religious.*

[42] See n. 34.

Part III
First Principles Applied

7
Abortion

Two subjects more than any others are at the heart of the American debate – they are the principal subtexts of the American debate – about the proper role of religion in the politics and law of a liberal democracy: abortion and same-sex unions. ("In a democracy, the people choose the questions they want to discuss, and in our time more of them want the religious spirit to concern itself with abortion and homosexuality rather than race relations or a just wage."[1]) In this chapter, I pursue the implications, for a ban on abortion, of the right to moral freedom – that is, the right to moral freedom read in conjunction with the principle that religion (religious rationales) may not serve as the basis of coercive and/or discriminatory lawmaking.

When I say, in this chapter, "a ban on abortion," I mean "a ban on most previability abortions."[2] There is no serious controversy about the legitimacy of a ban on postviability abortions. I say "most" previability abortions, because I assume that in a liberal democracy such as the United States, bans on previability abortions would typically, if not universally, include certain exceptions: in particular, abortions necessary to protect the life of the mother, or her physical health, from a serious threat; abortions to terminate a pregnancy that began with rape; and abortions to terminate a pregnancy that, because of a grave defect, would end with a child "born into what is certain to be a brief life of grievous suffering."[3]

A ban on abortion certainly implicates the right to moral freedom. For most women, at least, the decision to have an abortion is a *moral*

---

[1] Alan Wolfe, "Mobilizing the Religious Left," NEW YORK TIMES BOOK REV., Oct. 21, 2007.
[2] Over a decade ago, *The New York Times* reported that because of advances "in neonatology, most experts place the point of fetal viability at 23 or 24 weeks." Sheryl Gay Stolberg, "Shifting Certainties in the Abortion War," NEW YORK TIMES, Jan. 11, 1998.
[3] John Schwartz, "When Torment Is Baby's Destiny, Euthanasia Is Defended," NEW YORK TIMES, Mar. 10, 2005. Cf. Associated Press, "Study: Newborn Euthanasia Often Unreported," NEW YORK TIMES, Mar. 10, 2005.

decision: if not a decision they believe themselves morally obligated to make, nonetheless a decision they have weighty moral reasons to make. (Again, a choice one has moral reasons to make should not be confused with a choice one does not have moral reasons not to make; the right to moral freedom elaborated and defended in Chapter 5 protects only choices of the former sort.) But to implicate a right is not necessarily to violate the right. A ban on abortion does not violate the right to moral freedom if (a) the ban is is necessary to serve governmental interest that is both legitimate and sufficiently weighty to be proportionate to the weight of the burden imposed by the ban on those subject to the ban, and (b) there exists a plausible secular rationale that could account for the lawmakers' judgment that the ban is necessary to serve such an interest.

Is a ban on abortion necessary to serve a legitimate and sufficiently weighty governmental interest? We may safely assume that if the same question were asked about a ban on homicide, which protects human life, the answer would be yes. Similarly, we may safely assume that if the same question were asked about a ban on infanticide, which also protects human life – albeit, human life at an early stage of its development – the answer would be yes. Like the bans on homicide and infanticide, a ban on abortion protects human life – albeit, at a very early stage of its development. Why not then conclude that the ban, like the bans on homicide and infanticide, is necessary to serve a legitimate and sufficiently weighty governmental interest?

For those who believe that prior to viability unborn human beings do not have any moral status or, at least, sufficient moral status to warrant a ban on abortion, such a ban does not serve a sufficiently weighty governmental interest – and therefore violates the right to moral freedom. But for those who believe that even prior to viability unborn human beings *do* have sufficient moral status to warrant a ban on abortion, such a ban does serve a sufficiently weighty governmental interest: "Just as a ban on infanticide protects infants from unjust killing, a ban on abortion protects unborn human life from unjust killing."

But is there a reason, other than a religious reason or an implausible secular reason – that is, is there a plausible secular reason – that could account for the lawmakers' judgment that a ban on abortion serves a legitimate and sufficiently weighty governmental interest?

The principal rationale for a ban on abortion is twofold: (a) A human zygote, embryo, and fetus are each a human life, albeit an unborn human life, and (b) unborn human life has the same, or substantially the same, moral status as born human life. That rationale – at least, the version of it I elaborate here – does not depend on any religious premise whatsoever; hence, the rationale is secular. Moreover, it is a plausible rationale: a rationale that rational, well-informed, and thoughtful fellow citizens can affirm.

In the following section, I elaborate the rationale for a ban on abortion from the perspective of one who affirms the rationale; I elaborate the rationale *as if* I affirm it. But in fact I am presently agnostic about the rationale.

That a human zygote, embryo, and fetus are each a human life is beyond serious dispute. Although, as H. Tristram Engelhardt has observed, "many describe the status of the embryo imprecisely by asking when human life begins or whether the embryo is a human being... no one seriously denies that the human zygote is a human life. The zygote is not dead. It is also not simian, porcine, or canine."[4] Philosopher Peter Singer, who is famously and enthusiastically pro-choice, has acknowledged that "the early embryo is a 'human life.' Embryos formed from the sperm and eggs of human beings are certainly human, no matter how early in their development they may be. They are of the species *Homo sapiens*, and not of any other species. We can tell when they are alive, and when they have died. So long as they are alive, they are human life."[5] Similarly, constitutional scholar Laurence Tribe, a staunch pro-choice advocate, has written that "the fetus is alive. It belongs to the human species. It elicits sympathy and even love, in part because it is so dependent and helpless."[6]

The serious question, then, is not about the biological status of unborn human life, but about its moral status. The latter question is vigorously contested in contemporary liberal democracies, including the United States. Nonetheless, the claim that unborn human life, even unborn human life at the earliest stage of its development, has (substantially) the same moral status as born human life is both

---

[4] H. Tristram Engelhardt, Jr., "Moral Knowledge: Some Reflections on Moral Controversies, Incompatible Moral Epistemologies, and the Culture Wars," 10 CHRISTIAN BIOETHICS 79, 84 (2004).
[5] Peter Singer, *The President of Good and Evil: The Ethics of George W. Bush* 37 (2004).
[6] Laurence H. Tribe, "Will the Abortion Fight Ever End?; A Nation Held Hostage," NEW YORK TIMES, July 2, 1990.

secular and plausible, as I am about to explain. Nothing I am about to say, however, is meant to deny that there is also a plausible secular rationale for a public policy that permits rather than bans abortions, no less than for a public policy – a law – that bans abortions. That two competing public policies are each supported by a plausible secular rationale (each, of course, by a *different* plausible secular rationale) is scarcely remarkable.

Again, liberal democracy is committed to the proposition that each and every *born* human being has inherent dignity and is inviolable. (Moreover, liberal democracy's commitment to the inherent dignity and inviolability of every born human being grounds its commitment to certain fundamental rights.) What sense would it make to affirm that all *born* human beings have inherent dignity (and are inviolable) but that no *unborn* human beings have it? Some babies are born after a gestation period of nine months; some are born after a shorter gestation period. (Some babies are born after a shorter gestation period because they are removed from their mother's womb prematurely in order to protect the baby and/or the mother.) It seems quite arbitrary to hold that although a baby born, say, seven months after fertilization acquired inherent dignity the moment it was born, an eight-month-old fetus, because it has not yet been born, has not yet acquired inherent dignity. We who affirm that every born human being has inherent dignity do not all agree about why – in virtue of what – every human being has inherent dignity; we don't all agree about the ground of the inherent dignity we believe every human being to have. But whatever the ground, it seems fair to conclude that the acquisition of inherent dignity does not depend on the happenstance of whether or not one *has been* born if one *could be* born – that is, born as a *viable* infant, an infant *capable of survival outside the mother's womb*. Therefore, unless we want to be arbitrary – and it is surely arbitrary to suggest that whether one has inherent dignity depends on *where* one is located: inside the mother's womb? outside it? – we who affirm that every born human being has inherent dignity should also affirm that *at least* every unborn human being beyond the stage of fetal development known as "viability" has inherent dignity. The serious question, then, for those of us who affirm that every born human being has inherent dignity, is not whether we should also affirm that every unborn human being beyond viability has inherent dignity. We should: There is no good reason – no nonarbitrary reason – for us not to do so. The serious question is whether we should affirm that every unborn human being has inherent dignity from an even earlier point in pregnancy than viability – and if so, from what point?

Many opponents of abortion claim that the moral status that all born human beings have, they have had from the moment of fertilization, or at least from the moment of implantation. (The latter event – implantation – is often, but mistakenly, referred to as "conception."[7]) According to the morality to which liberal democracy is committed – the morality of human rights – the moral status all born human beings have is inherent dignity. Should we who affirm that all born human beings have inherent dignity also affirm that all born human beings have had this moral status from the moment of fertilization? Should we affirm, that is, that every unborn human being has inherent dignity from the moment of fertilization?

Assume that you believe that the ground of one's inherent dignity is that one is a beloved child of God, or is created in the image of God, or is "ensouled" by God. (Each of these propositions – that one is a beloved child of God, that one is created in the image of God, and that one is ensouled by God – is an effort to mediate in words substantially the same transcendent reality, a reality that cannot be captured or contained or domesticated by any particular formula or vocabulary.) Assume, too, that you also believe that one is ensouled by God from the moment of fertilization. Then you should affirm that every unborn human being has inherent dignity from the moment of fertilization.

---

[7] See Mary B. Mahowald, "Conception vs. Fertilization," COMMONWEAL, Sept. 9, 2005, at 40:

> Although these terms ["conception" and "fertilization"] are often used interchangeably, even in papal documents, "conception" refers to the beginning of a pregnancy within a woman's body, when the embryo is implanted within her uterus several days after an egg is fertilized. In contrast, "fertilization" refers to the process by which any embryo is formed either in vivo or in vitro through union of egg and sperm. (Cloned embryos are not formed through union of egg and sperm.) Infertility practitioners and some people who are publicly opposed to abortion (for example, [Utah Senator] Orrin Hatch) support stem-cell retrieval from in vitro embryos on grounds of this distinction, arguing that new life begins at conception or the onset of pregnancy. The Catholic position should be clearly stated as one that opposes termination of the life of any fertilized egg or embryo (even if the latter has been cloned) regardless of whether conception has yet occurred.

First Principles Applied

But many who believe that the ground of one's inherent dignity is that one is ensouled by God do not have a confident view about precisely when, during pregnancy, ensoulment occurs. One can be a person of deep religious faith without believing that humans can by dint of "reason" penetrate such a mystery. "Even St. Thomas Aquinas, who thought that a soul was infused into the body, could only guess at when that infusion took place (and he did not guess 'at fertilization')."[8] Some religious believers may be tempted to invoke

---

[8] Garry Wills, "The Bishops vs. the Bible," NEW YORK TIMES, June 27, 2004. For the views of some Roman Catholics on the issue, see Joseph F. Donceel, SJ, "Immediate Animation and Delayed Homonization," 31 THEOLOGICAL STUDIES 76 (1970); Joseph F. Donceel, SJ, "A Liberal Catholic's View," in Robert Hall, ed., *Abortion in a Changing World* 39 (1970); Thomas A. Shannon, "Human Embryonic Stem Cell Therapy," 62 THEOLOGICAL STUDIES 811, 814–21 (2001); Jean Porter, "Is the Embryo a Person? Arguing with the Catholic Traditions," COMMONWEAL, Feb. 8, 2002, at 8; John Haldane & Patrick Lee, "Aquinas on Ensoulment, Abortion and the Value of Life," 78 PHILOSOPHY 255 (2003); Robert Pasnau, "Souls and the Beginning of Life (A Reply to Haldane & Lee)," 78 PHILOSOPHY 521 (2003); John Haldane & Patrick Lee, "Rational Souls and the Beginning of Life," 78 PHILOSOPHY 532 (2003). Cf. Anthony Kenny, "The Soul Issue," TIMES LIT. SUPP., Mar. 7, 2003, at 12.

Consider these passages from an essay that Peter Steinfels, at the time the editor of the Catholic weekly *Commonweal*, published in *Commonweal* in 1981:

> [T]he right-to-life movement is naively overconfident in its belief that the existence of a unique "genetic package" from conception onwards settles the abortion issue. Yes, it does prove that what is involved is a human individual and not "part of the mother's body." It does not prove that, say, a twenty-eight-day-old embryo, approximately the size of this parenthesis (–), is *then and there* a creature with the same claims to preservation and protection as a newborn or an adult.... Although it is not *logically* impossible, for example, to consider the great number of fertilized eggs that fail to implant themselves in the uterus as lost "human beings," a great many people find this idea totally incredible. Similarly, very early miscarriage usually does not trigger the sense of loss and grief that miscarriage does. Can we take these instinctive responses as morally helpful? ... It is simply *not* the case that a refusal to recognize Albert Einstein or Anne Frank as human beings deserving of full legal rights is equivalent to the refusal to see the same status in a disc the size of a period or an embryo one-sixth of an inch long and with barely rudimentary features.

Peter Steinfels, "The Search for an Alternative," COMMONWEAL, NOV. 20, 1981, reprinted in Patrick Jordan & Paul Baumann, eds., *Commonweal Confronts the Century: Liberal Convictions, Catholic Tradition* 204, 209–11 (1999). Cf. Porter, supra this note, at 8:

> What can we [Catholics] say to convince men and women of good will who do not share our theological convictions or our allegiance to church teaching that early-stage embryos have exactly the same moral status as we and they do? It will not serve us to fall back at this point on blanket denunciations such as "the culture of death." Naturally, these tend to be conversation stoppers. What is worse, they keep us from considering the possibility that others may not be convinced by what we are saying because what we are saying is – not convincing.

"revelation" at this point, but revelation does not disclose when ensoulment occurs. ("[Saint] Augustine was [not] certain when the soul was infused.... On the whole subject of the origins of life, [Augustine] said: 'When a thing obscure in itself defeats our capacity, and nothing in Scripture comes to our aid, it is not safe for humans to presume that they can pronounce on it.'"[9]) So even if you are a theist, you might not have a confident view about when unborn human beings are ensouled by God (or become beloved children of God, or become in the image of God). Or you might not be a theist.

Even if you fit one of those two profiles – theist without a confident view; nontheist – you might nonetheless conclude not only that there is no good (nonarbitrary) reason for singling out any point between fertilization and viability as the moment when unborn human life acquires inherent dignity, but also that there is no good reason for selecting viability over fertilization as the moment when such life acquires inherent dignity. In that case, you should accept, by default, that unborn human beings have inherent dignity from the moment of fertilization.

But is it true that there is no good reason for singling out any point between fertilization and viability, or viability over fertilization, as the moment when unborn human beings acquire (substantially) the same moral status as newborns? In his important book *A Defense of Abortion*, philosopher David Boonin argues – persuasively, in my judgment – that several of the points after fertilization but before birth identified by some as the moment when unborn human life acquires moral status – implantation (generally six to eight days after fertilization); actual fetal movement (between five and six weeks after fertilization); perceived fetal movement, or quickening (approximately sixteen to seventeen weeks after fertilization); and viability – are not plausible candidates for the moment when unborn human life acquires moral status.[10] In Boonin's judgment, however, which he defends in an interesting, complex argument, there *is* a moment after fertilization but before birth when unborn human life acquires moral status: the moment when the fetus begins to display "organized cortical brain activity" (OCBA).[11]

---

[9] Garry Wills, *Papal Sin* 229 (2000).
[10] See David Boonin, *A Defense of Abortion* 91–115 & 129–32 (2003).
[11] See id. at 115–29.

First Principles Applied

Boonin reports that "there is no evidence to suggest that [organized cortical brain activity] occurs prior to approximately the 25th week of gestation, and ample evidence to suggest that it does begin to occur sometime between the 25th and 32nd week."[12] This means that the point when organized cortical brain activity begins to occur is not a point *between* fertilization and viability; it is a point *after* viability: Again, fetal viability occurs at twenty-three or twenty-four weeks. Boonin's argument supports the proposition that if we want to be cautious, we should assume that every fetus that has reached the twenty-fifth week of pregnancy has moral status. But I have already explained why we who affirm that every born human being has inherent dignity should affirm that at least every fetus that has reached the twenty-third week of pregnancy – viability – has inherent dignity. Therefore, we should not select the emergence of OCBA over viability as the moment when unborn human life acquires inherent dignity. Imagine two viable fetuses whose OCBA has not yet emerged; they are of the same gestational age; the first has been born, the second has not. It seems quite arbitrary for us who affirm that every born human being has inherent dignity to hold that although the first fetus has inherent dignity, the second lacks it.

In any event, there is a second, independent reason why Boonin's selection of the emergence of OCBA as the point at which unborn human life acquires moral status is problematic. In Boonin's argument, desires play the fundamental role: According to Boonin, one human being is the moral equal of another human being at least partly in virtue of having desires, and to respect another human being as a moral equal is to respect her desires – that is, her "ideal" (as distinct from "actual"), "dispositional" (as distinct from "occurrent") desires.[13] But, as Boonin explains, a fetus has no desires – in the relevant sense of "desires" – before the emergence of OCBA. However, according to a different argument that is at least as plausible as Boonin's, to respect another human being as a moral equal is to respect not her *desires*, not even her ideal, dispositional desires, but her (authentic) *well-being* – or, as it is sometimes put, her *welfare*.[14] And even before

---

[12] Id. at 115.
[13] For his careful presentation of the argument, one should read Boonin's impressive book.
[14] See David DeGrazia, "Identity, Killing, and the Boundaries of Our Existence," 31 PHILOSOPHY & PUBLIC AFFAIRS 414, 428–30 (2003).

the emergence of OCBA, unborn human life has well-being, even if in some cases that well-being happens to be compromised in one or more respects.[15]

I said that we who affirm that every born human being has inherent dignity should affirm that at least every fetus being who has reached the twenty-third week of pregnancy – viability – has inherent dignity. Notice the "at least." If we affirm that every born human being and every viable unborn human being has inherent dignity, and if we can discern no good reason for singling out any point between fertilization and viability, or viability over fertilization, as the moment when unborn human beings acquire inherent dignity, then we should accept, by default, that unborn human beings have inherent dignity from the moment of fertilization. Boonin is right, in my judgment, that there is no good reason for singling out any point between fertilization and the emergence of OCBA as the moment when unborn human life acquires moral status.[16] *A fortiori*, there is no good reason

---

[15] See Jeff McMahan, "Paradoxes of Abortion and Prenatal Injury," 116 ETHICS 625, 627 (2006):
> Some philosophers argue that a fetus cannot have an interest in continuing to live because it lacks a desire – and even the capacity to desire – to continue to live. But this view is hard to sustain. If a fetus is killed, it will have had a short life containing little of value. Suppose that if it is not killed, it will have a long life containing a great deal of value. The longer life would be the better life. Since each possible life would be the life of one and the same individual, it is better for that individual to have the better of the two lives. But if it would be better *for the fetus* to have the better of the two lives, it is hard to deny that the fetus has an interest in continuing to live.
>
> Assume that for a human being that, like a post-OCBA fetus, has desires, respecting her ideal, dispositional desires and respecting her well-being amount to the same thing as a practical matter, because her fundamental ideal, dispositional desire is to achieve, to the greatest extent possible, well-being. Nonetheless, for a pre-OCBA fetus, respecting her ideal, dispositional desires and respecting her well-being cannot amount to the same thing: The former is an impossible feat; the latter is not. One cannot respect a pre-OCBA fetus's desires; a pre-OCBA fetus has no desires. But one *can* respect a pre-OCBA fetus's well-being – by not acting to impair or destroy, or by acting to protect or improve, the fetus's well-being.

[16] In written comments, Cathy Kaveny has called to my attention "a possible position regarding the time at which individual human life begins: the early embryo possesses the possibility of twinning (one fertilized egg splits into two) and recombination (two fertilized eggs combine into one). So, eminent pro-life thinkers such as Paul Ramsey serious considered the possibility that the end of this phase (14 days or so) should mark the beginning of the life of an individual human being, since individual human beings, unlike individual human cells, don't possess this possibility – individual human beings don't a sexually reproduce or combine with one another." For a defense of this position,

First Principles Applied

for singling out any point between fertilization and viability, or viability over fertilization, as the moment when unborn human life acquires inherent dignity. So, we who affirm that every born human being has inherent dignity can reasonably affirm not only that every viable fetus has inherent dignity but also that every previable fetus has it, too.

Sometimes conclusions are counterintuitive; this one, however, is not: Why should we think that the fact that an unborn human being is viable – that it is capable of survival outside the mother's womb – is relevant to the question of whether he or she has inherent dignity? Why should we think that a six-month-old fetus, because it is capable of surviving outside its mother's womb, has inherent dignity, but that a five-month-old fetus, because it is not yet capable of surviving outside its mother's womb, does not have inherent dignity? Why should we think that one lacks inherent dignity just because one cannot yet survive outside the womb in which one has been gestating?[17] I cannot discern a satisfactory answer.[18] Readers who think they can should take a look at the note accompanying this sentence.[19]

see Mary Warnock, *An Intelligent Person's Guide to Ethics* 43–49 (1998) (giving reasons for drawing the line at "fourteen days from fertilisation").

[17] "We can distinguish between being dependent on a particular person and being dependent on some person or other. The viability criterion maintains that the former property [, not the latter,] is morally relevant...." Boonin, n. 10, at 130. "The proponent of the viability criterion is best understood as claiming that a fetus is viable if the technological means of keeping it alive outside of the womb are in principle available somewhere, even if not to this particular fetus." Id. at 131–32.

[18] See John Langan, "Observations on Abortion and Politics," AMERICA, Oct. 25, 2004: "[O]ur increased knowledge of embryology and human genetics... [make] clear the continuity and identity of human life from conception forward."

[19] Consider what Chris Eberle said in comments he provided me:

[T]he viability threshold makes the inherent dignity of human beings depend on temporal and perhaps spatial facts that are every bit as arbitrary as the spatial facts that scuttled the birth criterion. Why?

There doesn't seem to be any reason to believe that we can't develop technology that enables us to keep unborn human beings alive and developing long enough for them to [survive] outside the mother's womb *at any point from conception to birth*. We might not now be able to do so, but what of moral relevance is that? In fact, to claim that it's relevant is to claim that whether one has inherent dignity depends on when one happens to be lucky enough to be born. If we do not now have the requisite technology, but we develop that technology in ten years, then it will turn out that unborn human [beings] will be viable, and thus have inherent dignity, from conception on in ten years, but that those conceived now are just flat out of luck. Their clock doesn't start ticking till they're 24 weeks old. It's not clear that this kind of temporal arbitrariness is any less objectionable than the spatial arbitrariness that scuttled the birth criterion.

It bears emphasis, then, that some of us who affirm that all unborn human beings, previable as well as viable, have inherent dignity do so simply because we can discern no good reason not to affirm it, given that we *already* affirm that all born human beings have inherent dignity. ("The strongest case for personhood *ab initio* I have heard argues from the fact that there is no stage of nascent development that is so significant that it points to a major qualitative change: not implantation, not quickening, not viability, not birth."[20]) Now, one can certainly inquire, as I have elsewhere, at length, *why* one should affirm – *on what basis* one should affirm – that all born human beings have inherent dignity.[21] But the fact of the matter is that many of us *do* affirm it; for whatever reason, or for no articulable reason, we *do* affirm the morality of human rights. And the question for us is that *given* that we affirm that all born human beings have inherent dignity,

> Moreover, the viability criterion might be arbitrary in much the same way as the birth criterion. Consider a human being who would be able to live outside the mother's womb if that human being were conceived in the USA, but who happens to live in Darfur, which utterly lacks the technology that keeps American unborns alive. Is that child viable? It's not clear: must life – sustaining technology actually be available or must it be available only in principle?
>
> Suppose you take the former route – well, that seems arbitrary in the extreme. Whether one has inherent dignity seems to depend on chance facts about where one happens to be born.
>
> Suppose that you take the latter route – the in principle available route. Someone, somewhere has the technology necessary to [enable survival] outside the mother's womb. But this seems crazy: What if there are Aliens on another planet with the right technology, but who are not able to get that technology to us any more effectively than Americans can get their technology to the folks in Darfur? Are all unborn human beings viable from conception on if there are Aliens who live on Alpha Centauri who have the technology to keep babies alive from conception on until they [survive] outside the mother's womb?
>
> Maybe not – the technology has to be located here on earth – or at least in our solar system. Well, this is not going to work: do unborn human beings acquire human dignity if an Alien spaceship happens to pass through our solar system (or atmosphere) with the requisite technology? Even if we don't know they are passing through? So unborn [human beings] lose their inherent dignity when the Aliens leave the solar system?
>
> One could spin such silly stories for a long while longer....
>
> You get the picture: Making the inherent dignity of a human being depend on viability, which is in turn cashed out in terms of the existence and distribution of technology, is objectionably arbitrary.

[20] Richard A. McCormick, SJ, *Corrective Vision: Explorations in Moral Theology* 183 (1994).
[21] See Michael J. Perry, "Morality and Normativity," 13 LEGAL THEORY 211 (2007); Michael J. Perry, *Toward a Theory of Human Rights* 7–29 (2007).

is there any good reason not to affirm that all human beings, unborn as well as born, have it too?

What philosopher Michael Wreen has written recently about what he calls the Abortion Argument applies, with slight terminological modification, to the argument I am making here, namely, that it is *an indirect argument for its conclusion, one that simply piggybacks on the claim that every born human being – for example, a two-year-old – has inherent dignity. The fundamental grounds for possession of this moral status, "inherent dignity," are not mentioned, much less explored, in the argument. What this means is that it's a secondary, indirect argument, one that attempts to carry the day without itself tackling any of the weightier issues, both metaphysical and moral, that surround humanity and moral status.*[22] Wreen surmises that "such an argument is the best that can be done as far as the issue of foetal status and the morality of abortion is concerned."[23]

Nothing I have said to this point is meant to deny that there is, in many liberal democratic societies, including the United States, a deep and widespread controversy about the moral status of unborn human life in the earliest stages of its development. Moreover, there is little if any reason to doubt that this controversy will endure. Referring to "philosophy, neurobiology, psychology, [and] medicine," Garry Wills has observed that "[t]he evidence from natural sources of knowledge has been interpreted in various ways, by people of good intentions and good information. If natural law teaching were clear on the matter, a consensus would have been formed by those with natural reason."[24]

---

[22] See Michael J. Wreen, "The Standing Is Slippery," 79 PHILOSOPHY 553, 571–72 (2004): The Abortion Argument offers an indirect argument for its conclusion, one that simply piggybacks on the claim that a given being, a two-year-old, is a human being/person/etc. The fundamental grounds for, say, possession of a right to life are not mentioned, much less explored, in the argument. What this means is that it's a secondary, indirect argument, one that attempts to carry the day without itself tackling any of the weightier issues, both metaphysical and moral, that surround humanity, personhood, moral status, and the right to life. It could be that such an argument is the best that can be done as far as the issue of foetal status and the morality of abortion is concerned.

[23] Id. at 572. Wreen then adds: "but even so, we can hope for more, and try to find more. I, at least, would feel more confident if there were other, independent, and more fundamental arguments that also lead to the same conclusion." Id.

[24] Wills, "The Bishops vs. the Bible," n. 8. On the the enduring absence of a consensus to which Wills refers, compare Robert P. George & Patrick Lee, "Acorns and Embryos," THE NEW ATLANTIS, Fall 2004/Winter 2004, www.thenewatlantis.com/archive/7/georgeleeprint.htm, with Michael S. Gazzaniga, "The Thoughtful Distinction Between

Abortion

Nor is anything I have just said meant to deny – indeed, it is undeniable – that a ban on abortion can and often does impose serious costs on pregnant women who want to have an abortion but are prevented by the ban from doing so.[25] A ban on abortion is very different, in that regard, from, say, a requirement that motorcyclists wear protective headgear. Preventing a woman from having a previability abortion will profoundly affect the shape of her life for years to come, perhaps for the rest of her life. ("Let us not underestimate what is at stake: Having an unwanted child can go a long way toward ruining a woman's

---

Embryo and Human," THE CHRONICLE REVIEW, Apr. 8, 2005. See also Anthony Kenny, "Life Stories: When an Individual Life Begins – and the Ethics of Ending It," TIMES LIT. SUPP., Mar. 25, 2005, at 3. Jesuit moral theologian Richard McCormick foresaw that because of this dissensus about the moral status of the fetus – in particular, about the fetus's moral status during early pregnancy – "public policy [would] remain sharply contentious and the task of legislators correspondingly complex." Richard A. McCormick, SJ, "The Gospel of Life," AMERICA, Apr. 29, 1995, at 12, 13. See also John Langan, SJ, "Observations on Abortion and Politics," AMERICA, Oct. 25, 2004: "[T]he fact of continuing and intense public disagreement [underlines] how far we are from having a broad public consensus against the practice [of abortion] and of how difficult it would be to . . . enact a legal prohibition against it." Cf. Clifford Longley, "'The Church Hasn't Yet Made a Mature Appraisal of What Democracy Demands'," TABLET [London], May 7, 2005, at 11: "The criminal justice system . . . only works when there is at least a minimal degree of assent by the public to the moral framework in which it operates. . . . [W]hat you have to persuade the majority of is not just that your moral principle is correct but that it is right to insist that the minority which does not agree with it must nevertheless comply with it too."

[25] See *Roe v. Wade*, 410 U.S. 113, 153 (1973):
> The detriment that the State would impose upon the pregnant woman by denying this choice altogether is apparent. Specific and direct harm medically diagnosable even in early pregnancy may be involved. Maternity, or additional offspring, may force upon the woman a distressful life and future. Psychological harm may be imminent. Mental and physical health may be taxed by child care. There is also the distress, for all concerned, associated with the unwanted child, and there is the problem of bringing a child into a family already unable, psychologically and otherwise, to care for it. In other cases, as in this one, the additional difficulties and continuing stigma of unwed motherhood may be involved.

Did the Supreme Court overstate the costs? According to Richard Posner, the Court *understated* the costs:
> No effort is made to dramatize the hardships to a woman forced to carry her fetus to term against her will. The opinion does point out that "maternity, or additional offspring, may force upon the woman a distressful life and future," and it elaborates on the point for a few more sentences. But there is no mention of the woman who is raped, who is poor, or whose fetus is deformed. There is no reference to the death of women from illegal abortions.

Richard A. Posner, *Sex and Reason* 337 (1992).

life."[26]) However, that the costs are undeniably great does not entail that one cannot plausibly conclude that unborn human life has the requisite moral status and that therefore the public benefit achieved is sufficiently great to warrant the costs.

Now, the issue is not whether the secular rationale I have just elaborated is ultimately persuasive – again, I am presently agnostic about the rationale – but only whether the rationale is plausible. Perhaps one rejects the rationale because one sides with Boonin on this question: Does respect for another human being as a moral equal demand that one respect her ideal, dispositional desires; or, instead, does it demand that one respect her welfare? Be that as it may, that unborn human beings have the same, or substantially the same, moral status as newborns is certainly a plausible secular rationale; to many rational, well-informed, and thoughtful fellow citizens, it is a persuasive secular rationale. Therefore, it is not the case that the only discernible rationale for a ban on abortion is a religious rationale.[27]

Again, a ban on abortion does not run afoul of the right to moral freedom if (a) the ban is necessary to serve a governmental interest that is both legitimate and sufficiently weighty and (b) there is a plausible secular rationale that could account for the lawmakers' judgment that the ban serves such an interest. As I have explained here, there is a plausible secular rationale that could (and, indeed, does) account for the judgment of some lawmakers that a ban on abortion is necessary to serve a legitimate governmental interest, the

---

[26] John Hart Ely, "The Wages of Crying Wolf: A Comment on *Roe v. Wade*," 82 YALE L. J. 920, 923 (1973).

[27] By a parity of reasoning, there is a plausible secular rationale for laws and policies banning or otherwise regulating embryonic stem cell research.

Should one who affirms that every human being, unborn as well as born, has inherent dignity want government to ban all embryonic stem cell research? Not necessarily. Consider the position of Gene Outka, Dwight Professor of Philosophy and Christian Ethics at Yale University. Outka "take[s] conception and all that it alone makes possible as *the* point at which one should ascribe a judgment of irreducible value" and opposes the creation of embryos for use in stem cell research. But Outka would permit the use of "excess" embryos (i.e., embryos left over after infertility treatments have been completed). See Gene Outka, "The Ethics of Human Stem Cell Research," in Brent Waters & Ronald Cole-Turner, eds., *God and the Embryo: Religious Voices on Stem Cell and Cloning* 29 (2003). (The quoted language is on p. 55.)

weight of which is proportionate to the weight of the burden imposed by the ban.[28]

[28] Of course, not all lawmakers believe that prior to viability unborn human beings have sufficient moral status to warrant a ban on previability abortions. But even those lawmakers who do believe that all human life, unborn as well as born, has inherent dignity may nonetheless conclude, for prudential reasons, that the criminalization of previability abortions is not the optimal way for government to deal with the problem of unwanted pregnancies. See Perry, *Toward a Theory of Human Rights*, n. 21, at 61–64.

8

Same-Sex Unions[1]

In the preceding chapter, in pursuing the implications of the right to moral freedom for a ban on abortion, I illustrated the helpful role the right to moral freedom can play in shaping our discourse about the vexing, divisive controversy over whether goverment may ban abortion. In this chapter, I illustrate the discourse-shaping role the right to moral freedom can play in the context of another great, and greatly divisive, political-moral controversy: May government refuse to recognize – may it refuse to extend the benefit of law to – same-sex unions? Again, those two subjects – abortion and same-sex unions – are at the heart of the American debate; they are the principal subtexts of the American debate about the proper role of religion in the politics and law of a liberal democracy.

---

[1] In this chapter, I do not address the question whether government must or should recognize same-sex unions as "marriages," but only whether government may refuse to create civil unions for same-sex couples – that is, whether it may refuse to extend the benefit of law to same-sex unions. On the "marriage" versus "civil union" issue, compare David S. Buckel, "Government Affixes a Label of Inferiority on Same-Sex Couples When It Imposes Civil Unions & Denies Access to Marriage," 16 STANFORD L. & POL'Y REV. 73 (2005), with Andrew Koppelman, "Civil Conflict and Same-Sex Civil Unions," RESPONSIVE COMMUNITY, Spring/Summer 2004, at 20. In *Lewis v. Harris*, 908 A.2d 196 (NJ 2006), the New Jersey Supreme Court was unanimous in ruling that under the state constitution, all the benefits (and responsibilities) of civil marriage must be extended to same-sex unions, but was divided 4–3 over whether the title "marriage" must be extended to same-sex unions, with the majority declining to take that extra step. By contrast, the supreme courts of California and Connecticut each ruled that it violated the state constitution to refuse to call civil unions for homosexuals "marriages." See In re *Marriage Cases*, 183 P.3d 384 (California 2008); *Kerrigan v. Commissioner of Public Health*, 957 A.2d 407 (Connecticut 2008). On Nov. 4, 2008, however, a slim majority of voters in California (52%) voted to amend the state constitution to read: "Only a marriage between a man and a woman is valid or recognized in California." Cf. Adam Liptak, "Caution in Court for Gay Rights Groups," NEW YORK TIMES, Nov. 12, 2004; Alison Leigh Cowan, "Gay Couples Say Civil Unions Aren't Enough," NEW YORK TIMES, Mar. 17, 2008.

Same-Sex Unions

In the United States, most states refuse to extend the benefit of law to same-sex unions,[2] and in so doing a state

> effectively excludes [same-sex partners] from a broad array of legal benefits and protections incident to the marital relation, including access to a spouse's medical, life, and disability insurance, hospital visitation and other medical decisionmaking privileges, spousal support, intestate succession, homestead protections, and many other statutory protections.[3]

State refusals to extend the benefit of law to same-sex unions implicate *the right to moral equality* if there is good reason to suspect that such refusals are based on the view that gay men and lesbians are inferior human beings – the view, that is, that they do not have not equal inherent dignity, which includes the view that their interests do not merit the same respect and concern as the interests of others. State refusals to extend the benefit of law to same-sex unions *violate* the right to moral equality if they are based on such a view. Are such refusals based on that view?

The view that gays and lesbians are inferior human beings is not an unfamiliar one. Richard Posner has written of the "irrational fear and loathing of" homosexuals, who, like the Jews with whom they "were frequently bracketed in medieval persecutions[,] ... are

---

[2] As of July 2009, six states recognize same-sex marriage: Connecticut, Iowa, Maine, Massachusetts, New Hampshire, and Vermont; two states recognize same-sex unions (i.e., civil unions for same-sex couples): California (see n. 1) and New Jersey; and four more jurisdictions have enacted domestic partnerships laws that grant many or all of the benefits of marriage to registered domestic partners: Hawaii, Oregon, Washington State, and the District of Columbia. According to a 2007 Pew Research Center survey, a bare majority of Americans (55%) opposes, and a significant minority (36%) supports, recognizing same-sex marriage. However, a bare majority of Americans (54%) supports, and a large minority (42%) opposes, civil unions for same-sex couples, according to a 2006 Pew survey.

During the ten-year period from 1998 to 2008, voters in twenty-nine states approved state constitutional bans on same-sex "marriage." However, some of these bans are limited: They do not forbid states to extend the benefit of law to same-sex unions; they forbid only calling such unions "marriage." See "States with Voter-Approved Constitutional Bans on Same-Sex Marriage, 1998–2008," http://pewforum.org/docs/?DocID=370.

As of July 2009, seven countries – the Netherlands (since 2000), Belgium (2003), Spain (2005), Canada (2005), South Africa (2006), Norway (2009), and Sweden (2009) – recognize same-sex marriage.

[3] *Baker v. Vermont*, 744 A.2d 864, 870 (VT 1999). For a fuller specification of the benefits in question, see id. at 883–84. See also *Goodridge v. [Massachusetts] Department of Public Health*, 798 N.E.2d 941, 955–57 (MA 2003); *Hernandez v. Robles*, 855 N.E.2d 1, 6–7 (NY 2006).

despised more for who they are than for what they do."⁴ Andrew Koppelman has reminded us of

> the judge's famous speech at Oscar Wilde's sentencing for sodomy, one of the most prominent legal texts in the history of homosexuality, [which] "treats the prisoners as objects of disgust, vile contaminants who are not really people, and who therefore need not be addressed as if they were people." From this it is not very far to Heinrich Himmler's speech to his SS generals, in which he explained that the medieval German practice of drowning gay men in bogs "was no punishment, merely the extermination of an abnormal life. It had to be removed just as we [now] pull up stinging nettles, toss them on a heap, and burn them."⁵

It is certainly reasonable to suspect that states would not refuse to extend the benefit of law to same-sex unions in the absence of the "irrational fear and loathing" of homosexuals referenced by Judge Posner.⁶ In contemporary liberal democracies, however, including the United States, it is also not unreasonable to doubt that such fear and loathing is a basis of state refusals to extend the benefit of law to same-sex unions. True, some "of the antigay animus that exists in the United States is just like racism, in the virulence of the rage it bespeaks and the hatred it directs towards those who are its objects."⁷ Nonetheless, "[n]ot all antigay views...deny the

---

4 Richard Posner, *Sex and Reason* 346 (1992). Cf. Louis Crompton, *Homosexuality and Civilization* (2003). Crompton's book is discussed in Edward Rothstein, "Annals of Homosexuality: From Greek to Grim to Gay," NEW YORK TIMES, Dec. 13, 2003.

As history teaches, "an irrational fear and loathing" of *any* group "more for who they are than for what they do" has tragic consequences. The irrational fear and loathing of homosexuals – that is, the fear and loathing of them *more for who they are than for what they do* – is no exception. There is, for example, the horrible phenomenon of "gay bashing." "The coordinator of one hospital's victim assistance program reported that 'attacks against gay men were the most heinous and brutal I encountered.' A physician reported that injuries suffered by the victims of homophobic violence he had treated were so 'vicious' as to make clear that 'the intent is to kill and maim.'" Andrew Koppelman, *Antidiscrimination Law & Social Equality* 165 (1996). As "[a] federal task force on youth suicide noted[,] because 'gay youth face a hostile and condemning environment, verbal and physical abuse, and rejection and isolation from family and peers,' young gays are two to three times more likely than other young people to attempt and to commit suicide." Id. at 149.

5 Andrew Koppelman, "Are the Boy Scouts Being as Bad as Racists? Judging the Scouts' Antigay Policy," 18 PUBLIC AFFAIRS QUARTERLY 363, 372 (2004).

6 See *Kerrigan v. Commissioner of Public Health*, 957 A. 2d 407 (Connecticut 2008).

7 Andrew Koppelman, "You Can't Hurry Love: Why Antidiscrimination Protections for Gay People Should Have Religious Exemptions," 72 BROOKLYN L. REV. 125, 145 (2006).

Same-Sex Unions

personhood and equal citizenship of gay people."[8] Indeed, although the pope and the bishops of the Catholic Church are among the leading opponents of extending the benefit of law to same-sex unions, the pope and bishops' teaching "about the dignity of homosexual persons is clear. They must be accepted with respect, compassion, and sensitivity. Our respect for them means that we condemn all forms of unjust discrimination, harrassment or abuse."[9] Hate the sin, but love the sinner.[10]

State refusals to extend the benefit of law to same-sex unions implicate not only the right to moral equality; they also implicate *the right to moral freedom*: Such refusals interfere with one's ability to live one's life on the basis of – to integrate one's life with – one's moral convictions and commitments. For most people, the decision to live together with another person in marriage, or in a marriage-like union, is a decision animated by one's deepest moral convictions and commitments. Moreover, a government's refusal to recognize same-sex unions obviously impedes a gay or lesbian couple's living together in a marriage-like union. In his book *On Human Rights*, philosopher James Griffin has rightly observed that moral freedom (he calls it "liberty") "seldom requires" that government make it possible for everyone to live precisely the life one "has settled on. Most individual conceptions of a worthwhile life have alternatives, as good or nearly as good, and a person may reasonably be asked to fund an alternative, if the form first chosen is costly or reduces options for others."[11] Nonetheless:

> [I]f there are same-sex couples who want to form some sort of union and raise children – who want, that is, to have the rich, stable, recognized, respected relations that are at the heart of most people's conceptions of a worthwhile life – and, because of our ethical traditions, there are no social institutions to allow it, then we should create one or another form of them. *This too, I believe, is an issue of liberty. No matter how many options there are already, this one, because of its centrality to characteristic human conceptions of a worthwhile life, must be added....What is at stake for same-sex couples are several of the most important components of a good life available to*

---

[8] Id.
[9] USCCB Administrative Committee, "Promote, Protect, Preserve Marriage: Statement on Marriage and Homosexual Unions," 33 ORIGINS 257, 259 (2003).
[10] See Robert F. Nagel, "Playing Defense in Colorado," FIRST THINGS, May 1998, at 34, 35: "There is the obvious but important possibility that one can 'hate' an individual's behavior without hating the individual."
[11] James Griffin, *On Human Rights* 168 (2008).

human beings. . . . Some persons do not want deep personal relations or to raise children. But the great majority of us do, and the [refusal to extend the benefit of law to same-sex unions denies] same-sex couples some of the greatest, most widely distributed, and most deeply embedded – sometimes even genetically embedded – least easily substituted ends of human life there are.[12]

So state refusals to extend the benefit of law to same-sex unions implicate the right to moral freedom. And such refusals *violate* the right to moral freedom – that is, they violate the right to moral freedom read in conjunction with the principle that a religious rationale may not serve as the basis of coercive and/or discriminatory lawmaking – unless (a) such refusals are necessary to serve a legitimate governmental interest, the weight of which is sufficient to be proportionate to the weight of the burden imposed by the policy; and (b) there is a plausible secular reason that *could* account for the lawmakers' judgment that the refusal is necessary to serve such an interest – that is, *a reason we can realistically assume the lawmakers accept.*

If a state refusal to extend the benefit of law to same-sex unions is necessary to serve a legitimate (and sufficiently weighty) governmental interest, and if there is a plausible secular reason that could account for the lawmakers' judgment that the refusal is necessary to serve such an interest, then the refusal does not violate the right to moral freedom. Moreover, if a state refusal to recognize same-sex unions does not violate the right to moral freedom, then it does not violate the right to moral equality either: If a state refusal satisfies the test it must satisfy under the former right, necessarily it satisfies the test it must satisfy under the latter right, namely, that the refusal is necessary to serve a legitimate (and sufficiently weighty) governmental interest. Let's inquire, then, whether state refusals to extend the benefit of law to same-sex unions violate the right to moral freedom, read in conjunction with the principle that a religious rationale may not serve as the basis of coercive and/or discriminatory lawmaking.

---

[12] Id. at 163–64 (emphasis added). See also Kenji Yoshino, "Marriage Partners," NEW YORK TIMES MAGAZINE, June 1, 2008 (discussing "how much human flourishing is enabled by the [marriage] right and how much it is impeded by its denial"): "As many gay rights advocates have claimed, the issue is less one of gay equality than of individual liberty." The California Supreme Court agrees. See In re *Marriage Cases*, 183 P.3d 384, 440–42 (California 2008).

Same-Sex Unions

Several gay and lesbian couples claimed that the State of New York's nonrecognition policy – its refusal to extend the benefit of law to same-sex unions – violated the state constitution. On July 6, 2006, in the course of rejecting that claim, a majority of the New York Court of Appeals (New York's highest court) – in an opinion that within weeks was endorsed both by a three-judge panel of the U.S. Court of Appeals for the Eighth Circuit (July 14, 2006) and by a majority of the Supreme Court of the State of Washington (July 26, 2006) – argued that New York's refusal to extend the benefit of law to same-sex unions served two legitimate governmental interests: (a) minimizing the number of children born out of wedlock and (b) maximizing the number of children raised by their mother and father together.[13] Both are undeniably legitimate (and weighty) governmental interests.[14] But even if we assume that extending the benefit of law to *heterosexual* unions makes it more likely that children will be born in wedlock and raised by their mother and father together, it is not true that denying the benefit of law to *same-sex* unions serves either interest. Why extend the benefit of law *just* to heterosexual unions? Is it because New York marriage law is meant to serve *only* these two interests? That claim strains credulity past the breaking point: We all know that states extend the benefit of law to heterosexual unions *for a set of related reasons, some of which have nothing to do either with minimizing the number of children born out of wedlock or maximizing the number of children raised by their mother and father together*: to protect and nurture (by law) the solemn commitment each person makes to the other to unite

---

[13] See *Hernandez v. Robles*, 855 N.E.2d 1, 7–8 (New York 2006); *Citizens for Equal Protection v. Bruning*, 455 F.3d 859, 867–68 (8th Cir. 2006); *Andersen v. King County*, 138 P.3d 963, 982–85 (Washington 2006).

[14] Maximizing the number of children raised by two parents together is a legitimate governmental interest *without regard to whether the two parents are a heterosexual couple or a same-sex couple*. See *Lewis v. Harris*, 908 A.2d 196, 230 (New Jersey 2006) (Poritz, C.J., joined by Long & Zazzali, JJ., concurring in part & dissenting in part):

> Recent social science studies inform us that "same-sex couples increasingly form the core of families in which children are conceived, born, and raised." Gregory N. Herek, *Legal Recognition of Same-Sex Couples in the United States: A Social Science Perspective*, 61 Am. Pscychol. 607, 611 (2006). It is not surprising, given that data, that the State does not advance a "promotion of procreation" position to support limiting marriage to heterosexuals. Further, "[e]mpirical studies comparing children raised by sexual minority parents with those raised by otherwise comparable heterosexual parents have not found reliable disparities in mental health or social adjustment," *id.* at 613, suggesting that the "optimal environment" position is equally weak.

their lives in a lifelong, monogamous relationship of mutual love and support; to protect the individuals who have made that commitment and are living their lives accordingly; and to protect the children who have been born to or adopted by the couple. Those reasons simply do not explain denying the benefit of law to same-sex unions; indeed, by themselves those reasons call for the opposite policy. The point is so obvious that elaboration would be otiose: Don't same-sex partners who have made a commitment to one another to unite their lives in a lifelong, monogamous relationship of mutual love and support, and who are living their lives accordingly, need the protection of the law? Don't the children who have been born to or adopted by the same-sex couple need the protection of the law?[15]

Does New York's, or any other state's, nonrecognition policy serve a legitimate governmental interest? Why – for what reason or reasons – do states extend the benefit of law *just* to heterosexual unions; *why do they deny the benefit of law to same-sex unions?* One commonly stated reason is to protect traditional (i.e., heterosexual) marriage.

> In the 1990s, the opponents of same-sex marriage created a new line of argument critique.... The new line, which has been embraced within the White House and the most anti-gay circles of Capitol Hill, is this: "We love gays and lesbians – but as a society we cannot give them things that would undermine traditional marriage, which is the foundation of America's values and culture. Same-sex marriage would do precisely that – undermine marriage and the nuclear family. For that reason, neutral people should be skeptical of complete equality for these people.... We traditionalists love just about everyone – and look what we've done for homosexuals, we don't

---

[15] For answers to those and many other relevant questions – answers that led Professor McClain to support extending the benefit of law to same-sex unions – see Linda C. McClain, *The Place of Families: Fostering Capacity, Equality, and Responsibility* (2006); Linda C. McClain, "God's Created Order, Gender Complementarity, and the Federal Marriage Amendment," 20 BRIGHAM YOUNG UNIVERSITY J. PUBLIC LAW 313 (2006). See also In re *Marriage Cases*, 183 P.3d 384 (California 2008). Cf. The Brussels Declaration, https://www.iheu.org/v4e/html/the_declaration.html:
> Modern families come in a wide variety of forms: the traditional nuclear or extended families, single-parent families, unmarried couples with or without children, same-sex couples, even – in some AIDS-stricken societies – children with no parents at all. Whatever form the family may take, the primary responsibility of parents is to safeguard and nurture their children. No child should suffer discrimination because of his or her family circumstances. All are equally entitled to protection and support.

put them in jail anymore. But a positive and loving approach requires that we consider the public welfare, especially the welfare of children, our most vulnerable charges. So we cannot go along with the entire 'homosexual agenda,' for it sacrifices a great institution and the public welfare."[16]

Although protecting heterosexual marriage is undeniably a legitimate (and weighty) governmental interest, denying the benefit of law to same-sex unions does not serve that interest unless, as the pope and bishops of the Catholic Church, among others, claim, extending the benefit of law to same-sex unions would have, in the long run, subversive consequences for heterosexual marriage.[17] To avoid predictable misunderstanding, let me emphasize that I am not addressing in this chapter the question whether government must recognize same-sex unions as "marriages."[18] I am addressing here only the question

[16] William N. Eskridge Jr., Darren R. Spedale, & Hans Ytterberg, "Nordic Bliss? Scandinavian Registered Partnerships and the Same-Sex Marriage Debate" at 4, *Berkeley Electronic Press, Issues in Legal Scholarship, Symposium: Single-Sex Marriage* (2004), Article 4, www.bepress.com/ils/iss5/art4.

According to Peter Berkowitz, "conservatives' most important argument" against gay marriage is this: "Given the changes in the social meaning of marriage over the past forty years, conservatives worry that the legalization of same-sex marriage will further attenuate the connection between marriage and family that is crucial to a healthy society." Peter Berkowitz, "Illiberal Liberalism," FIRST THINGS, April 2007, at 50, 54. However, Berkowitz does not tell us how, and it is far from obvious that, "the legalization of same-sex marriage will further attenuate the connection between marriage and family that is crucial to a healthy society." Maybe the argument he has in mind is the argument pressed by the pope and the bishops of the Catholic Church. See nn. 30–31.

[17] See Stephen J. Pope, "The Magisterium's Arguments against 'Same-Sex Marriage': An Ethical Analysis and Critique," 65 THEOLOGICAL STUDIES 530, 559 (2004) (citing Judith S. Wallerstein & Sandra Blakeless, *The Good Marriage: How and Why Love Lasts* [1995]):

The magisterium [i.e., the pope and the bishops] fears that a purely nonprocreative, contractualized notion of marriage might lead to the elimination of the family and to anarchy in child-rearing practices. They believe that even conservative gays who want to have the monogamous commitments receive the social support that comes from legal validation are, unwittingly or not, pursuing a Trojan horse policy in which entry into the institution will eventually lead to its demise. Instead of helping matters, contractualism would leave them on their own and make it easier for fathers routinely to abandon their children.

Cf. Geoffrey Nunberg, "We the People? (In Order to Form a More Perfect Gay Union)," NEW YORK TIMES, Feb. 22, 2004: "For opponents [of recognizing same-sex unions as marriages], broadening the definition of marriage is like opening an exclusive hotel to package tours, with the result that the traditional clientele will no longer feel like checking in."

[18] See n. 1.

whether government may refuse to create civil unions for same-sex couples – whether, that is, it may refuse to extend the benefit of law to same-sex unions. Because the claim that creating civil unions for same-sex couples would have subversive consequences for heterosexual marriage is both bereft of empirical support[19] and, for many, deeply counterintuitive,[20] the claim is, for many, including myself, implausible. The New York and Washington justices previously referenced were conspicuously determined (desperate?) to lob the controversy over same-sex unions back into the lap of the legislators;[21] even so, the justices did not, in support of their ruling, go so far as to suggest that it would be plausible for lawmakers to believe that extending the benefit of law to same-sex unions may have, in the long run, subversive consequences for heterosexual marriage. Of course, one can disagree with a claim without thinking that the claim is implausible. And one should surely be wary about casually, and arrogantly, pronouncing that a claim with which one does not agree is implausible. In this case, however, I have been unable to resist the conclusion that the claim *is* implausible – the claim that creating civil unions for same-sex couples, even if the law does not recognize such unions as "marriages," would have, in the long run, subversive consequences for heterosexual marriage.

> The results of more than a century of anthropological research on households, kinship relations, and families, across cultures and through time, provide no support whatsoever for the view that either civilization or viable social orders depend upon marriage as an exclusively heterosexual

---

[19] See William N. Eskridge Jr. & Darren R. Spedale, *Gay Marriage: For Better or Worse?: What We've Learned from the Evidence* (2006).

[20] See, e.g., Jonathan Rauch, "Family's Value: Gay Marriage Is Good for Kids," NEW REPUBLIC, May 30, 2005, at 15; Rosemary Radford Ruether, "Marriage Between Homosexuals Is Good for Marriage," NATIONAL CATHOLIC RPTR., Nov. 18, 2005, at 20. Cf. Margaret A. Farley, *Just Love: A Framework for Christian Sexual Ethics* 293–94 (2006):

> The major argument against same-sex marriage has tended to be that it will weaken support for traditional heterosexual marriage and traditional notions of family. It is difficult to make sense of this reasoning, especially since the churches do not mount campaigns against laws that recognize divorce – arguably a greater threat to heterosexual marriage than gay marriages might be. A more persuasive position is that the possibility of gay marriage would actually reinforce the value of commitment for heterosexuals as well as for homosexuals.

[21] See *Hernandez v. Robles*, 855 N.E.2d 1, 22 (NY 2006); *Andersen v. King County*, 138 P.3d 963, 990 (Washington 2006).

institution. Rather, anthropological research supports the conclusion that a vast array of family types, including families built upon same-sex partnerships, can contribute to stable and humane societies.[22]

A different argument for denying the benefit of law to same-sex unions has been offered by British philosopher Roger Scruton. Here is the argument, as summarized by Roderick Hills:

> [O]ne might reasonably believe that men and women have different and complementary sexual "temperaments" such that sexual relationships between members of different sexes will be more psychologically satisfactory than relationships between members of the same sex. Scruton argues that men tend to be more sexually predatory and promiscuous than women; while women seek permanence in their sexual relationships, men tend to seek adventure. Therefore, if men form sexual relationships with other men rather than with women, those relationships will tend to have shorter duration and a greater concentration on physical self-gratification than heterosexual relationships. If one assumes that these characteristics are undesirable, then one might conclude that at least male homosexuality is undesirable.[23]

Scruton's argument fails as a plausible argument against extending the benefit of law to same-sex unions.

- First, the argument does not explain why government should refuse to recognize woman–woman unions.
- Second, there is good reason to doubt Scruton's generalization about man–woman unions being "more psychologically satisfactory"

---

[22] Press release, American Anthropological Association, Feb. 25, 2004, http://www.hrc.org/issues/5513.htm.
  Am I being too hasty here? See Pope, n. 17, at 562:
  It is hard to have confidence in predictions – pro or con – about the long-term effects that would follow from enacting same-sex marriage. In the absence of knowledge regarding matters of this magnitude, and involving courses of events that would be irreversible, the magisterium [of the Catholic Church] is not unreasonable to call for caution and even to resist the new social experiment proposed by advocates of same-sex marriage. It is possible for people of good faith to differ on this issue. At the very least, further discussion, investigation, and deliberation are in order.
[23] Roderick M. Hills, Jr., "You Say You Want a Revolution? The Case Against the Transformation of Culture Through Moral Equality Laws," 95 MICHIGAN L. REV. 1588, 1610–11 (1997) (citing Roger Scruton, *Sexual Desire: A Moral Philosophy of the Erotic* 305–11 [1986]).

than same-sex unions.[24] In 2008, the American Psychological Association reported that new research finds there is "an equal level of commitment and relationship satisfaction among same-sex couples and heterosexual couples."[25] But even if, for the sake of discussion, we credit the generalization, the argument does not explain why government should refuse to recognize same-sex unions given that those who form such unions are, because of their sexual orientation, incapable of forming man–woman unions.
- Third, there is good reason to doubt Scruton's generalization about man–man couples being more transitory than man–woman couples. "[E]ven in the present regime in which they are not permitted to marry, same-sex couples do not seem to be much less stable than heterosexual couples. [The] data suggests that same-sex couples are not all that different in terms of their capacity to function or to remain stable from heterosexual couples."[26] But even if, for the sake of discussion, we credit the generalization, the argument does not explain why government should refuse to recognize the man–man sexual relationships of those who are committed to, and seek public affirmation of, their relationships *as lifelong unions of faithful love*. After all, there is no reason to think that legal recognition of such

---

[24] See Martha C. Nussbaum, "Platonic Love and Colorado Law: The Relevance of Ancient Greek Norms to Modern Sexual Controversies," 80 VIRGINIA L. REV. 1515, 1601 (1994):
> Scruton's argument was always a peculiar one: for why should one believe that all individuals of one sex are more like each other in quality than any of them is like any member of the opposite sex? And would Scruton really wish to generalize his argument, as consistency seems to demand, preferring relationships between partners different in age, and race, and nationality, and religion? Even if he were to do so, Plato's dialogues offer good argument against him. Along with Aristotle's ethical thought, they argue that people who are alike in the goals they share and the aspirations they cherish may be more likely to promote genuine social goods than people who are unlike in character and who do not share any aspirations. In addition, the dialogues show that the kind of "otherness" that is valuable in love relationships – that one's partner is another separate and, to some extent, hidden world; that the body shows only traces of the soul within; and that lovers never can be completely welded together into a single person – is quite different from the "qualitative" otherness of physiology and character. Indeed, the "otherness" of mystery and separateness is actually defended in Scruton's argument, as it is in Plato's, as an erotic good.

[25] See Press Release, American Psychological Association, Jan. 22, 2008, http://www.apa.org/releases/satisfaction0108.html.

[26] Andrew Koppelman, "Three Arguments for Gay Rights," 95 MICHIGAN L. REV. 1636, 1666 (1997). See id. at 1664–66.

relationships would do the relationships any harm – and no reason to doubt that legal recognition would do the relationships good.[27]

Let's cut to the chase. The real and dominating reason for state refusals to extend the benefit of law to same-sex unions has nothing to do with protecting heterosexual marriage – or with minimizing the number of children born out of wedlock or maximizing the number of children raised by their mother and father together.[28] This is that reason:

- Government should not adopt policies that support, much less policies that encourage – incentivize – immoral conduct.
- To extend the benefit of law to same-sex unions would be to support and even incentivize same-sex sexual conduct.
- Same-sex sexual conduct is immoral.
- Therefore, government should not extend the benefit of law to same-sex unions.[29]

State refusals to extend the benefit of law to same-sex unions obviously succeed in serving the interest in not supporting or incentivizing same-sex sexual conduct, understood as immoral conduct. However, under the right to moral freedom, that interest is not a legitimate (or, much less, a weighty) governmental interest: I explained in Chapter 5 that given the right to moral freedom, *and beyond the point necessary to protect an interest government must be legally free to protect, such as the lives, health, and safety of the citizenry,* none of these governmental interests is legitimate: protecting (what the powers-that-be regard as) moral truth; protecting the moral unity of society; protecting the moral

---

[27] See Andrew Sullivan, "Three's a Crowd," NEW REPUBLIC, June 17, 1996, at 10, 12:
> [M]arriage acts both as an incentive for virtuous behavior – and as a social blessing for the effort. In the past, we have wisely not made nitpicking assessments as to who deserves the right to marry and who does not. We have provided it to anyone prepared to embrace it and hoped for the best.... For some, it comes easily. For others, its responsibilities and commitments are crippling. But we do not premise the right to marry upon the ability to perform its demands flawlessly. We accept that human beings are variably virtuous, but that, as citizens, they should be given the same rights and responsibilities – period.

See also David Brooks, "The Power of Marriage," NEW YORK TIMES, Nov. 22, 2003.

[28] See Ben Schuman, "Gods & Gays: Analyzing the Same-Sex Marriage Debate from a Religious Perspective," 96 GEORGETOWN L. J. 2103, 2121–24 (2008).

[29] See *Andersen v. King County*, 138 P.3d 963, 980 (WA 2006) (majority op'n); id. at 1032 et seq. (dissenting op'n).

"health" of the citizenry. So state refusals to extend the benefit of law to same-sex unions violate the right to moral freedom.

Moroever, and in any event, when read in conjunction with the principle that a religious rationale may not serve as the basis of coercive and/or discriminatory lawmaking, the right to moral freedom requires that there be a plausible secular reason that could account for the lawmakers' judgment that same-sex sexual conduct is immoral. Is there such a reason?

Again, the pope and the bishops of the Catholic Church are among the leading opponents of extending the benefit of law to same-sex unions: They "[strongly oppose] any legislative and judicial attempts, both at state and federal levels, to grant same-sex unions the equivalent status and rights of marriage – by naming them marriage, civil unions or by other means."[30] As it happens, when the pope or the bishops enter the public square (so to speak) to weigh in on political controversies, they rely on *nonreligious* arguments: arguments that presuppose the authority neither of Christianity (much less of Catholicism) nor, indeed, of any religious belief. The principal secular argument on the basis of which the Church opposes the legal recognition of same-sex unions holds that it is immoral for anyone to engage, voluntarily and intentionally, in any species of sex (genital) act that of its nature ("inherently") is not procreative – masturbation, for example; or oral copulation; or male–female sexual intercourse, even in marriage, in which the man uses a condom. According to the Administrative Committee of the U.S. Conference of Catholic Bishops, "[w]hat are called 'homosexual unions,' . . . *because they are inherently nonprocreative*, cannot be given the status of marriage."[31]

Most citizens of the United States – indeed, even most American Catholics – reject the Church's secular argument about the immorality of inherently nonprocreative sexual conduct, such as marital

---

[30] USCCB Administrative Committee, "Statement on Marriage and Homosexual Unions," 33 ORIGINS 257, 259 (2003).

[31] Id. (emphasis added). See also Congregation for the Doctrine of the Faith, "Considerations Regarding Proposals to Give Legal Recognition to Unions Between Homosexual Persons," http://www.vatican.va/roman_curia/congregations/cfaith/documents/rc_con_cfaith_doc_20030731_homosexual-unions_en.html. But cf. Farley, *Just Love*, n. 20, at 279: "[I]n official Roman Catholic negative assessments of homosexual activity[,] the procreative norm is relativized for heterosexual relationships (following the acceptance of some forms on contraception such as 'natural family planning'), but it is absolutized once again when homosexual relationships are at issue."

Same-Sex Unions

intercourse in which the husband uses a condom.³² Therefore, the Church's secular argument simply could not account for the judgment of state lawmakers that same-sex sexual conduct is immoral: We cannot realistically assume that the lawmakers accept the Church's argument; we know that most of them reject it.³³ No state – neither my predominantly Protestant state of Georgia nor any other state – would

---

³² For a recent elaboration of the Church's argument against the legal recognition of same-sex marriage, see Robert P. George, "Law and Moral Purpose," FIRST THINGS, January 2008, at 25–28.

³³ Even for one who does accept the Church's argument, it does not follow that *none* of the benefits of law should be extended to same-sex unions. Significantly, some Catholic bishops in the United States have recently expressed a willingness to consider supporting, as a matter of distributive justice, the extension of *some* of the benefits of law to same-sex unions. See Editorial, "Bishop Brings Reason to Issue of Gay Benefits," NATIONAL CATHOLIC RPTR., Nov. 7, 2003, at 24:

> [Daniel P.] Reilly[, Roman Catholic bishop of Worcester, Massachusetts,] told legislators that the Massachusetts Catholic Conference, made up of the dioceses of Boston, Worcester, Springfield and Fall River, was unequivocally opposed to legislation that would recognize gay "marriage" or "civil unions." But the church is open, he said, to discussing what public benefits should accrue to those in non-traditional relationships.... "If the goal is to look at individual benefits and determine who should be eligible beyond spouses, then we will join the discussion," said Reilly.... [Reilly] engaged the issue on the church's terms, saying such benefits are a matter of "distributive justice."
>
> ...
>
> "Some argue that it is unfair to offer only married couples certain socioeconomic benefits," Reilly told [a committee of Massachusetts legislators]. "That is a different question from the meaning of marriage itself. The civil union bill before this committee confuses the two issues, changing the meaning of spouse in order to give global access to all marital benefits to same-sex partners in a civil union. This alters the institution of marriage by expanding whom the law considers to be spouses. Let's not mix the two issues."

Even more recently, the papal nuncio to Spain, Archbishop Manuel Monteiro de Castro, "has surprised public opinion by defending legal same-sex unions as a 'right'." See "Nuncio Backs 'Right' to Gay Unions," TABLET [London], May 15, 2004, at 30: "The nuncio's words took commentators by surprise, as the Spanish bishops officially hold the view that homosexual relationships cannot receive any kind of approval.... 'It is right that other types of relationship are recognised,' the nuncio said. He added that those in such unions should have the same rights to social security 'as any other citizen.' But 'let's leave the term "marriage" for that to which it has always referred,' he added." See also "Sign of the Times," AMERICA, Nov. 15, 2004, at 4, 5:

> Bishop George H. Niederauer of Salt Lake City did not endorse the proposed constitutional amendment in Utah, saying that he believed that state law already prohibited same-sex marriages. He said he shared concerns voiced by all three candidates for attorney general about the amendment's stipulation that "no other domestic union may be recognized as a marriage given the same or substantially equal legal effect."

today even dream of trying to justify its nonrecognition policy on the basis of the Catholic Church's argument about the immorality of inherently nonprocreative sex.[34]

The argument that not only could but almost certainly does account – indeed, the only argument, other than an implausible

---

Cf. Jennifer 8. Lee, "Congressman Says Bush Is Open to States' Bolstering Gay Rights," NEW YORK TIMES, Feb. 9, 2004 ("President Bush believes states can use contract law to ensure some of the rights that gay parters are seeking through marriage or civil union, a South Carolina congressman said Sunday"); Brian Lavery, "Ireland: Premier Backs Rights for Gay Couples," NEW YORK TIMES, Nov. 16, 2004 ("Prime Minister Bertie Ahern said his government might consider giving same-sex couples more rights, which would allow them to benefit from cheaper tax rates and more favorable inheritance laws").

[34] For anyone who rejects the Church's argument about the immorality of inherently nonprocreative sex,

> it is no longer possible to argue that sex/love between two persons of the same sex cannot be a valid embrace of bodily selves expressing love. If sex/love is centered primarily on communion between two selves *rather than on biologistic concepts of procreative complementarity*, then the love of two persons of the same sex need be no less than that of two persons of the opposite sex. Nor need their experience of ecstatic bodily communion be less valuable.

Rosemary Ruether, "The Personalization of Sexuality," in Eugene Bianchi & Rosemary Ruether, eds., *From Machismo to Mutuality: Essays on Sexism and Woman–Man Liberation* 70, 83 (1976) (emphasis added). Cf. Edward Collins Vacek, SJ, "The Meaning of Marriage: Of Two Minds," COMMONWEAL, Oct. 24, 2003, at 17, 18–19: "When, after Vatican II, Catholics began to connect sexual activity more strongly with expressing love than with making babies, it became harder to see how homosexual acts are completely different from heterosexual acts." However, to conclude that same-sex sexual conduct is not inherently immoral does not entail that anything goes. As Margaret Farley, a Catholic sister and formerly Stark Professor of Christian Ethics at Yale University, has written:

> My answer [to the question of what norms should govern same-sex relations and activities] has been: the norms of justice – the norms which govern all human relationships and those which are particular to the intimacy of sexual relations. Most generally, the norms are respect for persons through respect for autonomy and rationality; respect for relationality through requirements of mutuality, equality, commitment, and fruitfulness. More specifically one might say things like: sex between two persons of the same sex (just as two persons of the opposite sex) should not be used in a way that exploits, objectifies, or dominates; homosexual (like heterosexual) rape, violence, or any harmful use of power against unwilling victims (or those incapacitated by reason of age, etc.) is never justified; freedom, integrity, privacy are values to be affirmed in every homosexual (as heterosexual) relationship; all in all, individuals are not to be harmed, and the common good is to be promoted.

Margaret A. Farley, "An Ethic for Same-Sex Relations," in Robert Nugent, ed., *A Challenge to Love: Gay and Lesbian Catholics in the Church* 93, 105 (1983). Farley then adds that "[t]he Christian community will want and need to add those norms of faithfulness, forgiveness, of patience and hope, which are essential to any relationships between persons in the Church." Id. See also Farley, *Just Love*, n. 20.

secular argument, that could account – for the judgment of state lawmakers that same-sex sexual conduct is immoral is not secular but religious: Such conduct (and therefore same-sex unions) is "in direct opposition to God's truth as He has revealed it in the Scriptures."[35] ("Absent credible data of harm, the secular arguments advanced by opponents of same-sex marriage appear increasingly insubstantial, and religious beliefs become a more plausible basis for such opposition."[36]) For many citizens of the United States – including many who self-identify as Christian, even as evangelical Christian – the argument that same-sex sexual conduct is contrary to the will of God is no longer credible.[37] Most other Americans, however, still affirm one or another version of just that argument.[38]

In the United States, however, that argument is not a permissible basis for refusing to extend the benefit of law to same-sex unions: As I explained in Chapter 6, the imperative that government not "establish" religion, properly understood, bans sectarian religious rationales as a basis of lawmaking – especially lawmaking that is coercive or discrmimatory – and the rationale that same-sex sexual conduct is contrary to the will of God is undeniably a sectarian religious rationale.[39] Indeed, it is a sectarian rationale, increasingly so, even as among just Christian denominations.[40] The claim is also contested

---

[35] So said the Rev. Ron Johnson, Jr., on Sept. 28, 2008. See Peter Slevin, "33 Pastors Flout Tax Law With Political Sermons," WASHINGTON POST, Sept. 29, 2008.

[36] Schuman, n. 28, at 2123.

[37] See, e.g., David G. Meyers & Letha Dawson Scanzoni, *What God Has Joined Together? A Christian Case for Gay Marriage* (2005). I have explained elsewhere why Christians, *as Christians*, have good reason to be wary about relying on this biblically based argument as a ground for opposing the legal recognition of same-sex unions. See Michael J. Perry, *Under God? Religious Faith and Liberal Democracy* 55–80 (2003). Cf. Nicholas D. Kristof, "Lovers Under the Skin," NEW YORK TIMES, Dec. 3, 2003: "A 1958 poll found that 96 percent of whites disapproved of marriages between blacks and whites.... In 1959 a judge justified Virginia's ban on interracial marriage by declaring that 'Almighty God . . . did not intend for the races to mix.'"

[38] See Schuman, n. 28, at 2109–13 & 2121–22.

[39] "Sectarian religious rationales" is not redundant: Not all religious rationales are "sectarian" in the relevant sense. The nonestablishment norm allows some religious rationales as a basis of lawmaking, but not sectarian religious rationales. See id.

[40] See Brian K. Blount, "Reading and Understanding the New Testament on Homosexuality," in Choon-Leong Seow, ed., *Homosexuality and Christian Community* 28 (1996); Victor Paul Furnish, "The Bible and Homosexuality: Reading the Texts in Context," in Jeffrey S. Siker, ed., *Homosexuality in the Church* 18 (1994); Daniel A. Helminiak, "The Bible on Homosexuality: Ethically Neutral," in John Corvino, ed., *Same Sex* 81 (1999); Patricia Beattie Jung & Ralph S. Smith, "The Bible and Heterosexism," in Patricia Beattie Jung &

among religious Jews: Some Jewish congregations now bless same-sex unions.⁴¹

But even if we put aside the nonestablishment norm, it remains the case that not only in the United States but in every liberal democracy, the argument that same-sex sexual conduct is contrary to the will of God is not a permissible basis for refusing to extend the benefit of law to same-sex unions. Every liberal democracy is, as such, committed to the right to religious freedom. As I explained in Chapter 6, if the only discernible rationale, other than an implausible secular rationale, for concluding that a coercive and/or discriminatory law serves a legitimate governmental interest is a religious rationale, then the law abridges freedom of religion, which includes not only freedom *to* practice one's own religion (if one has a religion) but also freedom *not* to practice someone else's religion – or, indeed, any religion at all. Freedom not to practice someone else's religion includes, of course, freedom not to be punished or discriminated against based on one's refusal to practice someone else's religion. For a liberal democracy – *any* liberal democracy, including one not constitutionally committed to "no 'establishment' of religion" – to enact, maintain, or enforce a law that is is bereft of a plausible secular basis contravenes the right to religious freedom: Such a law unacceptably

---

Ralph S. Smith, *Heterosexism: An Ethical Challenge* 61 (1993); Bruce J. Malina, "The New Testament and Homosexuality," in Patricia Beattie Jung, with Joseph Andrew Coray, eds., *Sexual Diversity and Catholicism: Toward the Development of Moral Theology* 150 (2001); Choon-Leong Seow, "A Heterosexual Perspective," in Choon-Leong Seow, ed., *Homosexuality and Christian Community* 14 (1996); Jeffrey S. Siker, "Homosexual Christians, the Bible, and Gentile Inclusion: Confessions of a Repenting Heterosexist," in Jeffrey S. Siker, ed., *Homosexuality in the Church* 178 (1994).

⁴¹ And the claim is beginning to be contested even among Muslims. See, e.g., Arash Naraghi, "Islam and the Moral Status of Homosexuality," http://www.arashnaraghi.org/articles/islamandminorities.htm.

Cf. Douglas Laycock, "Afterword," in Douglas Laycock, Anthony R. Picarello, Jr., & Robin Fretwell Wilson, eds., *Same-Sex Marriage and Religious Liberty: Emerging Conflicts* 189, 207 (2008):

> The nature of marriage is a question with profound religious significance and fundamentally disputed answers. The state has no more business imposing a single answer to that question than to any other religious question. Marriage is for the churches; government should confine itself to civil unions. And then we should try as best we can to create rules that enable Americans with fundamentally different views of marriage to live with peace and equality in the same society.

imposes religion on those the law coerces or against whom it discriminates.[42]

Let me recapitulate. State refusals to extend the benefit of law to same-sex unions are arguably aimed at serving one or more interests that are undeniably legitimate – but the refusals fail to serve those interests. State refusals are unarguably aimed at serving one interest they succeed in serving: the interest in not supporting or incentivizing same-sex sexual conduct, understood as immoral conduct. As I have just explained, however, that interest is not legitimate.[43]

---

[42] See Chapter 6, n. 34 and accompanying text. In the Iowa gay marriage case, decided in 2009, after I drafted this chapter, the Iowa Supreme Court made just this point. See *Varnum v. Brien*, 763 N.W. 2d 862 (Iowa 2009).

[43] Recall that state refusals to extend the benefit of law to same-sex unions implicate the right to moral equality as well as the right to moral freedom. I explained earlier in this chapter that if such refusals do not violate the right to moral freedom, they do not violate the right to moral equality either. But I have concluded here that state refusals to extend the benefit of law to same-sex unions *do* violate the right to moral freedom. Do such refusals also violate the right to moral equality? They do. As I have explained, such refusals do not serve a legitimate governmental interest: The interest in not supporting or incentivizing same-sex sexual conduct, understood as immoral conduct, is not legitimate.

Part IV
The Constitution of Liberal Democracy

9
Protecting Constitutionally Entrenched Rights
The Courts' – In Particular, the U.S. Supreme Court's – Proper Role

I. PRELIMINARIES

Again, a *liberal* democracy is, as such, committed to certain human rights, in the sense that in the legal system of the democracy the rights (understood as moral claims of a certain sort) are recognized and protected as fundamental legal rights (claims). As it happens, most liberal democracies, including the United States, recognize and protect, as fundamental legal rights, at least some of the human rights to which they are committed by entrenching the rights in their constitutions. In most liberal democracies, some human rights laws are both superior (lexically prior) to ordinary laws and entrenched: *exceedingly difficult, sometimes to the point of practically impossible, to amend or repeal.* A conspicuous example of such a law is the U.S. Constitution, which by its own terms can be amended only by a complex, supermajoritarian political act:

> In the [United States, a constitutional] amendment is permitted only upon completion of supermajority requirements both in Congress and in the states: an amendment must be proposed, either by 2/3 of each House of Congress or by a convention called at the request of the legislatures of 2/3 of the states, and then the proposed amendment must be approved by the legislatures of or conventions in 3/4 of the states. This makes the U.S. Constitution one of the most deeply entrenched [in the world].[1]

It is precisely because it is so difficult to amend or repeal an entrenched law that entrenching certain human rights makes sense. As a commentator on the transition to democracy in South Africa observed, an entrenched "bill of rights was crucial... to the whole question of legitimacy of a post-apartheid regime. For its powerful symbolism would establish an arena not just for law, *but would also be a*

---
[1] Vicki C. Jackson & Mark Tushnet, *Comparative Constitutional Law* 414 (1999).

definition of what is, and is not, legitimate in politics."² This is not to deny that in liberal democracies human rights that are not entrenched also have an important role to play in protecting human dignity and inviolability.³ In the United States, for example, many important human rights laws – the Civil Rights Act of 1964,⁴ to name just one – are not entrenched. But most liberal democracies, including the United States, understandably entrench – by constitutionalizing – some human rights.⁵

---

² Martin Chanock, "A Post-Calvinist Catechism or a Post-Communist Manifesto? Intersecting Narratives in the South Africa Bill of Rights Debate," in Philip Alston, ed., *Promoting Human Rights Through Bills of Rights: Comparative Perspectives* 392, 394 (1999) (emphasis added).
³ Cf. William N. Eskridge, Jr., "America's Statutory 'Constitution,'" 41 U. CALIFORNIA, DAVIS L. REV. 1 (2007).
⁴ The Civil Rights Act of 1964, P.L. 88–352, was enacted, *inter alia*, "[t]o enforce the constitutional right to vote...."
⁵ The U.S. Constitution consists mainly of two kinds of provisions:
  1. power-allocating provisions: (a) provisions that establish the national government – or, as it is typically called, the federal government – and allocate power (authority) among the three branches – the legislative, executive, and judicial branches – of the national government; and (b) provisions that allocate power between the national government and the governments of the states; and
  2. power-limiting provisions: provisions that limit the power of government. Most of the power-limiting provisions, such as the Eighth Amendment's ban on cruel and unusual punishments, articulate what we today recognize as human rights. (The Eighth Amendment states: "Excessive bail shall not be required, nor excessive fines imposed, nor cruel and unusual punishments inflicted.") So although it is more than a charter of human rights, the Constitution is a charter of human rights.
  Indeed, the Constitution, which is the earliest national charter of human rights in modern history, has been an inspiration for many later such charters (see William J. Brennan, Jr., "The Worldwide Influence of the United States Constitution as a Charter of Human Rights," 15 NOVA L. REV. 1 [1991]), including the Canadian Charter of Rights and Freedoms, which is Part 1 of the Canada's Constitution Act of 1982, and the South African Bill of Rights, which is Chapter 2 of the Constitution of the Republic of South Africa (1996). See Christina Murray, "A Constitutional Beginning: Making South Africa's Final Constitution," 23 U. ARKANSAS AT LITTLE ROCK L. REV. 809 (2001); Chanock, n. 2. In her essay, Murray reports these interesting details:
  > In March 1997, about seven million copies of the new constitution in pocket book size were distributed in South Africa. Four million went to high schools, two million were made available at post offices and another million were distributed to the police, army, prisons, and through civil organizations. These copies of the constitution were available in all eleven official languages and were accompanied by an illustrated guide, *You and the Constitution*, which, in thirty cheerfully illustrated pages, provided an introduction to the constitution.

  Murray, supra this note, at 837.

Even if it makes sense, all thing considered, for a liberal democracy to entrench (certain) human rights in its constitution, it does not necessarily follow that it also make sense for the democracy to empower its courts to protect (enforce) the rights. "One can have a constitution of entrenched rules but leave the interpretation of those rules to democratic decision making, and many countries do just that."[6] But why would a liberal democracy choose on the one hand to entrench norms and on the other not to empower its courts to protect the norms? Albert Venn Dicey suggested the answer in *An Introduction to the Study of the Law of the Constitution* (1885): "The restrictions placed on the action of the legislature under the French constitution are not in reality laws, since they are not rules which in the last resort will be enforced by the courts. Their true character is that of *maxims of political morality*, which derive whatever strength they possess from being formally inscribed in the constitution, and from the resulting support of public opinion."[7] Even if courts are not empowered to protect them (and, indeed, even if courts *are* so empowered), constitutionally entrenched human rights – qua "maxims of political morality" – can serve as shared, fundamental grounds of political-moral judgment in a political community.[8]

Nonetheless, contemporary liberal democracies typically empower their courts to protect constitutionally entrenched human rights.[9] Is it appropriate – is it a good idea, all things considered – for liberal

---

[6] Larry A. Alexander, "Constitutionalism," in Martin P. Golding & William A. Edmundson, eds., *The Blackwell Guide to the Philosophy of Law and Legal Theory* 248, 255 (2004).

[7] Quoted in James B. Thayer, "The Origin and Scope of the American Doctrine of Constitutional Law," 7 HARVARD L. REV. 129, 130 (1893) (emphasis added).

[8] See Michael J. Perry, *Morality, Politics, and Law* 153 et seq. (1988).

[9] Australia and New Zealand are exceptions. For a vigorous argument in defense of the status quo in Australia, see James Allan, "A Defense of the *Status Quo*," in Tom Campbell et al., eds., *Protecting Human Rights: Instruments and Institutions* 175 (2003). See also James Allan, "Rights, Paternalism, Constitutions and Judges," in Grant Huscroft & Paul Rishworth, eds., *Litigating Rights: Perspectives from Domestic and International Law* 29 (2002). For an argument in opposition to the status quo in Australia, see Dianne Otto, "Addressing Homelessness: Does Australia's Indirect Implementation of Human Rights Comply with Its International Obligations?" in Campbell et al., *Protecting Human Rights*, supra this note, at 281. For an argument that New Zealand should establish a system of judicial review, see Andrew S. Butler, "Judicial Review, Human Rights and Democracy," in Huscroft & Rishworth, supra this note, at 47. See also G. W. G. Leane, "Enacting Bills of Rights: Canada and the Curious Case of New Zealand's 'Thin' Democracy," 26 HUMAN RIGHTS QUARTERLY 152 (2004). But compare James Allan, "The Effect of a Statutory Bill of Rights Where Parliament Is Sovereign: The Lesson from New Zealand," in Tom Campbell et al., eds., *Sceptical Essays on Human Rights* 375 (2001).

democracies to do so?[10] I have argued elsewhere that the answer is yes; there is no need to rehearse my argument here.[11] The more serious – and more difficult – question is this: In a liberal democracy, how great should the courts' power to protect constitutionally entrenched human rights be; in particular, should it be the power to have the last word when the courts conclude that the law in question violates an entrenched human right (the last word, i.e., short of an extremely improbable event: a successful, supermajoritarian effort to amend or repeal the entrenched provision on which the court based its decision)? I have suggested elsewhere that there is good reason to doubt that the courts' power should be so great; in particular, I have suggested that a strong case can be made that the judicial power to protect constitutionally entrenched human rights should be the power of judicial "penultimacy," not the power of judicial "ultimacy": the power to have, not the last word, but only the penultimate word – for example, a word that may be overruled by ordinary legislation.[12] Canada, in 1982, and the United Kingdom, in 1998, each opted for a system (each for a different system) of judicial penultimacy.[13]

II. THAYER'S ARGUMENT FOR JUDICIAL DEFERENCE

In the United States, however, the Supreme Court exercises the power of judicial ultimacy: No state legislature nor even Congress may overrule by ordinary legislation a decision by the Court that a law (or other policy) is unconstitutional;[14] such a decision may be overruled only

---

[10] This question is distinct from the question whether it is a good idea, all things considered, for a liberal democracy to empower its courts to protect constitutionally entrenched norms other than human rights norms, such as, in the United States, separation-of-powers norms (i.e., norms allocating power among the three branches of the national government) or federalism norms (norms allocating power between the national government and the governments of the states). Cf. Jesse Choper, *Judicial Review and the National Political Process: A Functional Reconsideration of the Role of the Supreme Court* (1980).

[11] See Michael J. Perry, *Toward a Theory of Human Rights* 90 et seq. (2007).

[12] See id. at 98–102.

[13] See id. at 99–101 (Canada) & 113–17 (United Kingdom).

[14] Constitutional cases do not always seem to involve the constitutionality of a law or other government policy; constitutional cases sometimes involve the constitutionality of a government official's (e.g., a police officer's) behavior. Nonetheless, such cases do involve – they necessarily (if implicitly) involve – the constitutionality of a government policy, namely, the policy of permitting the government official to engage in the behavior at

(later) by the Court itself or by extraordinary, supermajoritarian lawmaking, in the form of constitutional amendment.[15] This important question therefore arises:

> Given that the Supreme Court of the United States exercises the power of judicial ultimacy, should the Court, in protecting constitutionally entrenched human rights – more precisely, *in specifying constitutionally entrenched but contextually underdeterminate human rights norms*[16] – exercise the power deferentially? (As it happens, most of the human rights norms entrenched in the constitutional law of the United States are underdeterminate in the context of most of the cases [a] in which they are invoked [b] that end up before the Supreme Court.) That is, in a case in which it is claimed that a law violates a constitutionally entrenched human rights norm, should the Supreme Court inquire merely whether the counterclaim that the law does not violate the norm is reasonable – and if the Court answers yes, uphold the law? Or, instead, should the Court exercise its power nondeferentially; should it determine for itself whether the law violates the norm – and if it answers yes, strike down the law?

A claim that a law does not violate a norm is reasonable if rational, well-informed, and thoughtful persons could affirm the claim. As James Bradley Thayer said: "The reasonable doubt... of which our judges speak is that reasonable doubt which lingers in the mind of a competent and duly instructed person who has carefully applied his faculties to the question. The rationally permissible opinion of which

---

issue. If a law or other government policy forbad the official to engage in the behavior at issue, the question of the constitutionality of the behavior would not need to be addressed; if, however, no government policy forbids the official to engage in the behavior, the constitutional question must be addressed. And to rule on the constitutionality of the behavior is necessarily to rule on the constitutionality of government's permitting the official to engage in the behavior.

[15] The doctrine of judicial supremacy should not be confused with the different and extremely problematic doctrine of judicial *exclusivity* that the present Supreme Court seems, implicitly, to have embraced. The Court has been acting as if it is not only the supreme but also the exclusive expositor of constitutional meanings. See Larry D. Kramer, "Foreword: We the Court," 115 HARVARD L. REV. 4 (2001); Robert C. Post & Reva B. Siegel, "Protecting the Constitution from the People: Juricentric Restrictions on Section Five Power," 78 INDIANA L. J. 1 (2003).

It bears mention that if legislators believe that an existing law is unconstitutional they may on that basis vote to repeal the law even if in the Supreme Court's judgment the law is not unconstitutional; similarly, if the legislators believe that a proposed law would be unconstitutional they may on that basis decline to enact the law even if in the Court's judgment the law would not be unconstitutional.

[16] In the postscript to this chapter, I explain what I mean by the "specification" of a "contextually underdeterminate" norm.

we have been talking is the opinion reasonably allowable to such a person as this."[17]

The choice here is best understood as a choice between two different judicial attitudes or orientations. For a judge to adopt a *deferential* attitude – for her to be oriented deferentially – is for her to be prepared to rule that a challenged law does not violate a constitutionally entrenched human rights norm if the claim that the law does not violate the norm is reasonable.[18] By contrast, for a judge to adopt a *nondeferential* attitude is for her to be prepared to rule that a challenged law violates a human rights norm if in the judge's own view the law violates the norm – even if, in the judge's view, the claim that the law does not violate the norm is reasonable. Put another way, for a judge to adopt a nondeferential attitide is for her to be prepared to rule that a challenged law violates a human rights norm if according to the judge's own specification of the norm the law violates the norm – even if according to a different but nonetheless reasonable specification the law does not violate the norm.

The most famous and influential argument for the sort of judicial deference I have in mind was made by James Bradley Thayer in the final decade of the nineteenth century, in an essay in the *Harvard Law Review*: "The Origin and Scope of the American Doctrine of Constitutional Law."[19] Even now, in the first decade of the twenty-first

[17] See Thayer, "The Origin and Scope of the American Doctrine of Constitutional Law," n. 7, at 149.

[18] See id. at 150: "[A] court cannot always, and for the purpose of all sorts of questions, say that there is but one right and permissible way of construing the constitution."

[19] See n. 7. See generally "One Hundred Years of Judicial Review: The Thayer Centennial Symposium," 88 NORTHWESTERN U. L. REV. 1–468 (1993).

> Felix Frankfurter described [James Bradley Thayer], his teacher, as "our great master of constitutional law." Thayer, said Frankfurter, "influenced Holmes, Brandeis, the Hands (Learned and Augustus) ... and so forth. I am of the view that if I were to name one piece of writing on American Constitutional Law – a silly test maybe – I would pick an essay by James Bradley Thayer in the *Harvard Law Review*, consisting of 26 pages, published in October, 1893, called 'The Origin and Scope of the American Doctrine of Constitutional Law'.... Why would I do that? Because from my point of view it's a great guide for judges and therefore, the great guide for understanding by non-judges of what the place of the judiciary is in relation to constitutional questions."

Leonard W. Levy, "Editorial Note," in Leonard W. Levy, ed., *Judicial Review and the Supreme Court: Selected Essays* 84 (1967). Paul Kahn reports:

> Thayer was a friend and professional colleague of Oliver Wendell Holmes, first in law practice and then at Harvard, where Thayer taught for thirty years. Louis Brandeis was a student of Thayer's, and Felix Frankfurter, who just missed

century, Thayer's essay remains the locus classicus of the argument that in the exercise of their great power to protect constitutional norms, the courts – including the Supreme Court – should proceed deferentially:

> [The court] can only disregard the [challenged] Act when those who have the right to make laws have not merely made a mistake, but have made a very clear one – so clear that it is not open to rational question. That is the standard of duty to which the courts bring legislative Acts; that is the test which they apply – not merely their own judgment as to constitutionality, but their conclusion as to what judgment is permissible to another department which the constitution has charged with the duty of making it. This rule recognizes that, having regard to the great, complex, ever unfolding exigencies of government, much which will seem unconstitutional to one man, or body of men, may reasonably not seem so to another; that the constitution often admits of different interpretations; that there is often a range of choice and judgment; that in such cases the constitution does not impose upon the legislature any one specific opinion, but leaves open this range of choice; and that whatever choice is rational is constitutional.[20]

In contending for judicial deference – for "the rule of the clear mistake," as Alexander Bickel called it[21] – Thayer did not argue that

---

Thayer at Harvard, acknowledged Thayer's substantial influence. Of Thayer's most famous essay in constitutional law, "The Origin and Scope of the American Doctrine of Constitutional Law," Holmes wrote, "I agree with it heartily and it makes explicit the point of view from which implicitly I have approached the constitutional questions upon which I have differed from some other judges."
Paul Kahn, *Legitimacy and History: Self-Government in American Constitutional Theory* 84 (1992).

[20] Thayer, n. 7, at 144.
According to Thayer, the deferential approach is fitting when a federal court reviews, for federal constitutionality, federal action or when a state court reviews, either for federal constitutionality or for state constitutionality, state action, but not when a federal court reviews, for federal constitutionality, state action, in which case (according to Thayer) a nondeferential approach is fitting. See Thayer, n. 7, at 154–55. This distinction makes little sense, however. See Sanford Gabin, *Judicial Review and the Reasonable Doubt Test* 5 (1980): "[T]he reasonable doubt test should be applied not just to all national legislation but, contrary to Thayer's prescription, to all state legislation as well." Most commentators who discuss Thayer's conception of proper judicial role fail even to note the distinction. See, e.g., Alexander M. Bickel, *The Least Dangerous Branch: The Supreme Court at the Bar of Politics* 35–46 (1962); Wallace Mendelson, "The Influence of James B. Thayer upon the Work of Holmes, Brandeis, and Frankfurter," 31 VANDERBILT L. REV. 71 (1978); but see Charles L. Black, Jr., *Decision According to Law* 34–35 (1981). Even Thayer's most prominent judicial disciple, Felix Frankfurter, failed to note the distinction – or to heed it. See *West Virginia State Board of Education v. Barnette*, 319 U.S. 624, 661–62, 666–67 (Frankfurter, J., dissenting) (1943).

[21] See Bickel, n. 20, at 34–46.

lawmakers are generally better than judges at resolving constitutional questions. Thayer's argument was simply that in the United States, a democracy, the citizens are supposed to be the ultimate political sovereign, and that they, therefore, not the judiciary, should have final responsibility for answering, through their elected representatives, contested constitutional questions – as long as their answers are reasonable. Otherwise "the people cease to function as the popular sovereign."[22]

Moreover, Thayer argued that in exercising their power to protect constitutional norms nondeferentially, courts would subvert the capacity of the people and their representatives to deliberate about contested constitutional questions as responsibly as they should. Thayer elaborated the point in his book on John Marshall, who served as chief justice of the United States from 1801 to 1835:

> [T]he exercise of [judicial review], even when unavoidable, is always attended with a serious evil, namely, that the correction of legislative mistakes comes from the outside, and the people thus lose the political experience, and the moral education and stimulus that comes from fighting the question out in the ordinary way, and correcting their own errors.... The tendency of a common and easy resort to this great function, now lamentably too common, is to dwarf the political capacity of the people, and to deaden its sense of moral responsibility.... [B]y adhering rigidly to its own duty, the court will help, as nothing else can, to fix the spot where responsibility lies, and... to bring the people and their representatives to a sense of their own responsibility.[23]

Many modern students of American judicial review have shared Thayer's concern. Alexander Bickel, for example, wrote that "[t]he search must be for a [judicial] function... whose discharge by the courts will not lower the quality of the other departments'

---

[22] Kahn, n. 19, at 87. For Kahn's commentary on Thayer's argument, see id. at 85–89.

[23] James Bradley Thayer, *John Marshall* 106–10 (1901). See also Thayer, n. 7, at 155–56. Keith Whittington reports:
> As the Supreme Court became increasingly activist in the late nineteenth century, James Bradley Thayer complained that this development "has tended to bereave our legislatures of their feeling or responsibility and their sense of honor.... It is a common saying in our legislative bodies when any constitutional point is raised, 'Oh, the courts will set that right.'" The courts "have often assumed a tone that tended to encourage these views," but Thayer warned that such complacency overlooked "how great is legislative power, and how limited is judicial power."

Keith E. Whittington, *Political Foundations of Judicial Supremacy* 138 (2007) (quoting James Bradley Thayer, "Constitutionality of Legislation: The Precise Question for a Court," THE NATION, Apr. 10, 1884, at 315).

performance *by denuding them of the dignity and burden of their own responsibility.*"[24]

Now, to insist that there is an obvious difference – and, in many cases, a consequential difference – between a judge asking whether the challenged law violates the right it is claimed to violate and asking whether the claim that the law does not violate the right is reasonable, is not to deny that reasonableness vel non – including the reasonableness vel non of the claim that the law does not violate the right it is claimed to violate – is a matter of degree. And, of course, we should not expect that every judge exercising Thayerian deference would draw the line between the reasonable and the unreasonable at precisely the same point – or, therefore, vote the same way in a case – as every other judge exercising Thayerian deference. Thayerian deference is not an algorithm; it is, again, a judicial attitude or orientation. As one of Thayer's interpreters, Sanford Gabin, explained:

> Thayer's rule, like all guideposts, is not self-applying. Even limited by the rule of administration, judges, like criminal juries, might differ over what constitutes a reasonable doubt; the possibilities, the stuff of which reasonable doubts are made, do not always strike all men, however reasonable, alike. Even under Thayer's rule of administration, then, the freedom and the burden of decisionmaking remain.[25]

Nonetheless, "that freedom is narrowed, and that was Thayer's aim. He sought to reduce the scope of judicial freedom without diminishing the judicial duty and burden of judging."[26]

In articulating the "duty and burden of judging," Thayer wrote: "The ultimate arbiter of what is rational and permissible is indeed always the courts, so far as litigated cases bring the question before them. This leaves to our courts a great and stately jurisdiction. It will only imperil the whole of it if it is sought to give them more. They

---

[24] Bickel, n. 20, at 24 (emphasis added). Cf. Allan C. Hutchinson, "Waiting for CORAF (or the Beatification of the Charter)," 41 U. TORONTO L. J. 332, 358 (1991): "By endlessly waiting for CORAF, we place ourselves *in waiting*; it inculcates a servile and sycophantic attitude in people. Such a practised posture of dependence is anathema to the democratic spirit. It is infinitely better to run the unfamiliar risks of genuinely popular rule than to succumb to the commonplace security of distant authority." For a more recent, but nonetheless critical, statement by Hutchinson, see Allan C. Hutchinson, "Supreme Court Inc: The Business of Democracy and Rights," in Gavin W. Anderson, ed., *Rights & Democracy: Essays in UK–Canadian Constitutionalism* 29 (1999).
[25] Gabin, n. 20, at 45–46.
[26] Id. at 46.

must not step into the shoes of the law-maker."[27] Should citizens of the United States want the Supreme Court to accede to Thayer's view of proper judicial role and exercise only the "great and stately jurisdiction" he defended? That is, should we want the Court to exercise its power of judicial ultimacy only deferentially; should we want the justices of the Court to defer to the claim that the challenged law does not violate the right it is claimed to violate if the claim is reasonable?[28] Which arrangement, for the United States today, is likely to serve us better:[29]

> A system of judicial ultimacy in which the Supreme Court is deferential (Thayerian) in the exercise of its power to protect constitutionally entrenched human rights – its power, that is, to specify constitutionally entrenched but contextually underdeterminate human rights norms?
>
> Or a system of judicial ultimacy in which the Court exercises its power nondeferentially?[30]

---

[27] Thayer, n. 7, at 152.
[28] I have explained elsewhere why the Thayerian argument for judicial deference has little if any power in the context of a system of judicial penultimacy, such as Canada's. See Perry, *Toward a Theory of Human Rights*, n. 11, at 105–06.
[29] The qualifier "for the United States" is important. Cf. Richard A. Posner, "Review of Jeremy Waldron, *Law and Disagreement*," 100 COLUMBIA L. REV. 582, 592 (2000):
> There is no reason to suppose that the issue [whether American-style judicial review is a good idea] should be resolved the same way in two different countries, even countries that share the same language and the same basic legal and political heritage. That depends on all sorts of emprical questions and judgmental imponderables involving the political and legal cultures of the two countries and the career path of judges and legislators in them.
[30] Whether a law violates the provision of the constitutional text it is claimed to violate – for example, the Eighth Amendment's cruel and unusual punishments clause – comprises two different questions: (a) What right (or other norm) does the provision entrench? (b) Does the law violate the entrenched right? Thayerian deference, as I elaborate and defend it here, pertains only to the second question. In most constitutional cases, the serious dispute is less likely to be about what right the provision entrenches than about whether the challenged law violates the right the provision is deemed to entrench. This is *either* because there is no serious doubt, in most constitutional cases, about what right the provision entrenches *or* because, even if there is a serious doubt, the issue has been settled by longstanding precedent. So I focus here on the question whether judges – in particular, Supreme Court justices – should exercise deference in addressing the second question: Should judges ask whether the challenged law violates the entrenched right it is claimed to violate? Or, instead, should they ask only whether it is reasonable to conclude that the law does not violate the right it is claimed to violate? Cf. Mitchell N. Berman, "Constitutional Decision Rules," 90 VIRGINIA L. REV. 1, 102–04 (2004): "[Thayerian deference,] if it is to exist, will find a more hospitable home at the level of applying constitutional meaning, not deriving it."

Richard Posner has observed, approvingly, that "American judges distinguish between how they might vote on a statute if they were legislators and whether the statute is unconstitutional; they might think it a bad statute yet uphold its constitutionality."[31] Thayer urged American judges to make a further distinction between whether the statute is unconstitutional and whether the claim that the statute is not unconstitutional is reasonable; the latter question, Thayer insisted, is the one judges should address. For Posner, judges usurp the legislators' authority if instead of asking whether a statute is unconstitutional they ask whether it is bad; for Thayer, judges usurp the legislators' authority – they "step into the shoes of the law-maker" – if instead of asking whether the claim that the statute is not unconstitutional is reasonable they ask whether in their own judgment the statute is unconstitutional. Judge Posner's position, understood as a statement not only about what American judges do *but should do*, represents the conventional wisdom. Professor Thayer's position, by contrast, goes well beyond the conventional wisdom.

Nonetheless, Thayer's position appears quite moderate next to the position Jeremy Waldron espouses. Waldron does not oppose, indeed he supports, constitutionalizing certain important rights;[32] however, Waldron argues that the citizens of "a free and democratic society" should not give to their courts the power to protect (enforce) the constitutionalized rights; more precisely, he argues that they should not give to their courts the power exercised by the U.S. Supreme Court, namely, the power of judicial ultimacy.[33] According to Waldron, as a general matter the citizens of "a free and democratic society should not" empower their courts to protect constitutionally

---

[31] Richard A. Posner, "Enlightened Despot," NEW REPUBLIC, Apr. 23, 2007, at 53, 55. Posner has himself been an "American judge" for more than 25 years. Cf. "Commemorating Twenty-Five Years of Judge Richard A. Posner," 74 U. CHICAGO L. REV. 1641–931 (2007).

[32] See Jeremy Waldron, "The Core of the Case Against Judicial Review," 115 YALE L. J. 1346, 1366 (2006).

[33] See id. at 1354:
> There are a variety of practices all over the world that could be grouped under the general heading of judicial review of legislation. They may be distinguished along several dimensions. The most important difference is between what I shall call strong judicial review and weak judicial review. My target is strong judicial review.

"Strong judicial review" is Waldron's name for the power of judicial ultimacy; "weak judicial review," his name for the power of judicial penultimacy.

The Constitution of Liberal Democracy

entrenched rights because, he says, disagreements about whether a law violates the constitutionally entrenched right it is claimed to violate are reasonable disagreements[34] and there is no good reason to empower the courts to override a reasonable claim to the effect that the law at issue – the challenged law – does not violate the right it is claimed to violate.[35]

---

[34] See, e.g., id. at 1360, 1368–69, 1406.

[35] Waldron writes that his "argument against [strong] judicial review is not unconditional but depends on certain institutional and political features of modern liberal democracies." Id. at 1353. He allows that strong judicial review may be "necessary as a protective measure against legislative pathologies relating to sex, race, or religion in particular countries." Id. at 1352. "But even if that is so," Waldron continues, "it is worth figuring our whether that sort of defense goes to the heart of the matter, or whether it should be regarded instead as an exceptional reason to refrain from following the tendency of what, in most circumstances, would be a compelling normative argument against [strong judicial review].... What is needed is some general understanding, uncontaminated by the cultural, historical, and political preoccupations of each society." Id. See also id. at 1406.

At one point in his essay Waldron writes: "There may be some countries – perhaps the United States – in which peculiar legislative pathologies have developed. If that is so, then Americans should confine their non-core argument for judicial review to their own exceptional circumstances." Id. at 1386. But how "exceptional" are the U.S. circumstances? Are most liberal democracies free of the pathologies to which Waldron refers? Speaking from a British perspective, Lord Scarman, in 1984, wrote: "[I]f you are going to protect people who will never have political power, at any rate in the foreseeable future (not only individuals but minority groups with their own treasured and properly treasured social customs, religion and ways of life), if they are going to be protected it won't be done in Parliament – they will never muster a majority. It's got to be done by the Courts and the Courts can do it only if they've got the proper guidelines." Lord Scarman, "Britain and the Protection of Human Rights," 15 CAMBRIAN L. REV. 5, 10 (1984). More recently, and speaking from a broader perspective, Mac Darrow and Philip Alston wrote that "there are ample grounds, based on experience in countries with constitutional human rights protections, to suggest that entrenchment of bills of rights can contribute significantly to the empowerment of disadvantaged groups, providing a judicial forum in which they can be heard and seek redress, in circumstances where the political process could not have been successfully mobilized to assist them." Mac Darrow & Philip Alston, "Bills of Rights in Comparative Perspective," in Philip Alston, ed., *Promoting Human Rights Through Bills of Rights: Comparative Perspectives* 465, 493 (1999). Such statements are quite common. For example, in a case in which the eleven justices of the Constitutional Court of the Republic of South Africa ruled unanimously that imposition of the death penalty was unconstitutional under the transitional 1993 constitution, the president of the Court wrote:

> The very reason for establishing the new legal order, and for vesting the power of judicial review of all legislation in the courts, was to protect the rights of minorities and others who cannot protect their rights adequately through the democratic process. Those who are entitled to claim this protection include the social outcasts and marginalized people of our society. It is only if there is a

The fundamental problem with Waldron's position is that in the past, including the recent past, *some* claims to the effect that "the challenged law does not violate the constitutionally entrenched right it is claimed to violate" were not reasonable, and there is no reason to doubt that in the future *some* such claims will not be reasonable. For example, the claim that anti-miscegenation legislation does not violate the constitutional right to moral equality (or, as the right is known in U.S. constitutional law, the right to equal protection) is not reasonable. Therefore, the following position is more realistic than Waldron's: Citizens *should* empower their courts to protect constitutionally entrenched rights, and *if* the power they give their courts is the power of judicial ultimacy rather than the power of judicial penultimacy, *then* the courts should exercise their power deferentially, striking down a law only when the claim that the law does not violate the right it is claimed to violate is, in the court's judgment, unreasonable.[36]

In any event, given that the Supreme Court, for better or worse, has and exercises the power of judicial ultimacy, Waldron should want, as second best, the Court to exercise that power deferentially; he should want the Court, in protecting constitutionally entrenched human rights, to take the path of Thayerian deference – and thereby avoid "step[ping] into the shoes of the law-maker."[37]

III. PROTECTING POPULAR SOVEREIGNTY AND INHERENT DIGNITY

So: In specifying constitutionally entrenched but contextually underdeterminate human rights norms, should the Supreme Court take the path of Thayerian deference? Given that the U.S. Supreme Court

> willingness to protect the worst and the weakest amonst us, that all of us can be secure that our own rights will be protected.
> Quoted in Henry J. Steiner & Philip Alston, *International Human Rights in Context* 48 (2d ed. 2000).

[36] I have explained elsewhere why the Thayerian argument for judicial deference has little if any power in the context of a system of judicial penultimacy, such as Canada's. See Perry, *Toward a Theory of Human Rights*, n. 11, at 105–06.

[37] See n. 27. Similarly, those who advocate on behalf of "popular constitutionalism" – such as Mark Tushnet and Larry Kramer – should want, as second best, the Court to take the path of Thayerian deference. See Mark Tushnet, *Taking the Constitution Away from the Courts* (1999); Larry D. Kramer, *The People Themselves: Popular Constitutionalism and Judicial Review* (2004).

exercises the power of judicial ultimacy, Thayer's argument for the Court taking the path of deference is quite powerful. Nonetheless, there is a powerful case *against* Thayerian deference with respect to two sorts of constitutional controversies.

A. Protecting Popular Sovereignty by Protecting the Right to Political Freedom

In the United States, Thayer insisted, the citizens are – at least, they are supposed to be – the ultimate political sovereign. Why, then, he asked, shouldn't the citizens, rather than the Supreme Court, have final responsibility for answering, through their elected representatives, contested constitutional questions – so long as their answers are reasonable? Thayer argued that to the extent the citizens are denied that responsibility, they have "cease[d] to function as the popular sovereign."[38]

Because the fundamental rationale for Thayerian deference is respect for the sovereignty of the citizenry, Thayerian deference is arguably inappropriate with respect to controversies about the constitutionality of laws that implicate the right to political freedom: the right, that is, to freedom to seek, receive, and share information and ideas; to vote, and to run for and hold office; and to petition the government for a redress of grievances. In adjudicating such controversies, the Supreme Court should exercise its own judgment

---

[38] Thayer, n. 7, at 87. Something Jeremy Waldron has written is relevant here:

> [T]hink what we might say to some public-spirited citizen who wishes to launch a campaign or lobby her [representative] on some issue of rights about which she feels strongly and on which she has done her best to arrive at a considered and impartial view. She is not asking to be a dictator; she perfectly accepts that her voice should have no more power than that of anyone else who is prepared to participate in politics. But – like her suffragette forbears – she wants a vote; she wants her voice and her activity to count on matters of high political importance.
>
> [I]magine ourselves saying to her: "You may write to the newspaper and get up a petition and organize a pressure group to lobby [the legislature]. But even if you succeed, beyond your wildest dreams, and orchestrate the support of a large number of like-minded men and women, and manage to prevail in the legislature, your measure may be challenged and struck down because your view . . . does not accord with the judges' view. When their votes differ from yours, theirs are the votes that will prevail." It is my submission that saying this does not comport with the respect and honor normally accorded to ordinary men and women in the context of a theory of rights.

Jeremy Waldron, "A Right-Based Critique of Constitutional Rights," 13 OXFORD J. LEGAL STUDIES 18, 50–51 (1993).

about the constitutionality of the challenged law – as distinct from its judgment about the reasonableness of the lawmaker's judgment that the law is constitutional – even though that means that the Court is prepared to rule against a law that (in the Court's judgment) the lawmakers reasonably regard as constitutional. In the long run, the cumulative effect of the Court exercising its own judgment – of it systematically resolving the benefit of the doubt in favor of a broader rather than a narrower specification of the right to political freedom – will be to enhance rather than to diminish the sovereignty of the citizenry; it will be to enhance rather than to diminish the capacity of the citizenry to deliberate in an optimally informed way about contested political questions, to hold their elected representatives accountable, and, in general, to participate in politics.[39] Or so we may reasonably speculate.[40]

B. Protecting Inherent Dignity by Protecting the Right to Moral Equality

Just as the right to political freedom is the most fundamental right to which democracy is, as such – as *democracy* – committed, the right to moral equality is the most fundamental right to which liberal democracy is, as such – as *liberal* democracy – committed. As I explained in Chapter 3, liberal democracy's commitment to the equal inherent dignity and inviolability of every human being entails its commitment to the right to moral equality, which, understood as a right against government, is the right of every human being to be treated by lawmakers and other government officials as one who has equal inherent dignity and is inviolable:

> Government may not enact, maintain, or enforce a law (or other policy) based on the view that some human beings do not have equal inherent dignity, including the view that the well-being (eudaimonia, flourishing) of some human beings does not merit the same respect and concern as the well-being of some other human beings.

Enactment, maintenance, or enforcement of a law is based on such a view if but for the view – if in the absence of the view – there would

---

[39] Cf. *United States v. Carolene Products Co.*, 304 U.S. 144, 152 n. 4 (1938); John Hart Ely, *Democracy and Distrust: A Theory of Judicial Review* 105–34 (1980).
[40] If laws that regulate "commercial" speech do not implicate the right to political freedom, as arguably they do not, then in adjudicating the constitutionality of such laws, the Court should take the path of Thayerian deference.

not be, or have been, enactment, maintenance, or enforcement of the law.

Sometimes it is obvious that a law not only implicates but violates the right to moral equality. (A law implicates the right to moral eqality if there is good reason to think that the law may be based on a view that under the right to moral equality may not serve as a basis of law.) For example, it was obvious that the laws struck down by the U.S. Supreme Court in *Brown v. Board of Education* (1954) (*de jure* racial segregation)[41] and in *Loving v. Virginia* (1967)[42] (anti-miscegenation law) not only implicated but violated the right to moral equality, which appears in U.S. constitutional law in the guise of the right to the equal protection of the laws.[43] And sometimes it is obvious that a law does not implicate, much less violate, the right to moral equality: for example, a law that denies driver's licenses to those who are not yet sixteen years old. Sometimes, however, although it is not obvious that a law that implicates also violates the right to moral equality, *there is nonetheless good reason to suspect that the law does violate the right*: for example, a law according to which no one who is homosexual may adopt a child.[44] In such a situation, two questions arise:

1. Does the law – that is, is the choice to single-out-and-treat-less-well, for example, if that is what is at issue, or the choice to adopt the policy that has the disproportionate impact rather than to forgo that

---

[41] 347 U.S. 483 (1954). For a compelling essay on the importance of the Supreme Court's decision in *Brown*, see Paul Finkelman, "Civil Rights in Historical Context: In Defense of *Brown*," 118 HARVARD L. REV. 973 (2005).

[42] 388 U.S. 1 (1967).

[43] This is not to say that the interpretation of the equal protection clause of the Fourteenth Amendment that has yielded, *inter alia*, the right to moral equality is a correct interpretation. In the postscript to this chapter, I discuss what it means – or should mean – to "interpret" the constitutional text.

[44] Cf. Robbie Brown, "Antipathy Toward Obama Seen as Helping Arkansas Limit Adoption," NEW YORK TIMES, Nov. 8, 2008; Dan Savage, "Anti-Gay, Anti-Family," NEW YORK TIMES, Nov. 12, 2008:

> [Arkansas's] Proposed Iniative Act No. 1, approved by nearly 57 percent of voters last week, bans people who are "cohabiting outside a valid marriage" from serving as foster parents or adopting children. While the measure bans both gay and straight members of cohabiting couples as foster or adoptive parents, the Arkansas Family Council wrote it expressly to thwart "the gay agenda." Right now, there are 3,700 children across Arkansas in state custody; 1,000 of them are available for adoption. The overwhelming majority of these children have been abused, neglected or abandoned by their heterosexual parents.

policy in favor of a different policy, if that is what is at issue – serve a legitimate governmental interest? In short, is the law necessary to serve a legitimate governmental interest?
2. If so, is that interest sufficiently weighty to be proportionate to the cost the law imposes on those subject to the law?

Assume that in a case before it, the Supreme Court has good reason to suspect that a law is based on the view that some human beings do not have equal inherent dignity – and that the law therefore violates the right to moral equality. Protecting the right to moral equality – protecting the equal inherent dignity and inviolability of every human being – is too important to the maintenance of the basic moral legitimacy of a liberal democracy for the Court to ask simply whether the judgment that such a law serves a legitimate, proportionate governmental interest is reasonable. The Court itself should determine whether the law – the "suspect" law – serves such an interest, and it should allocate the burden of proving that the law does serve such an interest to the party defending the law; that is, the Court should insist that the party defending the suspect law prove to the satisfaction of the Court that the law serves a legitimate, proportionate governmental interest; and if in the end it is not persuaded, the Court should rule against the law.[45]

And, indeed, in the modern period of U.S. constitutional law, the Supreme Court's practice has been to strike down a law that discriminates against a racial (or ethnic) minority unless the discrimination serves a "compelling" governmental interest that cannot otherwise be served.[46] Moreover, the Court treats its own judgment as determinative: The Court does not ask whether it is reasonable to conclude that the discrimination is necessary to serve a compelling governmental interest; instead, the Court asks whether in its own judgment the discrimination is necessary to serve a compelling governmental interest.

---

[45] Cf. *United States v. Carolene Products Co.*, 304 U.S. 144, 152 n. 4 (1938); John Hart Ely, n. 39, at 135–79.

[46] See, e.g., *McLaughlin v. Florida*, 379 U.S. 184 (1964); *Loving v. Virginia*, 388 U.S. 1 (1967); *Palmore v. Sidoti*, 466 U.S. 29 (1984). Cf. Stephen A. Siegel, "The Origin of the Compelling State Interest Test and Strict Scrutiny," 48 AMERICAN J. LEGAL HISTORY 355 (2006).

If a govermental interest is "compelling," *a fortiori* the interest is constitutionally legitimate, because no governmental interest that is not constitutionally legitimate is compelling. By contrast, a governmental interest that is constitutionally legitimate is not necessarily compelling.

(A law that does not overtly – "on its face" – discriminate against a racial minority may nonetheless do so covertly,[47] or those responsible for enforcing the law may be enforcing it in a racially discriminatory way.[48] The Supreme Court has developed a method for ferreting out covert racial discrimination.[49]) Since the end of World War II, no law that discriminates against a racial minority has been found by the Court to be necessary to serve a compelling governmental interest.[50]

Similarly, it has been the Court's practice for almost a quarter of a century to strike down a law that discriminates against women – or men[51] – unless in the Court's own judgment there is an "exceedingly persuasive" justification for the discrimination.[52] Moreover, the Court has made it clear that it will not be persuaded by any justification that relies on a gender stereotype.[53]

Although one might have thought that the Supreme Court would have adopted a hostile stance toward *all* discrimination that targets a group *whose members historically have been regarded and treated as inferior human beings*, the Court has not done so.[54] Homosexuals

---

[47] See, e.g., *Gomillion v. Lightfoot*, 364 U.S. 339 (1960).
[48] See *Yick Wo. v. Hopkins*, 118 U.S. 356 (1886).
[49] See *Arlington Heights v. Metropolitan Housing Development Corp.*, 429 U.S. 252 (1977). Cf. *Washington v. Davis*, 426 U.S. 229 (1976) (that a law has a disproportionate racial impact does not by itself entail that the law is racially discriminatory). Whether the Court's method for ferreting out covert racial discrimination is optimal is an open question. See Michael J. Perry, "The Disproportionate Impact Theory of Racial Discrimination," 125 U. PENNSYLVANIA L. REV. 540 (1977).
[50] Cf. *Johnson v. California*, 543 U.S. 499 (2005) (remanded to court below after ruling that strict scrutiny applies to state policy temporarily segregating prisoners by race to prevent racial gang violence).
[51] The Court has understood that laws that single out men and treat them less well than women are typically cut from the same ideological – sexist – cloth as laws that single out women and treat them less well than men. See, e.g., *Mississippi University for Women v. Hogan*, 458 U.S. 718 (1982).
[52] See *United States v. Virginia*, 518 U.S. 515 (1996).
[53] See id.
[54] In adjudicating the constitutionality of discrimination against groups whose members historically have *not* been regarded or treated as inferior human beings, the U.S. Supreme Court has typically adopted a quite deferential stance. For a collection of illustrative cases, see Kathleen M. Sullivan & M. Gerald Gunther, *Constitutional Law* 625–38 (16th ed. 2007). Cf. Stephen Breyer, *Active Liberty: Interpreting Our Democratic Constitution* 17 (2005): "[A] judge's 'agreement or disagreement' about the wisdom of a law 'has nothing to do with the right of a majority to embody their opinions in law.'" (Quoting Oliver Wendell Holmes's dissenting opinion in *Lochner v. New York*, 198 U.S. 45, 75 [1905].) See also id. at 18–19 (quoting Louis Brandeis, Felix Frankfurter, and Learned Hand to the same effect).

are undeniably a group whose members historically have been regarded and treated as inferior human beings;[55] nonetheless, the Court has refused to declare that discrimination against homosexuals is "suspect."[56] By contrast, the California Supreme Court recently declared that under California's constitution a law that discriminates against homosexuals – that singles homosexuals out and treats them less well – is suspect and therefore subject to strict scrutiny: Unless necessary to serve a compelling governmental interest, such a law will be adjudged unconstitutional.

> Because sexual orientation, like gender, race, or religion, is a characteristic that frequently has been the basis for biased and stereotypical treatment and that generally bears no relation to an individual's ability to perform or contribute to society, it is appropriate for courts to evaluate with great care and with considerable skepticism any statute that embodies such a classification. The strict scrutiny standard is therefore applicable to statutes that impose differential treatment on the basis of sexual orientation.[57]

A BRIEF COMMENT ON THE U.S. SUPREME COURT'S HOSTILE STANCE TOWARD RACE-BASED AFFIRMATIVE ACTION

There is undeniably good reason to suspect that race-based laws (and other policies) that disadvantage a racial minority violate the right to moral equality: U.S. constitutional history reveals that such laws have generally been racist.[58] And there is good reason too, therefore, for

---

[55] See *Rowland v. Mad River School District*, 470 U.S. 1009, 1014 (1985) (Brennan, J., joined by Marshall, J., dissenting from denial of petition for certiorari):

> [H]omosexuals constitute a significant and insular minority of this country's population. Because of the immediate and severe opprobrium often manifested against homosexuals once so identified publicly, members of this group are particularly powerless to pursue their rights openly in the political arena. Moreover, homosexuals have historically been the object of pernicious and sustained hostility, and it is fair to say that discrimination against homosexuals is "likely to reflect deep-seated prejudice rather than rationality." ... State action taken against members of such groups traditionally has been subjected to strict, or at least intermediate, scrutiny by this Court.

[56] See, e.g., *Romer v. Evans*, 517 U.S. 620 (1996).
[57] In re *Marriage Cases*, 183 P.3d 384, 444 (California 2008). Similarly, the Connecticut Supreme Court and the Iowa Supreme Court each recently ruled that under the state constitution, heightened scrutiny is applicable to differential treatment based on sexual orientation. See *Kerrigan v. Commissioner of Public Health*, 957 A. 2d 407 (Connecticut 2008); *Varnum v. Brien*, 763 N.W. 2d 862 (Iowa 2009).
[58] See, e.g., *McLaughlin v. Florida*, 379 U.S. 184 (1964); *Loving v. Virginia*, 388 U.S. 1 (1967).

the Supreme Court to adopt a hostile stance toward such laws. But is there good reason to suspect that race-based affirmative action – by which I mean government programs that single out members of some disadvantaged groups and give them a competitive advantage in gaining access to a scarce public resource, such as a job as a police officer in a large urban police department or a seat in the freshman class of a state university – violate the right to moral equality? Although they necessarily discriminate against members of those racial groups that are not given a competitive advantage, government programs of race-based affirmative action are clearly not based on the view that the discriminatees (or anyone else) lack equal inherent dignity. As one opponent of race-based affirmative action has acknowledged: "It is perfectly true – and pointless to deny – that affirmative action . . . does not stamp disappointed white candidates with a stigma of inferiority or signal that minority individuals cannot bear to mix with them."[59] One need not be a supporter of race-based affirmative action to acknowledge – as indeed even Antonin Scalia, who is a vigorous opponent of such programs, has acknowledged – that such programs are typically animated by "the most admirable and benign of purposes."[60]

Not only are government programs of race-based affirmative action not racist; they are obviously not on a par morally with racist laws and policies.[61] Indeed, the constitutions of India (1949), Canada (1982),

---

[59] Jeremy Rabkin, "Private Preferences: Why Affirmative Action Won't Disappear Anytime Soon," AMERICAN SPECTATOR, November 1998, 62, 63. See also J. M. Balkin, "The Constitution of Status," 106 YALE L. J. 2313, 2352–53 (1997):
> Admission preferences that attempt to increase the number of historically disadvantaged minorities . . . do not single out whites as social inferiors.
> . . .
>
> [They] clearly do not send the message that racial minorities are superior human beings by virtue of their identity. Whites may grumble that blacks and other minorities are getting "special treatment," but they would hardy view these preferences as a governmental assertion that blacks have higher social status or have a greater share of positive qualities and social esteem. To the contrary, so powerful are the social meanings of race and ethnicity in this country that affirmative action preferences often create the opposite social meaning among whites. They see these preferences as further evidence of the inferiority and unworthiness of racial and ethnic minorities.

[60] *Adarand Constructors, Inc. v. Pena*, 515 U.S. 200, 239 (1995) (Scalia, J., concurring in part and concurring in the judgment).

[61] Cf. Stephen L. Carter, "When Victims Happen To Be Black," 97 YALE L. J. 420, 433–43 (1988): "[T]o say that two centuries of struggle for the most basic of civil rights have been mostly about freedom from racial categorization rather than from freedom from

and South Africa (1996) all recognize and protect the right to moral equality, but they also all explicitly indicate that government programs of affirmative action, including government programs of race-based affirmative action, do not contravene – do not violate – the right to nondiscrimination.[62] For example, Article 15 of Canada's Charter of Rights and Freedoms (which is part of the Canadian Constitution) states, in Subsection (1), that "[e]very individual is equal before the law and has the right to the equal protection and equal benefit of the law without discrimination and, in particular, without discrimination based on race, national or ethnic origin, colour, religion, sex, age or mental or physical disability." Article 15 then goes on to state, in Subsection (2), that "[s]ubsection (1) does not preclude any law, program or activity that has as its object the amelioration of conditions of disadvantaged individuals or groups including those that are disadvantaged because of race, national or ethnic origin, colour, religion, sex, age or mental or physical disability."

It bears emphasis that the question of the constitutionality, under the right to moral equality, of a government program of race-based affirmative action and the question whether the program is, all things considered, good public policy are distinct questions. That such a program is not good public policy does not entail that the program is unconstitutional – that it violates the right to moral equality – any more than that the program is not unconstitutional entails that the program is good public policy. Moreover, whether such a program is good public policy is a question properly addressed, not by judges – not even by Supreme Court justices – but by citizens and their elected representatives, whose policymaking prerogatives the judiciary should not usurp. As it happens, the citizens of California, in 1996; the citizens of Washington, in 1998; the citizens of Michigan,

---

racial oppression, is to trivialize the lives and deaths of those who have suffered under racism."

Nor are those who support such programs on a par morally with those who support racist laws and policies. "It is one thing to question the wisdom of affirmative action programs.... It is another thing altogether to equate the many well-meaning and intelligent lawmakers and their constituents – whether members of majority or minority races – who have supported affirmative action over the years, to segregationists and bigots." *Adarand Constructors, Inc. v. Pena*, 515 U.S. 200, 247 n. 5 (1995) (Stevens, J., dissenting, joined by Ginsburg, J.).

[62] See Article 15 of Canada's Charter of Rights and Freedoms, which is a part of the Canadian Constitution; Article 15 of the Indian Constitution; and Article 9 of the South African Constitution.

in 2006; and, most recently, the citizens of Nebraska, in 2008; exercised their policymaking prerogatives by going to the polls and voting to add to the state constitution a provision forbidding the state to "discriminate against, or grant preferential treatment to, any individual or group on the basis of race, sex, color, ethnicity, or national origin in the operation of public employment, public education, or public contracting."[63] Ordinary politics seems to be working well enough; it doesn't need an assist – a *constitutionally unwarranted* assist – from the U.S. Supreme Court.

There is no constitutionally sound basis for the Supreme Court's hostile stance, not only toward government programs of race-based affirmative action,[64] but also toward other race-conscious but plainly nonracist government policies: for example, the race-conscious assignment of public school students to schools in an effort to decrease racial imbalance in the schools,[65] or the race-conscious drawing of congressional district lines in an effort to increase minority representation in electoral politics.[66] The response that "[t]he [United States] Constitution proscribes government discrimination on the basis of race...," *including discrimination that advantages rather than disadvantages a racial minority*,[67] is, in a word, false:

> The [Fourteenth] Amendment sought to bring into American society as full members those whom the Nation had previously held in slavery.... [There is a] legal and practical difference between the use of race-conscious criteria in defiance of that purpose, namely to keep the races apart, and the use of race-conscious criteria to further that purpose, namely to bring the races together.[68]

Because there is no constitutionally sound basis for the Supreme Court's hostile stance toward race-conscious but nonracist government programs – the same hostile stance it adopts toward race-based

---

[63] On November 4, 2008, the citizens of Colorado voted against – by 50.8% to 49.2% – adding such an amendment to their constitution.
[64] See *Gratz v. Bollinger*, 539 U.S. 244 (2003); *Grutter v. Bollinger*, 539 U.S. 306 (2003).
[65] See, e.g., *Parents Involved in Community Schools v. Seattle School District*, 551 U.S. 701 (2007).
[66] See, e.g., *Shaw v. Reno*, 509 U.S. 630 (1993).
[67] *Grutter v. Bollinger*, 539 U.S. 306, 349 (2003) (Scalia, J. joined by Thomas, J., concurring in part & dissenting in part).
[68] *Parents Involved in Community Schools v. Seattle School District*, 551 U.S. 701 (2007) (Breyer, J. joined by Stevens, Souter, & Ginsburg, J., dissenting).

government programs that disadvantage a racial minority – the Court has arrogated to itself a power that does not rightfully belong to it: the power to veto those race-conscious but nonracist programs that do not satisfy its *policy* predilections and preferences.[69] Against the background of what the citizens of California, Washington, Michigan, and Nebraska did, we may say: How fitting it would be, in a democracy, if citizens and their elected representatives, and not Supreme Court justices, had the final authority to decide whether it's good public policy to permit government sometimes to utilize – for what Justice Scalia called "the most admirable and benign of purposes"[70] – race-conscious but nonracist government programs and policies.[71]

[69] Cf. Associated Press, "Thomas: Best Policy Colorblind," Sept. 10, 2008 (reporting on Justice Clarence Thomas' longstanding opposition to race-based affirmative action).
[70] See n. 60.
[71] Cf. *Adarand Constructors, Inc. v. Pena*, 515 U.S. 200, 243, 245 (1995) (Stevens, J., dissenting, joined by Ginsburg, J.):
> [The Court] assumes that there is no significant difference between a decision by the majority to impose a special burden on the members of a minority race and a decision by the majority to provide a benefit to certain members of that minority notwithstanding its incidental burden on some members of the majority. In my opinion that assumption is untenable. There is no moral or constitutional equivalence between a policy that is designed to perpetuate a caste system and one that seeks to eradicate racial subordination. Invidious discrimination is an engine of oppression, subjugating a disfavored group to enhance or maintain the power of the majority. Remedial race-based preferences reflect the opposite impulse: a desire to foster equality in society....
> ...
> [The Court disregards] the difference between a "No Trespassing" sign and a welcome mat. It would treat a Dixiecrat Senator's decision to vote against Thurgood Marshall's confirmation in order to keep African Americans off the Supreme Court as on a par with President Johnson's evaluation of his race as a positive factor. It would equate a law that made black citizens ineligible for military service with a program aimed at recruiting black soldiers. An attempt by the majority to exclude members of a minority race from a regulated market is fundamentally different from a subsidy that enables a relatively small group of newcomers to enter that market.

The following year, Justice Stevens made much the same point in a different context: "[T]he Court's aggressive supervision of state action designed to accommodate the political concerns of historically disadvantaged minority groups is seriously misguided. A majority's attempt to enable the minority to participate more effectively in the process of democratic governance should not be viewed with the same hostility that is appropriate for oppressive and exclusionary abuses of political power." *Shaw v. Hunt*, 517 U.S. 899, 116 S.Ct. 1894, 1907 (1996) (Stevens, J., dissenting, joined by Ginsburg & Breyer, J.).

C. Protecting Other Constitutionally Entrenched Rights

I said that although Thayer's argument is quite powerful, the case *against* Thayerian deference is powerful, too – with respect to two sorts of constitutional controversies: controversies about the constitutionality of laws that implicate the right to political freedom and controversies about the constitutionality of laws that implicate, and that the courts have good reason to suspect violate, the right to moral equality. But U.S. constitutional law contains many human rights in addition to the right to political freedom and the right to moral equality, and with respect to each of the rights it contains – for example, the right to religious freedom, the various rights concerning the operation of the criminal process, and the right not to be subjected to cruel and unusual punishment – we may, and should, ask: In adjudicating controversies about the constitutionality of laws that implicate the right, should the Supreme Court take the path of Thayerian deference? The answer that makes the most sense (all things considered) with respect to constitutional controversies that implicate one right – for example, the right to political freedom – does not necessarily make the most sense with respect to constitutional controversies that implicate a different right – for example, the right to moral freedom.

Just as the right to moral equality appears in American constitutional law in the guise of the right to the equal protection of the laws, a variant of the right to moral freedom has emerged in American constitutional law in the guise of what the Supreme Court calls "the right of privacy."[72] In *Eisenstadt v. Baird* (1972),[73] in which the

---

[72] See, e.g., *Griswold v. Connecticut*, 381 U.S. 479 (1965); *Eisenstadt v. Baird*, 405 U.S. 438 (1972); *Roe v. Wade*, 410 U.S. 113 (1973); *Planned Parenthood of Southeastern Pennsylvania v. Casey*, 505 U.S. 833 (1992). Cf. *Washington v. Glucksberg*, 521 U.S. 702 (1997); *Lawrence v. Texas*, 539 U.S. 558 (2003).

This is not to say that the interpretation of the constitutional text that has yielded the right of privacy is a correct interpretation. In the postscript to this chapter, I discuss what it means – or should mean – to "interpret" the constitutional text.

It bears mention that the European Court of Human Rights enforces a right "to respect for [one's] private life" that functions much like the right to moral freedom. See, e.g., *Dudgeon v. United Kingdom*, no. 7525/76 (1981); *Norris v. Ireland*, no. 10581/83 (1988). For a similar decision, decided by the Human Rights Committee under the ICCPR, see *Toonen v. Tasmania*, CCPR/C/50/D/488/1992 (1992).

[73] 405 U.S. 438.

Court ruled that a law banning the use of contraceptives was unconstitutional, the Court stated: "If the right of privacy means anything, it is the right of the *individual*, married or single, to be free from unwarranted governmental intrusion into matters so fundamentally affecting a person as the decision whether to bear or beget a child."[74] One year later, the Court invoked the right of privacy as the basis of its ruling in *Roe v. Wade* (1973)[75] that a state may not ban abortion in the period of pregnancy prior to viability. Almost twenty years later, in *Planned Parenthood of Southeastern Pennsylvania v. Casey* (1992),[76] the Court reaffirmed the basic holding of *Roe v. Wade* and, in so doing, stated:

> [Our] law affords constitutional protection to personal decisions relating to marriage, procreation, contraception, family relationships, child rearing, and education. [These] matters, involving the most intimate and personal choices a person may make in a lifetime, choices central to personal dignity and autonomy, are central to the liberty protected by the Fourteenth Amendment. At the heart of liberty is the right to define one's own concept of existence, of meaning, of the universe, and of the mystery of human life. Beliefs about these matters could not define the attributes of personhood were they formed under compulsion of the State.[77]

Although judicial deference was notably absent in *Roe v. Wade* – a decision I have criticized at length elsewhere[78] – almost twenty-five years after its decision in *Roe v. Wade* the Court was appropriately deferential in *Washington v. Glucksberg* (1997),[79] declining to rule that state bans on physician-assisted suicide are unconstitutional.[80] Although in *Glucksberg* the Court did not mention the right of privacy, *Glucksberg*, no less than *Eisenstadt*, *Roe*, and *Planned Parenthood*, fit the profile of a "right of privacy" case. *Glucksberg*, no less than *Eisenstadt*, *Roe*, and *Planned Parenthood*, implicated the right to moral freedom.

---

[74] Id. at 453.
[75] 410 U.S. 113.
[76] 505 U.S. 833.
[77] Id. at 851.
[78] See Michael J. Perry, *We the People: The Fourteenth Amendment and the Supreme Court* 151–66 (1999); Michael J. Perry, *Constitutional Rights, Moral Controversy, and the Supreme Court* 131–67 (2009). See also John Hart Ely, "The Wages of Crying Wolf: A Comment on *Roe v. Wade*," 82 YALE L. J. 920 (1973).
[79] *Washington v. Glucksberg*, 521 U.S. 702.
[80] See Perry, *We the People*, n. 78, at 168–77 (1999).

The following passage, written by David Souter in his concurring opinion in *Glucksberg*,[81] is substantially a statement of the Thayerian approach to judicial enforcement of the right to moral freedom – and of its American variant, the right of privacy:

> [This Court] has no warrant to substitute one reasonable resolution of the contending positions for another, but authority to supplant the balance already struck between the contenders only when it falls outside *the realm of the reasonable*.... [We should] respect legislation within *the zone of reasonableness*.... It is no justification for judicial intervention merely to identify a reasonable resolution of contending values that differs from the terms of the legislation under review. It is only when the legislation's justifying principle, critically valued, is so far from being commensurate with the individual interest as to be arbitrarily or pointlessly applied that the statute must give way.[82]

POSTSCRIPT TO CHAPTER 9

"Interpreting" the Constitution

The U.S. Constitution is a written document; it is a text. What human rights are entrenched in the U.S. Constitution? In addressing that question, we must do more than quote the constitutional text; we must interpret it. But what does it mean to "interpret" the constitutional text?[83] What is constitutional "interpretation"? That is, what is constitutional "interpretation" *as that concept – textual interpretation – has generally been understood in our (i.e., American) legal practice?*

---

[81] *Washington v. Glucksberg*, 521 U.S. 702.
[82] 521 U.S. at 764–65, 768 (Souter, J., concurring in the judgment) (emphasis added). Compare this statement by the Canadian Supreme Court:
> Parliament has enacted this legislation after a long consultation process that included a consideration of the constitutional standards outlined by this Court.... While it is the role of the Court so specify such standards, there may be a range of permissible regimes that can meet these standards. It goes without saying that this range is not confined to the specific rule adopted by the Court pursuant to its competence in the common law.

Regina v. Mills, 3 S.C.R. 668 at para. 59 (1999).
[83] Cf. Jeffrey Goldsworthy, "Raz on Constitutional Interpretation," 22 LEGAL PHILOSOPHY 167, 193 (2003) (discussing "judicial law-making masquerading as interpretation, rather than genuine interpretation as that concept is generally understood in legal practice"). On how the cencept has generally been understood in our legal practice, see Richard S. Kay, "Original Intention and Public Meaning in Constitutional Interpretation," 103 NORTHWESTERN L. REV. 703 (2009) See also Goldsworthy, supra this note.

Protecting Constitutionally Entrenched Rights

I. WHAT IS CONSTITUTIONAL "INTERPRETATION"?

The U.S. Constitution is a "text" in the ordinary sense of the term: a writing by one or more human beings intended to communicate a message to one or more other human beings. In particular, the Constitution is a *normative text*: a text intended to communicate one or more norms (imperatives, directives) – one or more prescriptive statements about what acts are forbidden, required, or authorized.

Who are the human beings whose writing the U.S. Constitution is? The Preamble to the Constitution answers that question: "We the People of the United States ... do ordain and establish this Constitution for the United States of America." But, as we know, in 1787–89, when the Constitution was drafted and ratified; in 1789–91, when the Bill of Rights was drafted and ratified; and ever since, right up until the present, not all the citizens of the United States got (get) to decide what norms the Constitution shall comprise, but only a relative few.[84] In the case of the unamended Constitution that entered into force in 1789, the few consisted of "the people comprising the majorities in the nine state conventions whose ratification preceded the Constitution entering into force."[85] In the case of the amendments to the Constitution, the few consisted of "the people comprising the majorities in the houses of Congress proposing the amendments and in the ratifying legislatures of the necessary three-quarters of the states."[86]

Let's consider, for illustrative purposes, the Eighth Amendment to the Constitution, which states (in part) that "cruel and unusual

---

[84] Cf. Vicki C. Jackson & Mark Tushnet, *Comparative Constitutional Law* 414 (1999): "In the [United States, a constitutional] amendment is permitted only upon completion of supermajority requirements both in Congress and in the states: an amendment must be proposed, either by 2/3 of each House of Congress or by a convention called at the request of the legislatures of 2/3 of the states, and then the proposed amendment must be approved by the legislatures of or conventions in 3/4 of the states."

[85] Kay, n. 83, at 709 n. 28.

[86] Id.

> In American constitutional history, the legitimating source of the Constitution is settled. The Constitution is binding because it is the expression of the will of "the people." The constituent authority of the people was universally acknowledged at the end of the eighteenth century by both proponents and opponents of the proposed constitution. It was, for example, the basis from which its advocates dismissed objections about the illegality of the constitution-making process. The founding generation regarded the approval of the ratifying conventions *to be* the approval of the people.
>
> Id. at 716.

punishments shall not be inflicted."⁸⁷ The quoted language was clearly intended to communicate a norm of the "Don't do this" sort. But precisely what norm? Several possibilities come to mind. Here are three:

1. Don't inflict punishments the English common law has regarded as cruel and unusual.
2. Don't inflict punishments we (i.e., we who are adding this amendment to the Constitution) regard as cruel and unusual.
3. Don't inflict punishments that are in fact cruel and unusual, in the ordinary sense – the conventional sense – of "cruel" and "unusual."

Before we can use the "cruel and unusual punishments" language of Eighth Amendment as a premise in an argument about the constitutionality of a contested punishment, such as the death penalty, we must ascertain what norm, of the various possible ones, those who added the Eighth Amendment to the Constitution – let's call them "the Eighth Amenders" – understood the "cruel and unusual punishments" language to mean – and, therefore, to communicate. (I concur in Richard Kay's compelling argument that in our legal practice, the object of textual, including constitutional, interpretation has generally been what the enactors of the text – both those who drafted the text and those who ratified it – understood the text to mean.⁸⁸) In short, we must "interpret" the language – the

---

[87] The Eighth Amendment states: "Excessive bail shall not be required, nor excessive fines imposed, nor cruel and unusual punishments inflicted." Although the cruel and unusual punishments clause, like the rest of the Bill of Rights, originally applied only to the federal government, it is now constitutional bedrock that the clause – like much (although not all) of the rest of the Bill of Rights – applies to state government, too. See nn. 105–106 and accompanying text.

[88] See Kay, n. 83.

If what those who drafted the text understood it to mean was different from what those who ratified the text understood it to mean, then it would make sense to bow to the understanding of those who ratified the text, for they were the ones empowered to add the text to the Constitution. But I know of no constitutional provision about which we can say: The evidence suggests that what those who drafted the text understood it to mean was different from what those who ratified the text understood it to mean. So we may say that the enactors of the text include both those who drafted the text and those who ratified it.

In rejecting the "original public meaning" of constitutional language as the object of constitutional interpretation, Kay writes:

> In practice, however, this divergence [between original intention and original public meaning interpretation] will be very rare. Constitutional enactors chose words for the purpose of communicating the meaning that they wished to

text – of the Eighth Amendment: We must try to discern whether the Eighth Amenders understood (or, if you prefer, meant) "cruel and unusual punishments" to communicate "punishments the common law has regarded as cruel and unusual"? Or "punishments we regard as cruel and unusual"? Or "punishments that are in fact cruel and unusual, in the ordinary sense of 'cruel' and 'unusual'"? (Of course, the sense of "cruel" and "unusual" that was ordinary at the time the Eighth Amendment was added to the Constitution may differ significantly from the sense that is ordinary today. One way to test that possibility: Consult the dictionaries in common use at the

> express. The enterprise of rulemaking is, after all, an attempt to influence the future conduct of those subject to the rules made. It follows that public meaning will be a critical source – and sometimes the only source – for the determination of intended meaning....
>
> It follows that the public meaning of the constitutional text will mirror the intentions of the human beings who drafted and approved it....
>
> Only in the most inventive academic hypotheticals... will these two methods employ different techniques or yield different results.

Id. at 712–14. Later in his essay, Kay goes on to observe that

> [t]o the extent that we are interested in people who were fluent in language, conversant with the historical and constitutional discourse of the time and fully familiar with the issues at stake in any particular act of constitution-making, we seem to have constructed a person who pretty much exemplifies the real enactors. For example, in discussing the relevance of the published debates of the state ratifying conventions, Vesan Kesavan and Michael Stokes Paulsen say, "[It] matters not what (much less all) of the Ratifiers actually intended or understood but what the hypothetical reasonably well-informed Ratifier would have objectively understood the legal text to mean with all the relevant information in hand." Reducing the reasonable person to the reasonably well-informed ratifier with all the relevant evidence in hand more or less collapses the difference between intended and public meaning.

Id. at 722–23. Id. (quoting Vesan Kesavan & Michael Stokes Paulsen, "The Interpretive Force of the Constitution's Secret Drafting History," 91 GEORGETOWN L. J. 1113, 1162 [2002–03]). Cf. Robert G. Natelson, "The Founders' Hermeneutic: The Real Original Understanding of Original Intent," 68 OHIO STATE L. J. 1239, 1305 (2007):

> The Founders' hermeneutic – how they expected the Constitution to be construed – rested on the text, of course, but also on the subjective understanding of the ratifiers. Where subjective understanding was not retrievable, the preferred substitute was original public meaning.
>
> The founding generation inherited this view from Anglo-American jurisprudence, which treated "intent of the makers" – subjective intent, where recoverable – as the ultimate guide for statutory construction. Judges and lawyers sought that intent from the text and from a wide range of extrinsic evidence, including legislative history. The records of the Ratification Era richly confirm American acceptance of this approach to constitutional interpretation.

time the Eighth Amendment was added to the Constitution.[89]) After we weigh all the available evidence, one answer will dominate the others. Or so we may hope.

Assume, for the sake of discussion, that the available evidence supports the proposition that the Eighth Amenders most likely understood (and, therefore, meant) the "cruel and unusual punishments" language to communicate this norm: *Do not inflict punishments that are in fact cruel and unusual, in the ordinary sense of "cruel" and "unusual."* Assume too that at the time the Eighth Amendment was added to the Constitution: (a) the ordinary meaning of "cruel" was "significantly harsher than necessary to serve the legitimate aims of criminal punishment," and (b) the ordinary sense of "unusual" was "not commonly used." Given those two assumptions – which I have defended elsewhere[90] – capital punishment may be "cruel and unusual" within the meaning of the Eighth Amendment even though neither the English common law nor the Eighth Amenders regarded capital punishment as cruel and unusual.[91] Antonin Scalia is famously fond of pointing out that those who added the Eighth Amendment to the Constitution did not regard capital punishment as cruel and unusual.[92] But Justice Scalia's point is not determinative unless the

---

[89] See Michael J. Perry, *Constitutional Rights, Moral Controversy, and the Supreme Court* 57, n. 10 (2008) (consulting Samuel Johnson's *A Dictionary of the English Language*, first published in 1756). Johnson's dictionary was "'the standard authority at the time when the Constitution was drawn up in 1787.'" Andrew O'Hagan, "Word Wizard," NEW YORK REV. BOOKS, Apr. 27, 2006, at 12, 12 (quoting and reviewing Henry Hitchings, *Defining the World: The Extraordinary Story of Dr. Johnson's Dictionary* [2006]). Johnson's dictionary "is a beautiful read, and its influence is unending. . . . Without it, English-speakers would not be English-speakers as we think of them." Id.

[90] See Perry, *Constitutional Rights*, n. 78, 58–60.

[91] See id. 61–64.

[92] See, e.g., Antonin Scalia, *A Matter of Interpretation: Federal Courts and the Law* 46, 132, 145–47 (1997). See also *Baze v. Rees, Commissioner, Kentucky Department of Corrections*, 128 S.Ct. 1520, 1552 (2008) (Scalia, J. joined by Thomas, J., concurring in the judgment).

Both the due process clause of the Fifth Amendment, which was added to the Constitution at the same time the Eighth Amendment was added (1791), and the due process clause of the Fourteenth Amendment, which was added in 1868, state that government may not deprive a person of life without due process of law. Moreover, the grand jury clause of the Fifth Amendment states that government may not prosecute a person for a "capital" crime – a crime for which the penalty of death may be imposed – unless a grand jury authorizes it to do so. Clearly, then, neither the Eighth Amenders nor

Eighth Amenders most likely intended the "cruel and unusual punishments" language to communicate "Do not inflict punishments *we* regard as cruel and unusual."[93] So far as I am aware, Scalia has not defended that interpretation.[94]

> the Fourteenth Amenders regarded capital punishment as cruel and unusual. Still, as Justice Brennan emphasized, the Fifth Amendment
>> does not, after all, declare that the right of Congress to punish capitally shall be inviolable; it merely requires that when and if death is a possible punishment, the defendant shall enjoy certain procedural safeguards.... [W]hat one can fairly say is that they sought to ensure that *if* there was capital punishment, the process by which the accused was to be convicted would be especially reliable.
>
> William J. Brennan, Jr., "Constitutional Adjudication and the Death Penalty: A View from the Court," 100 HARVARD L. REV. 313, 324 (1986). See generally Shannon D. Gilreath, "Cruel and Unusual Punishment and the Eighth Amendment as a Mandate for Human Dignity: Another Look at Original Intent," 25 THOMAS JEFFERSON L. REV. 559, 571–84 (2003).

[93] Cf. Andrew Oldenquist, "Retribution and the Death Penalty," 20 U. DAYTON L. REV. 335, 340–43 (2004) (criticizing Scalia's interpretive approach to the Eighth Amendment).
> Scalia points out that the Framers did not think that capital punishment was cruel because they allude to it as an option in the same document in which they prohibit cruel and unusual punishments. But why does it matter whether they thought capital punishment was cruel. What should guide us is what they explicitly prohibit or mandate in the Constitution. And if the Framers' opinions about capital punishment do not count, surely neither do the opinions of late eighteenth century reasonable bystanders. Where is the evidence that the Framers intended that their own acceptance of capital punishment should determine our interpretation of the Eighth Amendment? And even if they, or the reasonable bystanders of the time, considered burying alive but not hanging to be cruel, it doesn't follow that this is what the Eighth Amendment means or implies. It certainly isn't what it *says*.... Awe at writing a document to guide a new nation through future generations, together with respect for the judgment of future generations, may well have moved them not to want to restrict us by their personal opinions about what is cruel or what is an unreasonable search, and this awe and respect may account for the abstractness of much of the Bill of Rights.
>
> Id. at 341.

[94] I do not mean to deny that the fact that the Eighth Amenders did not regard capital punishment as cruel and unusual bears on the question what directive, of the various possible ones, they intended the language of the Eighth Amendment to communicate. "The scope beliefs that particular drafters might have had about the application of [a] constitutional principle may be useful to understanding what principle they actually intended to convey with their language...." Keith E. Whittington, "The New Originalism," 2 GEORGETOWN J. L. & PUBLIC POLICY 599, 610 (2004). Nonetheless, "the textual principle should not be reduced to the founders' scope beliefs about that principle. The founders could be wrong about the application and operation of the principles that they intended to adopt." Id. at 610–11. "[I]n a defensible version of originalism, authorial expectations about how the text will be applied are not the important measure of textual meaning." Id. at 610. And yet, in *Baze v. Rees, Commissioner, Kentucky Department of Corrections,*

Although I have used the "cruel and unusual punishments" language of the Eighth Amendment for illustrative purposes, I could just as well have used any of a number of other provisions of the constitutional text – for example, the "freedom of speech" language of the First Amendment:[95] Before we can use that language as a premise in an argument about the constitutionality of a contested restriction on speech, we must ascertain what norm, of the various possible ones, the First Amenders understood the "freedom of speech" to communicate.

II. DISPELLING TWO LARGE MISUNDERSTANDINGS

The answer I have just given to the "What is constitutional 'interpretation'?" question is easily misunderstood.

A. Specifying Constitutional Norms

Resolving a constitutional controversy – a controversy over whether government is acting unconstitutionally – involves more than just interpreting a constitutional text (e.g., the Eighth Amendment's "cruel and unusual punishments" language); it also typically involves specifying an underdeterminate constitutional norm:[96] either a norm that is the yield of the process of interpreting the constitutional text or a norm that is, in any event, constitutional bedrock.

We must distinguish among (a) "interpreting" a legal text, (b) "applying" a determinate legal norm, and (c) "specifying" an

---

[95] 125 S. Ct. 1520, 1556 (2008), Justice Thomas, in a concurring opinion joined by Justice Scalia, wrote as if authorial expectations about how the text will be applied *are* the important measure of textual meaning. Justices Thomas and Scalia seem blind to the possibility that a provision of the constitutional text, such as the Eighth Amendment, "embod[ies] principles or general rules.... [M]uch of the constitutional text does exactly that. The point for an originalist should be to understand [what] those original principles or rules [are], to understand what principle was entrenched in the Constitution." Whittington, supra this note, at 610. See also Kay, n. 83: "The intentions in which we are interested are those relating to the elements that should mark an instance as within or without an intended category. The defining elements are fixed; the instances are not. New ones can qualify and existing ones may become disqualified as facts, or our knowledge about facts, change. How fluid the contents are depends on a prior determination as to the criteria for inclusion intended by the rule-makers."

[95] The First Amendment states, in relevant part: "Congress shall make no law... abridging the freedom of speech."

[96] See Lawrence B. Solum, "On the Indeterminacy Crisis: Critiquing Critical Dogma," 54 U. CHICAGO L. REV. 462 (1987).

underdeterminate legal norm. (I have elaborated and defended the distinction elsewhere.[97]) A legal norm is *determinate* in the context of a controversy in which the norm is invoked – a controversy in which, let us assume, the relevant facts are clear and beyond dispute – if there is no room for a reasonable difference of judgment about whether the norm forbids (or requires) what the party invoking the norm claims the norm forbids. "In countless litigations, the law is so clear that judges have no discretion. They have the right to legislate within gaps, but often there are no gaps. We shall have a false view of the landscape if we look at the waste spaces only, and refuse to see the acres already sown and fruitful."[98] By contrast, a legal norm is *underdeterminate* in the context of a controversy in which the norm is invoked – a controversy in which the relevant facts are clear and beyond dispute – if there is room for a reasonable difference of judgment about whether the norm forbids what the party invoking the norm claims the norm forbids.

The process of interpreting a legal text is the process of trying to discern what norm the enactors of the text understood the text to communicate. The process of interpreting a legal text should not be confused with the process of specifying an underdeterminate legal norm, which is the process of deciding what the norm shall mean – that is, what the norm shall require, forbid, or authorize – in a particular context. A specification "of a principle for a specific class of cases is not a deduction from it, nor a discovery of some implicit meaning; it is the act of setting a more concrete and categorical requirement in the spirit of the principle, and guided both by a sense of what is practically realizable (or enforceable), and by a recognition of the risk of conflict with other principles or values."[99] In *The Federalist* No. 37, James Madison emphasized the need for specification: "All

---

[97] See Michael J. Perry, *We the People: The Fourteenth Amendment and the Supreme Court* 23–35 (1999).

[98] Benjamin N. Cardozo, *The Nature of the Judicial Process* 129 (1921). See also Kent Greenawalt, "How Law Can be Determinate," 31 UCLA L. REV. 1, 29 (1990): "Few, if any, writers have asserted the most extreme thesis about indeterminacy – that no legal questions have determinate answers – in clear terms, and almost no one may actually believe that thesis."

[99] Neil MacCormick, "Reconstruction after Deconstruction: A Response to CLS," 10 OXFORD J. LEGAL STUDIES 539, 548 (1990). Where I have used the term *specification*, MacCormick uses the Latin term *determinatio*, borrowing it from John Finnis. "John Finnis has to good effect re-deployed St Thomas' concept of *determinatio*; Hans Kelsen's translators used the term 'concretization' to much the same effect." Id. (Citing J. M.

new laws, though penned with the greatest technical skill and passed on the fullest and most mature deliberation, are considered as more or less obscure and equivocal, until their meaning be liquidated and ascertained by a series of particular discussions and adjudications."[100]

If a norm that is entrenched in U.S. constitutional law – either a norm that is the yield of the process of interpreting the constitutional text or a norm that is, in any event, constitutional bedrock – is underdeterminate in the context of a constitutional controversy, then the norm must be specified in that context; if the norm is underdeterminate in many such contexts, then there are many contexts in which the norm must be specified. Assume, for example, that a norm to this

---

Finnis, "On the Critical Legal Studies Movement," 30 AMERICAN J. JURISPRUDENCE 21, 23–25 (1985), and Hans Kelsen, *The Pure Theory of Law* 230 [1967].)

What Anthony Kronman has said of the process of "judgment" aptly describes the process of specifying a constitutional norm. Such specification is a species of judgment.

> Good judgment, and its opposite, are in fact most clearly revealed in just those situations where the method of deduction is least applicable, where the ambiguities are greatest and the demand for proof most obviously misplaced. To show good judgment in such situations is to do something more than merely apply a general rule with special care and thoroughness, or follow out its consequences to a greater level of detail. Judgment often requires such analytic refinement but does not consist in it alone. That this is so is to be explained by the fact that we are most dependent on our judgment, most in need of *good* judgment, in just those situations that pose genuine dilemmas by forcing us to choose between, or otherwise accommodate, conflicting interests and obligations whose conflict is not itself amenable to resolution by the application of some higher-order rule. It is here that the quality of a person's judgment comes most clearly into view and here, too, that his or her deductive powers alone are least likely to prove adequate to the task.

Anthony T. Kronman, "Living in the Law," 54 U. CHICAGO L. REV. 835, 847–48 (1987).

[100] In *Truth and Method*, Hans-Georg Gadamer commented on the process of specification both in law and in theology:

> In both legal and theological hermeneutics there is the essential tension between the text set down – of the law or of the proclamation – on the one hand and, on the other, the sense arrived at by its application in the particular moment of interpretation, either in judgment or in preaching. A law is not there to be understood historically, but to be made concretely valid through being interpreted. Similarly, a religious proclamation is not there to be understood as a merely historical document, but to be taken in a way in which it exercises its saving effect. This includes the fact that the text, whether law or gospel, if it is to be understood properly, i.e., according to the claim it makes, must be understood at every moment, in every particular situation, in a new and different way. Understanding here is always application.

Hans-Georg Gadamer, *Truth and Method* 275 (1975).

effect is entrenched in U.S. constitutional law: *Government may not ban (or otherwise impede) one's saying what one wants, when one wants, where one wants, or how one wants, unless the ban is necessary to serve a legitimate governmental interest, the weight of which is proportionate to the weight of the burden imposed by the ban on those subject to the ban.* There are many contexts – very many! – in which that norm must be specified.

Constitutional interpretation – that is, the interpretation of a constitutional text – is one thing, constitutional specification – the specification of an underdeterminate constitutional norm – another.[101] To answer the "What is constitutional 'interpretation'?" question as I have in this postscript is not to discount the importance of the role constitutional specification typically plays in resolving constitutional controversies.

B. Respecting Constitutional Bedrock

Nor does my answer entail that each and every time it must resolve a constitutional controversy, the U.S. Supreme Court should do so on the basis of constitutional interpretation – that is, on the basis of what it believes to be the correct interpretation of the constitutional text. It is one thing to say what constitutional "interpretation" is; it is another thing altogether to say that constitutional adjudication should always be based on constitutional interpretation. There is no inconsistency in (a) answering the "What is constitutional 'interpretation'?" question as I have in this postscript and (b) holding that constitutional adjudication should *not* always be based on what the adjudicators believe to be the correct interpretation of the Constitution.

And, in my judgment, constitutional adjudication should *sometimes* be based on a (major) premise[102] *without regard to whether the premise is the yield of an accurate interpretation of the Constitution*: namely, when

---

[101] Cf. Kim Lane Scheppele, *Legal Secrets* 94–95 (1988): "Generally in the literature on interpretation the question being posed is, What does a particular text (or social practice) *mean*? Posed this way, the interpretive question gives rise to an embarrassing multitude of possible answers, a cacophony of theories of interpretation.... [The] question that (in practice) is the one actually asked in the course of lawyering and judging [is]: what ... does a particular text mean *for the specific case at hand?*"

[102] Major premise: Instances of X are forbidden (required, authorized). Minor premise: The challenged law is an instance of X. Conclusion: The challenged law is forbidden.

the premise has achieved the status of (what we may call) "constitutional bedrock," by which I mean that the the premise, in the words of Robert Bork, has "become so embedded in the life of the nation, so accepted by the society, so fundamental to the private and public expectations of individuals and institutions," that the premise should be maintained without regard to whether it is an accurate interpretation of the Constitution.[103] Listen, too, to Michael McConnell: "[M]any decisions, even some that were questionable or controversial when rendered, have become part of the fabric of American life; it is inconceivable that they would now be overruled.... This overwhelming public acceptance constitutes a mode of popular ratification...."[104]

One of the foremost examples of a premise that has achieved the status of constitutional bedrock – perhaps *the* foremost example – is this: The most important provisions of the Bill of Rights are applicable to state government as well as to the federal government.[105] According to some scholars, that premise rests on a mistaken interpretation of the Fourteenth Amendment.[106] Even if we assume

---

[103] Robert Bork, *The Tempting of America: The Political Seduction of the Law* 158 (1989).

[104] Michael W. McConnell, "Active Liberty: A Progressive Alternative to Textualism and Originalism?," 119 HARVARD L. REV. 2387, 2417 (2006).

[105] See, e.g., Sullivan & Gunther, n. 54, at 354–61. Cf. Charles L. Black, Jr., "'One Nation Indivisible': Unnamed Human Rights in the States," 65 ST. JOHN'S L. REV. 17, 55 (1991): "[W]ithout such a corpus of national human rights law good against the States, we ought to stop saying, 'One nation indivisible, with liberty and justice for all,' and speak instead of, 'One nation divisible and divided into fifty zones of political morality, with liberty and justice in such kind and measure as these good things may from time to time be granted by each of these fifty political subdivisions.'"

[106] More precisely, it rests (according to some scholars) on a mistaken interpretation of the second sentence of Section 1 of the Fourteenth Amendment, which states: "No State shall make or enforce any law which shall abridge the privileges or immunities of citizens of the United States; nor shall any State deprive any person of life, liberty, or property, without due process of law; no deny to any person within its jurisdiction the equal protection of the laws." For example, even though it has long been held and is now well established that the Fourteenth Amendment makes the takings clause of the Fifth Amendment – "nor shall private property be taken for public use, without just compensation" – applicable to the states (see *Chicago, B. & Q. R. Co. v. Chicago*, 166 U.S. 226 [1897]; *Kelo v. City of New London*, 545 U.S. 469, 472 n. 1 [2005]), there is at best only scant support for that interpretation of the Fourteenth Amendment. See Aviam Soifer, "Text-Mess: There Is No Textual Basis for Application of the Takings Clause to the States," 28 U. HAWAII L. REV. 373 (2006).

arguendo that those scholars are right, or probably right, the premise, because it has achieved the status of constitutional bedrock, should be maintained.[107]

Perhaps, however, I (along with Bork, McConnell, and countless others) am wrong in holding that constitutional adjudication should sometimes be based on a premise without regard to whether the premise is the yield of a correct interpretation of the constitutional text. Still, the answer I have given here to the "What is constitutional 'interpretation'?" question does not entail – indeed, no answer to the question entails – that constitutional adjudication should *always* be based on constitutional interpretation. Indeed, strictly speaking, neither my answer nor any other answer to the question entails even that constitutional adjudication should *generally* be based on constitutional interpretation.[108]

---

[107] By contrast, the Supreme Court's ruling in *Roe v. Wade*, 410 U.S. 113 (1973), has never achieved the status of constitutional bedrock: That ruling has been widely contested since the day it was handed down.

[108] Let me dispel a third misunderstanding: Neither my answer nor any other answer to the "What is constitutional 'interpretation'?" question entails that as a moral matter judges may never lie about what they believe to be the correct interpretation of the constitutional text.

May judges sometimes lie? Jeff Goldsworthy has suggested that "[j]udges may sometimes be morally justified in lying about what they are doing, but in a democratic and tolerably just society, only in rare and exceptional circumstances." Goldsworthy, n. 83, at 193. (Cf. id.: "Insofar as Raz argues that, as a matter of morality, judges are sometimes permitted or even required to use innovative interpretation in order to mitigate injustice, my defence is ... to argue that even if this is occasionally justified, it really involves judicial law-making masquerading as interpretation, rather than genuine interpretation as that concept is generally understood in legal practice.") Richard Kay has said:

[I]n theory, a judge who values constitutionalism may still sometimes depart from constitutional norms and (just because he/she believes in constitutional values) conceal that departure. But a judge committed to constitutionalism will understand the enormous danger of that course of action for at least three reasons. 1) The judge understands that his/her own priorities may be exactly the thing which long-term constitutions properly exclude. He/she will have an acute sense of the fallibility of ad hoc judgments. 2) He/she knows that his/her deception will not be perfectly successful and thus will set a precedent of repeated adventures of the same kind. Or it will be converted into evidence for some new theory of "interpretation." 3) The decision will necessarily have ripple effects in the adjudication of other cases invoking the same or related rules. If in those cases stepping out is not the right thing to do, either legally or morally, the risk of unjustifiable decisions is increased. A sincerely constitutionalist judge,

The voluminous literature about constitutional interpretation is rife with misunderstandings. So I have emphasized here that nothing I have said in this postscript discounts the importance of the role constitutional specification plays in resolving constitutional controversies or entails that constitutional adjudication should always be based on constitutional interpretation – that is, on what the adjudicators believe to be the correct interpretation of the constitutional text.

III. A CONCLUDING COMMENT

Recall the question-in-chief; recall it in full: What is constitutional "interpretation" *as that concept – textual interpretation – has generally been understood in our legal practice?* In my judgment, the only plausible answer to that question is the one I have given here.

Now, consider a different question: not what "interpretation" of the constitutional text has generally meant in our legal practice, but what it *should* mean. Consider this claim:

> Our legal practice should be revised so that to "interpret" a constitutional text means more than it has generally meant in our legal practice; it means more, that is, than trying to discern what norm the enactors of the text – those who made the text a part of the Constitution – meant to communicate and thereby establish as constitutionally authoritative. Our legal practice should be revised so that to "interpret" a constitutional text also means

therefore, will work under a near-irrebuttable presumption that his/her moral convictions are to be subordinated to the constitutional norm.
E-mail from Richard Kay to Michael Perry, May 19, 2008.
  Imagine that it is 1953 and *Brown v. Board of Education*, 347 U.S. 483 (1954), which would be decided one year later, is before the Supreme Court. Imagine, too, that according to what a justice of the Court sincerely believes to be the correct interpretation of the second sentence of Section 1 of the Fourteenth Amendment, racially segregated public schools do not violate the Fourteenth Amendment. All things considered, perhaps the justice may – indeed, perhaps he should – lie about what he believes to be the correct interpretation of the Fourteenth Amendment. But whether he may/should do so, nothing I have said in this postscript about what constitutional "interpretation" is entails that he may not lie; it does not entail that he may not pretend that racially segregated public schools violate the Fourteenth Amendment, correctly intepreted.

to use the text as a vehicle for establishing as constitutionally authoritative a norm the enactors of the text did *not* mean to communicate/establish.

I cannot discern a plausible argument in support of that claim.[109]

[109] In correspondence, Larry Alexander has asked:
> What do we think we're doing when we "interpret" a normative document if not searching for the intended meaning of the author(s)? Treat it as if it were a poem? A secretly coded message? Written in a language in which the meaning of the words just happens to correspond to our policy preferences? In other words, once you unhinge a document like the Constitution from its authorially intended meaning, everything's up for grabs, and "interpretation" becomes a matter of "interpreter" preference. Notice that when we are asked to interpret a normative document that is now normatively dead – such as the Articles of Confederation of the Constitution of the Confederate States – everyone looks to authorial intent. No one would interpret those documents the way most constitutional law academics "interpret" the Constitution.

E-mail from Larry Alexander to Michael Perry, May 19, 2008.

I have written this postscript without once, until now, using the terms "originalism" and "originalist" (other than when I was either (a) citing an article the title of which included one of the terms or (b) quoting someone else). Am I an originalist? The question puts me in mind of the Christian theologian who, when asked whether he was a Catholic, responded: "I will tell you what I believe, then you can decide whether I am a Catholic." Compare Mitchell N. Berman, "Originalism Is Bunk," 84 NYU L. REV. 1, 33–36 (2009) (arguing that it may not be possible to overcome the tension between authentic originalism and *stare decisis*) with Kurt T. Lash, "Originalism, Popular Sovereignty, and *Stare Decisis*," 93 VIRGINIA L. REV. 1437, 1481 (2007): "Making room for stare decisis in the practice of originalism does not make one unprincipled or inconsistent; it merely reflects a normatively grounded theory of constitutional interpretation."

Conclusion
In the Matter of the Adoption of John Doe and James Doe

My overarching aim in this book has been to elaborate and defend an account of the political morality of liberal democracy. I have focused, in particular, on four aspects of the political morality of liberal democracy: content, grounding, implications for two moral controversies (abortion and same-sex unions), and judicial enforcement. Along the way, I addressed the question of the proper, and properly limited, role of religious faith in the politics and law of a liberal democracy.

Liberal democracy is, as such – as *liberal* democracy – committed to the proposition that each and every human being has inherent dignity and is inviolable: In the political culture of a liberal democracy, the proposition is axiomatic. Moreover, liberal democracy is (as such) committed to certain human rights: In the legal system of a liberal democracy, the rights are recognized and protected as fundamental legal rights. Liberal democracy is committed to certain human rights *because* it is committed to the inherent dignity and inviolability of every human being; the former commitment grounds – it is a principal warrant for – the latter commitment. Among the human rights to which liberal democracy is committed are the right to moral equality and the right to religious freedom.

And among the rights to which liberal democracy *should be* committed is the right to moral freedom. As I argued in Chapter 5, the right to moral freedom is a compelling extension of the right to religious freedom – an extension animated by the logic, so to speak, of the fundamental warrant for liberal democracy's commitment to the right to religious freedom: *Government – a political majority – is not to be trusted (i.e., beyond a certain point) as an arbiter of moral truth any more than it is to be trusted (beyond that same point) as an arbiter of religious truth; moreover, the coercive imposition of moral uniformity, like the coercive imposition of religious uniformity, is (beyond a certain point) more likely to corrode than to nurture the strength of a democracy.* According to the right to moral freedom – that is, the right to moral freedom read in conjunction with the principle that a religious rationale may not serve as the basis of coercive and/or discriminatory lawmaking – government may not ban (or otherwise impede) a moral practice unless (a) the ban is necessary to serve a governmental interest that is both legitimate and sufficiently weighty to be proportionate to the weight of the burden imposed by the ban; and (b) there is a plausible secular reason that could account for the lawmakers' judgment that the ban is necessary to serve such an interest.

The account of the political morality of liberal democracy I have elaborated and defended in this book is not meant to be exhaustive: Liberal democracy is committed to more human rights than those I have discussed here. Two important examples: the right to certain protections when one is criminal defendant; the right not to be subjected to torture or to cruel, inhuman, or degrading treatment or punishment.[1] Moreover, a powerful argument can be made – in my judgment, a conclusive argument – that liberal democracy should affirm, as a fundamental political-moral norm, the right to freedom from severe poverty: the right, that is, to freedom from the most debilitating consequences of severe poverty.[2] Whether a liberal democracy should constitutionalize such a norm – and if so, whether it should authorize its judiciary play a role in enforcing the norm – are separate, and more difficult, questions.[3]

Except for some fine-tuning, I finished this book in Fall 2008. In November 2008, a few weeks after the election of Barack Obama to the presidency of the United States, Cyndy S. Lederman, a Florida judge, decided an adoption case: *In the Matter of the Adoption of John Doe and James Doe*.[4] When I read Judge Lederman's opinion

---

[1] See Article 7 of the ICCPR.
[2] See Thomas Pogge, ed., *Freedom from Poverty as a Human Right* (2007).
[3] The literature addressing these questions is voluminous. A good place to start: Cecile Fabre, *Social Rights Under the Constitution: Government and the Decent Life* (2000); Frank I. Michelman, "Socioeconomic Rights in Constitutional Law: Explaining America Away," 6 INTERNATIONAL J. CONSTITUTIONAL L. 663 (2008).
[4] For Judge Lederman's opinion, see http://www.aclu.org/images/asset_upload_file16_37906.pdf. For more information on the case, see http://www.aclu.org/lgbt/parenting/37875res20081124.html.

Conclusion

in the case, I was struck by the fact that she was addressing, both explicitly and implicitly, some of the very issues at the heart of this book.

A Florida law, enacted in 1977 during Anita Bryant's successful campaign to repeal a gay rights ordinance that had recently been adopted by Dade County (Miami), declares that no one otherwise eligible to adopt under Florida law "may adopt if that person is a homosexual."[5] That a state refuses to create civil unions for same-sex couples – or that a state creates such unions but refuses to recognize them as "marriages" – does not prevent a same-sex couple from being a couple and living together as such and, along with their families, friends, and community, recognizing their union as a marriage. But the Florida adoption law prevents gays and lesbians from becoming adoptive parents – and, so, imposes a much more severe hardship on gays and lesbians; it effects a more grievous assault on gays and lesbians, than does a state's refusal to create civil unions for same-sex couples.[6]

Judge Lederman concluded that the Florida law violates the Florida Constitution's guarantee of equal protection. As I write this conclusion, the attorney general of Florida has filed an appeal in the case,[7] and by the time this book has been published, Judge Lederman's ruling may have been – or may be on its way to being – reversed. Nonetheless, her ruling is correct as a matter of the political morality of liberal democracy. And because the relevant part of that morality – the right to moral equality – is embedded in the constitutional law of Florida (in the guise of the right to equal protection),[8] Judge Lederman's ruling is also correct as a matter

---

[5] "Florida is the only state with a law prohibiting gay men and lesbians – couples and individuals – from adopting children." Yolanne Almanzar, "Florida Gay Adoption Ban Is Ruled Unconstitutional," Nov. 26, 2008. Cf. Robbie Brown, "Antipathy Toward Obama Seen as Helping Arkansas Limit Adoption," NEW YORK TIMES, Nov. 9, 2008: "Arkansas is not the first state with such a policy [i.e., "preventing unmarried cohabiting couples from adopting or fostering children"]. Florida prohibits adoption by applicants who identify themselves as gay, Utah prevents unmarried cohabiting couples from adopting and Mississippi specifically bans same-sex couples from adopting."

[6] See Dan Savage, "Anti-Gay, Anti-Family," NEW YORK TIMES, Nov. 12, 2008.

[7] See Almanzar, n. 5.

[8] Indeed, the right to moral equality is embedded in the constitutional law of every state (in the guise of the right of equal protection or of an equivalent right).

Conclusion

of Florida constitutional law. Because the right to moral equality is also embedded in the constitutional law of the United States (in the guise of the right to equal protection), the Florida law invalidated by Judge Lederman also violates U.S. constitutional law. (As I read her opinion, Judge Lederman ruled only as to Florida constitutional law.)

The Florida law clearly implicates the right to moral equality: There is a undeniably a serious question whether the law is based on the view that homosexuals are inferior – second-class, or worse – human beings: that they do not have equal inherent dignity; that their well-being does not merit the same respect and concern as the well-being of some other human beings. Answering that question – and thereby deciding whether the law not only implicates but violates the right to moral equality – requires answering this question: Is the Florida law – specifically, the singling out of homosexuals and treating them less well – necessary to serve a legitimate (and sufficiently weighty) governmental interest?[9]

Judge Lederman's opinion patiently and thoroughly explained that the evidence presented to the court demonstrates a robust social-scientific consensus to the effect that parenting by homosexuals, whether as biological, foster, or adoptive parents, is no less healthy for

---

[9] Does the Florida law also implicate the right to moral freedom? By making homosexuals ineligible to adopt, Florida diminishes the moral freedom of homosexuals, just as Florida diminishes the moral freedom of homosexuals by refusing to create civil unions for same-sex couples. The following passage, which I quoted in Chapter 8, is as applicable to the issue of legal eligibility to adopt as it is to the issue of legal eligibility to live in a legally recognized civil union:

> [I]f there are same-sex couples who want to form some sort of union and raise children – who want, that is, to have the rich, stable, recognized, respected relations that are at the heart of most people's conceptions of a worthwhile life – and, because of our ethical traditions, there are no social institutions to allow it, then we should create one or another form of them. *This too, I believe, is an issue of liberty. No matter how many options there are already, this one, because of its centrality to characteristic human conceptions of a worthwhile life, must be added.... What is at stake for same-sex couples are several of the most important components of a good life available to human beings....* Some persons do not want deep personal relations or to raise children. But the great majority of us do, and the [refusal to extend the benefit of law to same-sex unions denies] same-sex couples some of the greatest, most widely distributed, and most deeply embedded – sometimes even genetically embedded – least easily substituted ends of human life there are.

See Chapter 8, n. 12.

children – no less in the "best interests" of children – than parenting by heterosexuals.[10] The sole interest the Florida law succeeds in serving, then, is the interest in affirming the traditional moral view that homosexual sexual conduct is immoral. As I explained in Chapter 8, however, that interest is not a legitimate governmental interest.

I can anticipate a response along these lines: "Although the right to moral equality (in the guise of the right to equal protection) is part of the constitutional law both of Florida and of the United States, a court should adopt a deferential stance – a Thayerian stance – in enforcing the right. And this Judge Lederman did not do." I argued in Chapter 9 that a court should *not* adopt a Thayerian stance in enforcing the right to moral equality if there is good reason for the court to suspect that the challenged law is based on the view that those whom the law treats differently and less well are morally inferior. Put that point aside, however. The fact remains that Judge Lederman, constrained by established judicial precedent, *did* adopt a Thayerian stance: She did not ask whether in her own judgment the Florida law served a legitimate governmental interest; instead, she asked whether a lawmaker could plausibly think that the law served a legitimate governmental interest. (In the parlance of constitutional law, she asked whether the Florida law had a "rational basis.") Judge Lederman's answer, which was no, was more than amply supported – indeed, it was overdetermined – by the social-scientific evidence presented to the court.

The Florida law not only violates the political morality of liberal democracy. The law – according to which, again, no one otherwise eligible to adopt under Florida law "may adopt if that person is a homosexual" – is unconstitutional. The law is unconstitutional even from the perspective of Thayerian deference: Given the robust social-scientific consensus that has emerged to the effect that parenting by homosexuals is no less healthy for children – no less in the "best interests" of children – than parenting by heterosexuals, Judge Lederman was right to conclude that no lawmaker could any longer plausibly think that the Florida law serves a legitimate governmental interest.

---

[10] According to that scientific consensus, parenting by homosexuals is no more likely than parenting by heterosexuals to cause children to be homosexuals.

Conclusion

Sometimes a court's rejection of a constitutional challenge to a law is not merely incorrect; sometimes it is shameful. So shameful as to later warrant both embarassment and apology. Two infamous examples:

1. *In Plessy v. Ferguson*,[11] the U.S. Supreme Court's rejection of a constitutional challenge to a law requiring racially segregated ("separate but equal") railroad accommodations.
2. In *Korematsu v. United States*,[12] the Court's rejection of a constitutional challenge to the forced relocation of persons of Japanese ancestry, many of whom were American citizens, from their homes on the west coast of the United States to internment camps, during World War II.[13]

By the time this book has been published, Judge Lederman's constitutional ruling may have been reversed by the Florida Supreme Court. If so, that reversal – that rejection of the constitutional challenge to the Florida adoption law – will be not merely incorrect; it will be shameful. So shameful as to later warrant both embarassment and apology.

---

[11] 163 U.S. 537 (1896).
[12] 323 U.S. 214 (1944).
[13] It is also shameful that the Court waited until 1967 to strike down antimiscegenation legislation. See *Loving v. Virginia*, 388 U.S. 1 (1967).

Index

abortion, 123–137
    Abortion Argument, 134
    ban on, definition of, 123
    beginning of human life argument and, 125
    conception of life v. fertilization and, 127
    dignity of unborn and, 16
    "ensoulment" by God and, 127–129
    as government interest, 124
    laws banning, 2
    moral freedom and, 123–124, 136
    Roe v. Wade and, 135
    viability of fetus and, 131–133
Abortion Argument, 134
Ackerman, Bruce, 47–48
ACLU of Ohio v. Capitol Square Review & Advisory Board, 108
Adarand Constructors, Inc. v. Pena, 181
adoption bans
    for homosexuals, 174, 199–200, 202
    moral freedom and, 201
affirmative action, 177–181
    arguments against, 178–179
    white treatment under, 178
African Americans, lynching of, 12
After Theory (Eagleton), 34
agape, religious belief and, 36–37
    Nietzsche and, 46
'age of genocide,' 13
agent-neutrality, 41, 50
agent-relativity, 50
Alexander, Frank S., 5
Alexander, Larry, 197
alienation, 110
Alston, Philip, 170
altruism, 31
    Tawney on, 50

Amar, Akhil, 103
amendments, to U.S. Constitution
    First Amendment, 173, 190
    Fifth Amendment, 188–189
    Eighth Amendment, 160, 168, 185–186, 188, 190
    Fourteenth Amendment, 174, 180, 188, 196
    process for, 159, 185
American Constitutional Law, 164
American Law Institute, 96
American Psychological Association, 148
Amnesty International, 14
analogy, 32
anti-miscegenation laws, 63. *See also Loving v. Virginia*
    moral equality and, 171
Appleby, R. Scott, 83
Aquinas, Thomas, 30, 32, 98, 128
Aristotle, 148
atheism, 49
    of Nietzsche, 46, 51
    nonestablishment norm and, 115
Augustine (Saint), 40
authenticity, in religious belief, 39
authoritarianism, human rights under, 9, 26

Barry, Brian, 111
Bayle, Pierre, 52
Baze v. Rees, Commissioner, Kentucky Department of Corrections, 189
Benedict XVI (Pope), 70
Bentham, Jeremy, 22
Berkowitz, Peter, 145

Index

The Bible
  commandments in, 34–35
  Corinthians, 36
  John, 33–35
  Matthew, 35
Bickel, Alexander, 165, 166
Bill of Rights
  in South Africa, 159, 160
  in U.S., 185, 194
Bloody Tenent (Williams, R.), 67
Bokser, Baruch M., 31
Bokser, Ben Zion, 31
Bonhoeffer, Dietrich, 19
Boniface VIII (Pope), 70
Boonin, David, 129–131
Bork, Robert, 194
Bosnia, genocide in, 12
Brandeis, Louis, 164
Brennan, William, 102, 112
Brown v. Board of Education, 63, 174, 196
Bryant, Anita, 200
Buddhism, 89
Burma, 9, 25
Bush, George H. W., 15, 71

California Supreme Court, 177
Cambodia, genocide in, 12
Canada
  Charter of Rights and Freedoms for, 160, 179
  Constitution Act of 1982 in, 160
  Constitution of, 90
  Supreme Court of, 73, 162, 178–179
capital punishment, 189
  Eighth Amenders on, 189–190
Carter, Jimmy, 15
Castro, Manuel Monteiro de, 151
Catholicism. *See* Roman Catholic Church
Charter of Rights and Freedoms, in Canada, 160, 179
China
  government perception of religion in, 76
  socialist democracy in, 9, 26
Christian Jurisprudence Project, 1, 5
Christian Science, as religion, 74
Christianity, 27, 45
  concept of love and, 33, 45
  doctrine of, 35
Christopher, Warren, 56

Church of England, 101, 111
civil rights, denial of, by Roman Catholic Church, 83–84
Civil Rights Act of 1964 (U.S.), 160
civil unions, 146. *See also* same-sex unions
  traditional marriage v., 146–147
Civil War, in Spain, 85
coercion. *See* religious coercion
commercial speech, 173
Commonweal, 128
community, religious belief and, 43
conception of life, fertilization v., 127
  OCBA and, 130
  viability of fetus and, 131–133
concretization, 191
Congo, genocide in, 12
Connecticut Supreme Court, 177
Constitution Act of 1982 (Canada), 160
Constitution of Canada, moral freedom under, 90
Constitution of the Republic of Ireland, 110
  religion in, 110–111
Constitution of the Republic of South Africa, 160, 170–171
"constitutional bedrock," 194
constitutional interpretation, 184–197
  from "constitutional bedrock," 194
  constitutional norms in, 190–193
  definition of, 185–190
  of Eighth Amendment, 168
  of Fourteenth Amendment, 174, 196
  of right to privacy, 182, 184
  specification in, 191–192
  specifications of, 190–191
constitutional norms, 190–193
constitutionality
  morality and, 2
  of political behavior, 162–163
  of racial discrimination, 175–176
  of same-sex unions, 177
constitutions. *See* Constitution of Canada, moral freedom under; Constitution of the Republic of Ireland; U.S. Constitution
Corinthians, Book of, 36
Corvino, John, 63
court system, in U.S., religion in, 103–104
crimes against humanity, under international law of human rights, 14

Index

crimes of aggression, 14
cruel and unusual punishment. *See* Eighth Amendment, to U.S. Constitution

Darfur. *See* Sudan, genocide in
Darrow, Clarence, 48–49
Darrow, Mac, 170
death penalty. *See* capital punishment
Declaration of Independence (of U.S.), 105–106
Declaration of Independence to the Universal Declaration of Human Rights of the United Nations, 17
Declaration on Religious Freedom, 80
Declaration of the Relation of the Church to Non-Christian Religions, 44
Declaration on the Elimination of All Forms of Intolerance and of Discrimination Based on Religion Belief, 72
  nonestablishment norm in, 112
A Defense of Abortion (Boonin), 129–131
democracy. *See also* liberal democracy
  definition of, 9–10
  Roman Catholic Church and, 86
  socialist, 9, 26
  in Spain, 84–85
Dicey, Albert Venn, 161
Die Linke, 78
Dignitatis Humanae, 80–87. *See also* Second Vatican Council
  criticism of, 83
  religious coercion in, 82
  right to religious freedom under, 81–82
dignity
  as concept, 17
  definition of, 16–17
  under ICCPR, 62
  as inherent, 28, 30
  as inviolable, 54, 126–127
  liberal democracy and, 10–11, 27
  moral freedom and, 92
  in morality of human rights, 46
  religious belief and, as factor in inherent nature of, 51–52
  under secularism, 52–53
  Smith on, 54
  of unborn, 16
  under U.S. Constitution, protection of, 173–177
  viability of fetuses and, 131
discrimination. *See also* religious coercion
  antimiscegenation laws as, 63
  constitutionality of, 175–176
  under ICCPR, 16–17, 62
  against racial minorities, 63, 175–176
  from religious coercion, 114
  toward homosexuality, 139–140, 199–202
  toward women, 63
  U.S. Supreme Court and, 175–177
  against women, 175–176
Divine Command Theory, 42
Doctrine of Faith, 103
doctrine of judicial supremacy, 163
domestic partnerships, 139
duty, rights v., 24

Eagleton, Terry, 34
East Germany, 9
Eberle, Chris, 132–133
Eighth Amenders, 188
  on capital punishment, 189–190
Eighth Amendment, to U. S. Constitution, 160, 185–186, 188, 190
  interpretation of, 168
Einstein, Albert, 128
Eisenstadt v. Baird, 182
"Elements of a Theory of Human Rights" (Sen), 19
Elk Grove Unified School District v. Newdow, 112–113
emotional suffering, 19
Encyclopedia of Genocide, 13
Engelhardt, H. Tristram, 125
equal protection clause. *See Brown v. Board of Education*; Fourteenth Amendment, to U.S. Constitution
equality. *See* moral equality
ethics
  in natural law, 39–40
  philosophical, 45, 47
eudaimonia, happiness v., 40
European Court of Human Rights, 182
evil, as concept, 38–39
extra ecclesian nulla salus ("outside the church no salvation"), 69
  for Roman Catholic Church, 70

Index

families, contemporary forms for, 144
Farley, Margaret, 152
The Federalist Papers (Madison), 191
fertilization, conception of life v., 127
   OCBA and, 130
   viability of fetus and, 131–133
Fides et Ratio (John Paul II), 44
Fifth Amendment, to U.S. Constitution, 188–189
Finke, Roger, 65
Finnis, John, 24, 191
First Amendment, to U.S. Constitution, 190
   commercial speech under, 173
The First Letter of John, 30
Fitzgerald, F. Scott, 56
Foot, Philippa, 46
forced labor. *See* slave labor
forgiveness, in religious belief, 37
Fourteenth Amenders, 189
Fourteenth Amendment, to U.S. Constitution, 180, 188
   interpretation of, 174, 196
Fourth Lateran Council, 32
France, nonestablishment of religion in, 100–101
Frank, Anne, 128
Frankfurter, Felix, 164, 165
Free Exercise clause, of U.S. Constitution, 96
freedom. *See* moral freedom, as right
fulfillment, 40

Gabin, Sanford, 167
Gadamer, Hans-Georg, 192
Gaita, Raimond, 45, 47
gender
   discrimination by, 175–176
   same-sex unions by, 147–149
genocide
   in Bosnia, 12
   in Cambodia, 12
   in Congo, 12
   Encyclopedia of Genocide, 13
   under Hitler, 12
   under international law of human rights, 14
   loss of life from, 12–13
   under Mao Tse Tung, 12
   under Ottoman Turks, 12
   in Rwanda, 12
   in Sudan, 12
   in Yugoslavia, 14
George, Robert, 52, 95
German Democratic Left Party (PDS), 78
Gettysburg Address, 105
global morality, 28
God
   in concept of love, 30
   in Divine Command Theory, 42
   "ensoulment" by, 127–129
   as supreme legislator, 41–42
government interests
   ban on abortion as, 124
   legitimacy of, 92
   moral freedom and, 91–94
   moral health as, 94
   moral truths and, 92–93
   moral unity as, 93–94
   protection of marriage as, 145
   religious freedom and, 75–77, 79
   same-sex unions and, 143
governments
   affirmation of religions by, 101–114
   autonomy of religion under, 84–85
   ban of religion by, under international law of human rights, 71–72, 75
   human rights regulation by, 21
   moral equality and, as right against, 62
   moral freedom under, 91
   protection of religious truth by, 75–78, 84–85
   protection of religious unity of society by, 78–79
   right to religious freedom and, interests of, 75–79
   Second Vatican Council on, 85
   suffering imposed by, 19
Greenawalt, Kent, 101, 114
Greene, Graham, 38
Griffin, James, 25, 26, 141
Grim, Brian, 65
Guess, Raymond, 23
Gysi, Gregor, 78

Habermas, Jürgen, 36, 42–43, 45
happiness, eudaimonia v., 40
Harvard Law Review, 164
hate, as concept, 38–39. *See also* evil, as concept

Index

Herero peoples, 12
Heschel, Abraham, 48
Hills, Roderick, 147
Himmler, Heinrich, 140
Hitler, Adolph, genocide under, 12
Holmes, Oliver Wendell, 164
the Holocaust, 12
homosexuality, 94. *See also* same-sex unions
    California Supreme Court and, 177
    historical discrimination against, 139–140, 199–202
    religious lawmaking and, 114–115
    religious view of, 115
    Roman Catholic Church on, 140–141, 150
    U.S. Supreme Court rulings, 176–177
homosexuals, as adoptive parents, 174, 199–200, 202
    In the Matter of the Adoption of John Doe and James Doe, 199–200, 202
    moral equality for, 201
    scientific support for, 201–202
human life, beginning of
    abortion and, 125
    conception v. fertilization and, 127
human right foundationalism, 54–55
human rights. *See also* international law of human rights; universality, of human rights
    activists for, 53
    under authoritarianism, 9, 26
    denial of, 57
    dignity and, 16
    foundationalism for, 54–55
    government regulation of, 21
    indetermination of, 18–19
    International Bill of Human Rights, 15–18, 28
    inviolability and, 17–18, 28
    Judaism and, 29
    in law, 20
    liberal democracy and, 7–26, 159
    morality of, 11–16, 18–19, 28, 46–57
    perfect v. imperfect duties for, 18–19
    religious belief and, 36–40
    Sen on, 19
    treaties for, 14
    under United Nations guidelines, 18
    universality of, 9, 26
Human Rights Watch, 9, 26

ICCPR. *See* International Covenant on Civil and Political Rights
ICESCR. *See* International Covenant on Economic, Social, and Cultural Rights
imago Dei, 32
Immigration Act of 1995 (U.S.), 3
In the Matter of the Adoption of John Doe and James Doe, 199–200, 202
India, constitution of, 178–179
International Bill of Human Rights, 15–18, 28
    components of, 15–16
    international law of human rights and, 56
International Covenant on Civil and Political Rights (ICCPR), 15
    development of, 71
    dignity concept under, 62
    discrimination under, 16–17, 62
    moral freedom under, 96–97
    right to religious freedom under, 71–73
    Siracusa Principles in, 72, 97
International Covenant on Economic, Social, and Cultural Rights (ICESCR), 15
International Criminal Court, 14
    Rome Statute of, 14
international law of human rights, 56–57
    crimes against humanity under, 14
    crimes of aggression under, 14
    development of, 13–18
    genocide under, 14
    governmental ban of religion under, 71–72, 75
    human rights treaties and, 14
    International Bill of Human Rights and, 56
    moral equality under, 62
    rules of, 14–15
    UN role in, 14
    war crimes under, 14
An Introduction to the Study of the Law of the Constitution (Dicey), 161
intuition, moral, 42–43
inviolability
    definition of, 17
    of dignity, 54, 126–127
    human rights and, 17–18, 28
    in morality of human rights, 46, 50–51
Iowa Supreme Court, 177

Index

Ireland. *See* Constitution of the Republic of Ireland
Islam, religious freedom and, 85

Jefferson, Thomas, 67, 68
Jesus, as moral guide for human rights, 36–40
Jews, genocide of, 12
John, Book of, 33–35
John Paul II (Pope), 44, 75, 90, 103
John XXIII (Pope), 86
Johnson v. California, 176
Judaism
  ethic of justice under, 45
  morality of human rights and, 29
  same-sex unions under, 153–155
  universality of human rights in, 31
judicial deference, 162–171
judicial nondeference, 164
judicial review, 168–169
  arguments against, 170–171
judicial supremacy, 168
  doctrine of, 163
  Waldron on, 169
justice as concept, under Judaism, 45

Kahn, Paul, 164
Kant, Immanuel, 18, 36–37
Kaveny, Cathy, 131
Kay, Richard, 195–196
Kelsen, Hans, 191
Kesavan, Vesan, 187
King, Martin Luther Jr., 20
Koppelman, Andrew, 140
Korematsu v. United States, 203
Kramer, Larry, 171
Kronman, Anthony, 192
Kundera, Milan, 43

labor. *See* slave labor
Larmore, Charles, 10
law(s), 3
  antimiscegenation, 63
  human rights in, 20
  illicit view as basis for, 62–64
  moral equality violated by, 174–175
  morality and, 18–21, 98
  racial minorities under, 63
  religion as basis for, 4, 100–119
  as rights violation, 167
  as unconstitutional, 162, 168
  women under, disadvantages of, 63
Laycock, Douglas, 70
Lederman, Cyndy S., 199–202
Lee, Patrick, 52
legal cases
  ACLU of Ohio v. Capitol Square Review & Advisory Board, 108
  Adarand Constructors, Inc. v. Pena, 181
  Baze v. Rees, Commissioner, Kentucky Department of Corrections, 189
  Brown v. Board of Education, 63, 174, 196
  Eisenstadt v. Baird, 182
  Elk Grove Unified School District v. Newdow, 112–113
  Johnson v. California, 176
  Korematsu v. United States, 203
  In the Matter of the Adoption of John Doe and James Doe, 199–200, 202
  Planned Parenthood of Southeastern Pennsylvania v. Casey, 183
  Plessy v. Ferguson, 203
  Roe v. Wade, 135
  Rowland v. Mad River School District, 177
  for same-sex unions, 142–144
legal rights, 22
  fundamental, 61
  under international law of human rights, 9, 26
Leopold II (King), 11–12
Letter Concerning Toleration (Locke), 66, 68
Levi, Primo, 20, 43
"us-ism" for, 43
liberal democracy
  dignity as part of, 10–11, 27
  fundamental legal rights under, 61
  governmental interests under, for religious freedom, 77
  human rights and, 7–26, 159
  moral equality and, 61
  as pluralistic, 79
  political morality of, 1, 202
  as post-Nuremberg democracy, 11
  principles of, 11
  religion and, 27–45
  religious freedom and, 65, 70–80
  religious lawmaking in, 118–119
  right to religious freedom under, 65–87
Lincoln, Abraham, 105
Linker, Damon, 4–5

Index

Locke, John, 66, 68, 76, 95
   on religious tolerance, 66–67
love, as concept, 33, 45
   God and, 30
   for strangers, 38
Lovin, Robin, 93
Loving v. Virginia, 63, 174
Lutheran Church, 111
lynching, 12

MacIntyre, Alasdair, 24
Madison, James, 67–68, 76, 191
males, same-sex unions between, 147–148
Mao Tse Tung, genocide under, 12
Maritain, Jacques, 28–29
marriage, traditional, 154
   civil unions v., 146–147
   as healthy for society, 145
   for procreative purposes, 150, 152
   same-sex unions v., 144–146
   social purpose of, 149
Marshall, John, 166
Marshall, Thurgood, 112, 181
Martino, Renato (Cardinal), 83
Marx, Karl, 53
Matthew, Book of, 35
maxims of political morality, 161
McCabe, Herbert, 35
McConnell, Michael, 95, 194
McCormick, Richard, 135
McDonald, Alonzo, 5
meaning, as religious, 48
Melville, Herman, 10
Memorial and Remonstrance against Religious Assessments (Madison), 67–68, 76
Milosz, Czeslaw, 55–56
Model Penal Code, 96
moral equality, 61–64
   antimiscegenation laws and, 171
   as desirous ideal, 130–131
   for homosexuals as adoptive parents, 201
   under international law of human rights, 62
   liberal democracy and, 61
   as right against government, 62, 200
   for same-sex unions, 139
   violation of, by laws, 174–175
moral freedom, as right, 88–99, 198–199
   adoption ban as violation of, 201

ban on abortion and, 123–124, 136
   under Canadian Constitution, 90
   as commitment, 93
   dignity and, 92
   government interests and, 91–94
   under governments, 91
   under ICCPR, 96–97
   religious freedom v., 89, 98
   for same-sex unions, 141, 142, 149, 155
   under Supreme Court of Canada, 90
   under U.S. Constitution, 96
moral health, 94
   psychological health and, 94
moral intuition, 42–43
moral rights
   as enforceable, 23–25
   language of, 24–25
   of the unborn, 125–126, 128, 137
   utility of, 24
moral truths, 92–93
moral unity, 93–94
morality. *See also* moral equality; political morality
   biological roots of, 33
   constitutionality and, 2
   as global, 28
   law and, 18–21
   legal regulation of, 98
   religion-based, legal issues and, 4
morality of human rights, 11–16, 18–19, 28, 46–57
   dignity claim in, 46
   inviolability claim in, 46, 50–51
   Judaism and, 29
morals legislation, 98
Murdoch, Iris, 37
Murray, John Courtney, 85, 86, 88, 98
Mussolini, Benito, 78

Nagel, Thomas, 10, 49
Nama peoples, 12
Namibia, 12
National Association to Secure the Religious Amendment to the Constitution, 109
natural law
   ethics in, 39–40
   Thomistic theory of, 33
Natural Law and Natural Rights (Finnis), 24
"natural" rights, 22–23

Index

Nazis, Jewish genocide under, 12
"negative" religious freedom, 105. *See also* atheism
The New Jerusalem Bible, 38
Nickel, James, 22–23
Niederauer, George H., 151
Nietzsche, Friedrich
   agape and, 46
   atheism of, 46, 51
nihilism, 47–48
nonestablishment norm, 104, 107–112
   atheism and, 115
   in Declaration on the Elimination of All Forms of Intolerance and of Discrimination Based on Religion Belief, 112
   for religious lawmaking, 104, 107–109, 112, 115, 117
   same-sex unions and, 154
   U.S. Supreme Court enforcement of, 109
Noonan, John, 85
normative agents, 53
North Korea, 9
Novak, William, 96
Nozick, Robert, 48

Obama, Barack, 199
OCBA. *See* organized cortical brain activity
O'Connor, Sandra Day, 112
On Human Rights (Griffin), 141
O'Neill, Aidan, 11
organized cortical brain activity (OCBA), 129–130
"The "Origin and Scope of the American Doctrine of Constitutional Law" (Thayer), 164–165
originalism, 197
other-regard, in religious belief, 40
Ottoman Turks, genocide under, 12
Outka, Gene, 136
The Oxford English Dictionary, 16–17

Parable of the Good Samaritan, 37–38
Paul VI (Pope), 80, 86
Paulsen, Michael Stokes, 187
PDS. *See* German Democratic Left Party
philosophical ethics, 45
   concepts of, 47

Planned Parenthood of Southeastern Pennsylvania v. Casey, 183
Plato, 148
Pledge of Allegiance (U.S.), 106
   religious addition to, 103–107
Plessy v. Ferguson, 203
pluralism, liberal democracy and, 79
political freedom, popular sovereignty and, 172–173
political morality, 1
   definition, 1, 202
   maxims of, 161
politics, religion and, role in, 2, 51
Pope, Stephen, 33
popular constitutionalism, 171
popular sovereignty, right to political freedom and, 172–173
   for citizenry, 172
Posner, Richard, 49, 139, 168
   on *Roe v. Wade*, 135
post-Nuremberg democracy, 11
Price, T. W., 50
privacy rights, 182, 184
Proposed Initiative Act No. 1, 174
Protestants, distrust of Catholic Church by, 81
Putnam, Hilary, 31

racial minorities
   antimiscegenation laws and, 63
   discrimination against, 63, 175–176
Rahner, Karl, 34
Ratzinger, Joseph 70. *See also* Benedict XVI
reductionism, 49
Rehnquist, William, 112
Reilly, Daniel P., 151
religion
   affirmation of, by governments, 101–104, 114
   analogy in, 32
   autonomy of, under government rule, 84–85
   in Constitution of the Republic of Ireland, 110–111
   "ensoulment" by God and, 127–129
   homosexuality and, 115
   imago Dei in, 32
   laws based on, 4, 100–119
   liberal democracy and, 27–45
   in national currency, 103

Index

in Pledge of Allegiance, 103–107
role in politics for, 2, 51
same-sex unions and, 152–153
in U.S. court system, 103–104
in U.S., diversity of, 3–4
under U.S. Constitution, establishment of, 101
violence as result of, 13
religious belief
  agape and, 36–37
  atheism v., 49
  authenticity in, 39
  community and, 43
  dignity as concept and, 51–52
  forgiveness in, 37
  hate and, 38–39
  Jesus as moral guide for human rights and, 36–40
  origin questions in, 43
  other-regard in, 40
  problem of meaning and, 48
  reasons for action in, 50–51
  role of God in, 41–42
  self-fulfillment in, 41
  self-regard in, 40
religious coercion, 72
  in *Dignitatis Humanae*, 82
  discrimination as result of, 114
  through lawmaking, 114, 118
religious freedom, as right, 65–87
  belief in inferiority of other faiths as, 75–76, 103
  Christian Science and, 74
  coercion and, 72
  as conditional, 73–75
  under Constitution of Republic of Ireland, 110
  denial of, 69
  under *Dignitatis Humanae*, 81–82
  government bans and, 71–72, 75
  governmental interests in, 75–77, 79
  under ICCPR, 71–73
  Islam and, 85
  liberal democracy and, 70–80
  moral freedom v., 89, 98
  "negative," 475
  for nonbaptized, 82
  religious practices under, 73
  religious truth under, 75–78
  under Roman Catholic Church, 88

Second Vatican Council on, 103
Smith on, 68–69
under U.S. Constitution, 74, 85–86
religious lawmaking, 4, 100–119
  as coercive, 114, 118
  in France, 100–101
  homosexuality under, 114–115
  in liberal democracy, 118–119
  for national currency, 103
  nonestablishment norm for, 104, 107–109, 112, 115, 117
  rationale for, 115–116
  Ten Commandments and, 104
  in U.K., 118, 119
  in U.S., 100–118
  under U.S. Constitution, 100
religious truth, 75–78
  government as arbiter of, 84–85
  Second Vatican Council on, 85
religious unity, protection of, 78–79
right to privacy, 182, 184
rights, 21–26. *See also* human rights
  duty v., 24
  legal, 22
  moral, 23–25
  moral freedom, 88–99, 198–199
  "natural," 58
  to privacy, 182, 184
  to religious freedom, 65–87
  under U.S. Constitution, 182–184
  violations of, through laws, 167
Roe v. Wade, 135, 183–184
  Posner on, 135
  U.S. Supreme Court and, 135
Roman Catholic Church
  as arbiter of religious truth, 78
  democracy and, 86
  denial of civil rights by, for non-Catholics, 83–84
  Dignitatis Humanae and, 80–87
  extra ecclesian nulla salus for, 70
  on homosexuality, 140–141, 150
  on inferiority of other faiths, 81
  on moral rights of unborn, 128
  on nonprocreative sex, 150, 152
  Protestant distrust of, 81
  religious freedom under, 88
  on same-sex unions, 145, 150–152
  Second Vatican Council, 44, 78, 80

213

Index

Rome Statute, of International Criminal Court, 14
Rorty, Richard, 55–56
Roth, Kenneth, 9
Rowland v. Mad River School District, 177
Rwanda, genocide in, 12

same-sex unions, 138–155
　Christian arguments for, 153
　constitutionality of, 177
　domestic partnerships and, 139
　gender differences and, 147–149
　government interests and, 143
　government interests v., 145
　under Judaism, 153–155
　legal cases for, in U.S., 142–144
　legality of, in U.S., 138–139
　moral freedom of, 141, 142, 149, 155
　nonestablishment norm and, 154
　prediction of effects of legalization of, 147
　religious arguments against, 152–153
　right to moral equality for, 139
　Roman Catholic Church on, 145, 150–152
　sectarian religious rationales against, 153
　secular arguments against, 150–152
　state bans on, 139
　traditional marriage v., 144–146
　U.S. legal cases for, 142–144
Scalia, Antonin, 109, 178
Scarman (Lord), 170
Schulz, William, 57
Scruton, Roger, 147–148
Second Vatican Council, 44, 78, 80, 81, 84, 86
　Declaration of Religious Freedom in, 80
　democracy under, 86
　governments as arbiters of religious truth and, 85
　on religious freedom, 103
secularism, dignity under, 52–53
self-fulfillment, in religious belief, 41
self-regard, in religious belief, 40
Sen, Amartya, 18–19, 23
　on human rights, 19
Senturk, Recep, 42
separation-of-powers, under U.S. Constitution, 162

Shiffrin, Steven, 110
Shumpeter, Joseph, 9
Singer, Peter, 125
Siracusa Principles, 72, 97
slave labor, 12
Smith, Steve, 33, 54, 108
　on alienation, 110
　on dignity, 54
　on right to religious freedom, 68–69
socialist democracy, 9, 26
Souter, David, 184
South Africa
　Bill of Rights in, 159, 160
　Constitution of, 160, 170–171
　Supreme Court of, 179
Spain
　Civil War in, 85
　democracy in, 84–85
Spellman, Francis (Cardinal), 86
Stalin, Josef, 12
Sudan, genocide in, 12
suffering, 20
　emotional, 19
　government-imposed, 19
Sullivan, Andrew, 149
Supreme Court of Canada, 73, 162, 178–179
　constitutional standards for, 184
　moral freedom under, 90

Tawney, R. H., 49
　on altruism, 50
Taylor, Charles, 27, 52
Ten Commandments, 104
Thayer, James Bradley, 163–166
　on judicial deference, 162–171
Thomas, Clarence, 103
Thomistic theory of natural law, 33
torture, 9, 25
Tractatus Logico-Philosophicus (Wittgenstein), 31
Tracy, David, 44
traditional marriage. *See* marriage, traditional
Tribe, Laurence, 125
Truth and Method (Gadamer), 192
Tushnet, Mark, 171

U.K. *See* United Kingdom
Ullendorff, Edward, 34

Index

Unam Sanctam (Boniface VIII), 70
The Unbearable Lightness of Being (Kundera), 43
the unborn. *See also* abortion
  dignity of, 16
  moral status of, 125–126, 137
  Roman Catholic Church on, 128
  viability of, 131–133
United Kingdom (U.K.)
  court system in, 162
  nonestablishment of religion in, 118, 119
United Nations (UN)
  Declaration of Independence to the Universal Declaration of Human Rights of, 17
  human rights under, 18
  international law of human rights and, 14
United States (U.S.). *See also* U.S. Constitution
  Bill of Rights in, 185, 194
  Brown v. Board of Education in, 63
  Civil Rights Act of 1964 in, 160
  Declaration of Independence of, 105–106
  diversity of religion in, 3–4
  Immigration Act of 1995 in, 3
  international law violations by, 14–15
  Loving v. Virginia in, 63
  Pledge of Allegiance in, 103–107
  political theology in, 5
  religious belief in, 27
  religious lawmaking in, 100–118
  same-sex unions in, legality of, 138–139
  Supreme Court in, 109
Universal Declaration of Human Rights, 15–16
universality, of human rights, 9, 25–26
  in Judaism, 31
U.S. Constitution. *See also* constitutional interpretation
  First Amendment, 173, 190
  Fifth Amendment, 188–189
  Eighth Amendment, 160, 168, 185–186, 188, 190
  Fourteenth Amendment, 174, 180, 188
  amendment process for, 159, 185
  capital punishment under, 189
  Establishment Clause in, 117–118
  establishment of religion under, 101
  founders of, 185
  free exercise clause in, 96
  inherent dignity protected under, 173–177
  interpretation of, 184–197
  legitimating source of, 185
  maxims of political morality in, 161
  moral freedom under, 96
  "original meaning" of, 186–187
  popular constitutionalism and, 171
  popular sovereignty protected under, 172–173
  protecting of rights under, 182–184
  provisions in, 160
  religious freedom under, 74, 85–86
  religious lawmaking under, 100
  right to privacy under, 184
  separation-of-powers under, 162
U.S. Supreme Court, 159–184
  affirmative action under, 177–181
  discrimination laws and, 175–177
  gender discrimination cases, 175–176
  homosexuality and, legal treatment under, 176–177
  judicial deference for, 162–171
  judicial nondeference for, 164
  judicial review for, 168–169
  judicial ultimacy of, 168
  nonestablishment norm under, 109
  racial discrimination cases, 175–176
  Roe v. Wade and, 135
"us-ism," 283

violence, from religion, 13
Virginia Statute for Religious Freedom (Jefferson), 67, 68

Waldron, Jeremy, 169–170, 172
  on judicial ultimacy, 169
Walsh, Michael, 81
war crimes, 14
Washington v. Glucksberg, 183
Watson, Micah, 5

Index

We Hold These Truths: Catholic Reflections on the American Proposition (Murray), 88
Weil, Simone, 30–31
Whittington, Keith, 166
Wilde, Oscar, 140
Williams, Bernard, 51
Williams, Roger, 67
Wills, Garry, 134
Witte, John, 5
Wittgenstein, Ludwig, 31

women
    disadvantages under the law, 63
    discrimination against, 175–176
    same-sex unions and, 147–148
Workers' Educational Association, 50
World Conference on Human Rights, 57
Wreen, Michael, 134

Yugoslavia, genocide in, 14